POTTERSFIELD PRESS

# The Dark Side of Life in Victorian Halifax

## Judith Fingard

Pottersfield Press

*For my daughter Clio Burroughs and my parents Susan and Irwin Fingard whose love and understanding are always with me.*

Copyright 1989   Judith Fingard
Second Printing 1991

Typesetting: Dal Graphics, Halifax

Cover Illustration: *Address on the Effects of Ardent Spirits,*
        (J.J. Stewart Collection, Dalhousie University).

**Canadian Cataloguing in Publication Data**
Fingard, Judith, 1943-

    The dark side of life in Victorian Halifax

    Bibliography: p.
    Includes index.
    ISBN 0-919001-58-0

1. Poor — Nova Scotia — Halifax — History — 19th century.
2. Halifax (N.S.) — Social conditions. 3. Halifax (N.S.) — History
— 19th century. I. Title

FC2346.4.F56   1989          971.6  ʹ22          C89-098591-X
F1039.5.H17F56   1989

---

On-going assistance is provided to Pottersfield Press by The Canada Council
and the Nova Scotia Department of Culture and Tourism.

Pottersfield Press
RR 2, Porters Lake
Nova Scotia   B0J 2S0

# CONTENTS

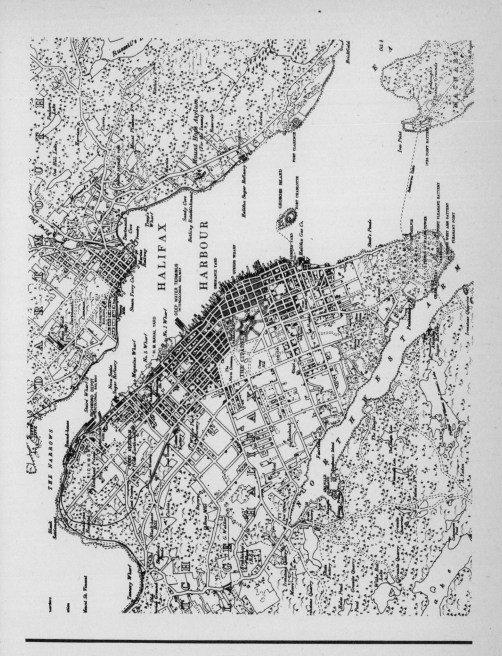

Map of Halifax-Dartmouth showing the location of such important landmarks as Rockhead Prison and the Penitentiary. (Public Archives of Nova Scotia)

# PREFACE

On a promontory in the extreme north end of the city of Halifax, where luxury apartments now stand, the Victorians built Rockhead. An octagonal block of granite flanked by two 180-foot wings, it was in appearance "every inch a Prison." Somewhat incongruously, the site offered its inmates a spectacular view of Bedford Basin, thought to be "one of the handsomest in the Province."[1] As a short-term jail, Rockhead seldom accommodated residents in its eighty-four cells for more than a few months at a time. But some of them returned frequently. This book is a study of 92 of those repeat offenders, who were intimately acquainted with the prison, and of the world in which they lived in the second half of the nineteenth century. To their contemporaries they were not just names on the police court docket or numbers in the prison registers. They were prominent in the annals of the city; prominent, that is, for their notoriety.

The group of 92 was compiled by identifying the most persistent of the approximately 640 imprisoned repeat offenders—known as recidivists—during a ten-year period and consulting prison records previous and subsequent to the decade in order to finalize the list and round out the profile. All those who qualified for inclusion went to jail on average at least twice a year for at least five consecutive years, an arbitrary definition admittedly, but one which proved to be serviceable. Together the 92 accounted for 1506 (31.7 per cent) of the 4749 committals to city prison between 1864 and 1873, ten years chosen because they represented the second decade of jail register keeping and therefore provided sufficient scope for identifying those offenders whose incarcerations dated from the 1850s.

Unfortunately the available qualitative evidence concerning the 92 and their peers is largely second-hand since jail habitués seldom had occasion, even if they were literate, to contribute to the written record. They often spoke in their own defence in court. Some of those comments have been preserved verbatim in so far as we can trust the presiding clerk; others have been embellished by newspaper reporters. Sometimes the press reports convey an objectivity consistent with good journalism but all too often the weaknesses of the defendants, based on their speech or their appearance, were mocked or criticized. Paul Craven's analysis of the melodrama of the Toronto police court reporting in the same period suggests that press coverage, the richest source, "is clearly not a neutral one."[2] In Halifax the daily papers insisted on referring to the regular police court proceedings as the 'Huckleberry,' an unflattering colloquialism which meant persons of no consequence who provoked laughter and ridicule.[3] These 'jailbirds' were beneath the contempt of most observers of the urban scene, only occasionally evoking a response as positive as pity. More often they were labelled as incorrigible misfits. In terms of both the scorn they incurred and the position they occupied, they were members of the underclass of their society.

The use of the American sociological term 'underclass' in a historical study requires an explanation since it is normally applied to present-day black residents of large urban slum-ghettoes. It has been criticized as a cultural rather than an economic concept and has also rekindled the debate between behaviourists and environmentalists as to the causes and solutions of poverty, deviancy and dependency.[4] In terms of both definition and controversy, however, it is a useful description of the types of people who fall within the net of this study, allowing, of course, for nineteenth-century differences. They were the residents of specific, rough and disreputable streets of the city, limited in their lifetime opportunities because of racial prejudice, gender inequalities, educational deprivation, chronic poverty, pathological disorders, or, by association with those so limited. They even developed a welfare dependency in their attitude towards the few public services available. For those who prefer neo-Marxist jargon, they could equally well be described as the sub-proletariat.[5] Both terms are more descriptively accurate than working-class identities such as casual labourers or labouring poor. They are also less pejorative than the Victorian favourites of 'dangerous classes' and 'undeserving poor.'[6]

Since the population chosen for analysis seldom held steady jobs and did not frequent 'respectable' institutions like churches, temperance societies and sports clubs, we are severely limited in the contexts in which

10

to place their lives beyond the prison and the poorhouse. Some of the analysis in Part One focuses on the tavern and the family, institutions which played significant roles in the lives of many of the offenders, and on prostitution as employment, which was important to thirty-eight of the forty-three women among the 92. In each of these three contexts we meet additional people closely associated with the core group but, for a variety of reasons, most of them did not share the same fate. The reason why some members of the underclass became jailbirds and others did not is one of the questions with which this study is concerned. Within a family, the difference was sometimes generational, sometimes a matter of degree; within a tolerated but disreputable occupation like prostitution, repeat offenders tended to be the more brazen women, quite open in their approach to their work; within the world of drink, alcoholism often provided the dividing line between those who went to jail and those who escaped the heavy hand of the law. While the notion of the 'underclass' implies inescapable circumstances associated with the 'culture of poverty,' class lines were not rigidly fixed for many of the associates of the prison population considered here. In the mobile and extremely uncertain world of the nineteenth century, people sometimes moved out of the underclass from one generation to another, or from one set of associations to another, or even from one part of the city to another. The low-life society which surrounded the 92 repeat offenders was not therefore completely devoid of the chances for social mobility. Underclass hustlers, in the form of tavernkeepers and brothel-keepers, for example, might have also been repeat or occasional offenders but they did not go to jail for their transgressions. Without a jail record and with the accumulation of capital they were sometimes able to move completely out of underclass life.

The other context is explored in Part Two where we shift our focus from the members of the underclass and their struggle for survival to the middle-class assessment of the problems of the disrespectable lower classes. This is not meant to be a comprehensive study of middle-class reform. It does not deal directly with such crucial issues as health, education or temperance. Instead, the focus has been confined to those charitable enterprises which directly touched, however tangentially, the lives of the core group of 92 and their families. As a result, the evangelical, rescue, poor relief and anti-cruelty movements receive the bulk of the attention. Given the lack of commitment to social reform in a small and relatively poor city, the new solutions proposed during the period were piecemeal and unsystematic. But in the measures haltingly adopted the environmentalist approach predominated, as evidenced in proposals to clean up the slums, separate children from 'unsatisfactory' parents and provide religion and education. It was also a period for opening institutions of reform and rehabilitation where the separation from the offensive areas of society was augmented by instilling notions of correct behaviour.

Although the period featured in this study was determined by the careers of particular underclass individuals, who became active as early as the 1850s and lived in some cases until the new century, and not by the response to those individuals by the society around them, we can distinguish a shift in attitude on the part of that society in the second half of the nineteenth century. In 1850 the residents of the slums were relatively free of interference with their rough and ready way of life. The traditional institutions of the jail and poorhouse, dating from pre-Victorian times, were ever present realities for the casualties of the social system. None the less the custodial nature and relative flexibility of these public institutions of 'social control' by mid-century meant that the inmates could move in and out of them much as they needed. They were, in a very real sense, their own welfare institutions. They became much less so by the end of the century. Nothing the members of the underclass themselves did contributed to the alteration of social attitudes and social policy. Rather the change must be traced to both the fears and aspirations of the mid-Victorian middle class.

Evangelical millenarianism and Catholic social action combined with new notions of urban order, domestic ideology and industrial discipline to focus attention on the social problems of the city. As a result of outside intervention, much of the autonomy in the lives of the lower classes was lost. In some important respects this was a good thing. Wife and child abuse, which was more readily detected among the working class and the underclass than the classes higher on the social scale, became recognized as unacceptable behaviour, for example. But in other ways the peculiar survival skills of underclass community life were threatened by the forces of reform. Hardened attitudes undoubtedly encouraged hardened responses in both directions and the gap between the classes was widened as a result. At the same time, the evolution of racial prejudices made it more difficult for Halifax's poor black population than for their white associates to escape from the cycle of poverty and dependence.

In order to place the underclass and its critics within the specific context of Halifax, the introductory chapter is designed to familiarize the reader with the city's marginalized population, low-life geography and reform impulses in the nineteenth century. As historians have observed, cities have both common and unique features. Comparative history has its limits and we should not be tempted to document conclusions about nineteenth-century Halifax "by citing evidence which may not be applicable from another time and place.''[7] Structural changes affecting Halifax outcasts which were shared by urban populations elsewhere in this period include the reform of the police force and the magistracy, the tightening of discipline in public institutions ranging from jails to schools, the invention of juvenile delinquency, the campaign against the retail drink trade and the intervention in the family to prevent and punish cruelty.[8] Halifax did, however, also have distinct features which set it apart from most cities its size or bigger. It was a military society, unique in Canada in this regard after 1871. It did not attract poor immigrants from Europe, which distinguished it from most of its American counterparts. Its rapid industrialization in the 1880s failed to transform social relations and geographical patterns in the city. It was characterized more by static than dynamic development. This may have meant that new ideas had less impact on urban problems or that the city was spared the worst features of urbanization in the industrial age. If problems did not exist, local citizens were not above inventing them as they continued to derive much of their inspiration for change and renewal from the larger urban centres to which they looked for guidance. Even though the headlines in the newspapers and the clichés of the moralizers were the standard for the day—'The Dangerous Classes'; 'The Dark Side of City Life'; 'Halifax: Its Sins and Sorrows'— middle-class observers were quick to point out that Halifax's social problems paled when compared to those of larger cities.[9] This was small comfort for those who were forced through various circumstances to spend most of their lives poor, homeless, sick, persecuted and unloved.

********

All of the research for this study was undertaken in Halifax over the past ten years. I am indebted for their kind assistance to archivists, librarians and curators in half a dozen city institutions, especially those at the Public Archives of Nova Scotia (PANS). Penny Hoover, Stephen Brooke and Sue Brown helped with the research and Mary Wyman and Becky Grant with the production of the computerized text. For reading all or part of the manuscript my heartfelt thanks go to Peter Burroughs, Ian McKay and David Sutherland. The book has been published with the help of a grant from the Social Science Federation of Canada, using funds provided by the Social Sciences and Humanities Research Council of Canada.

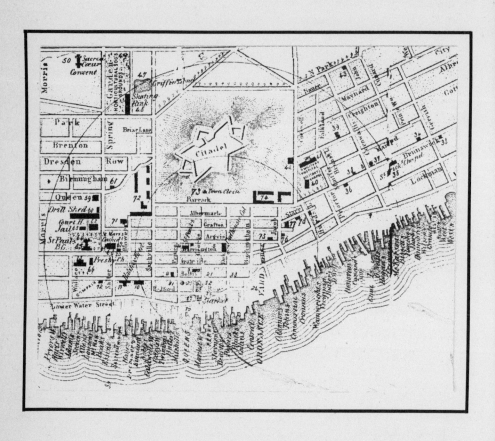

Map of Victorian Halifax showing the upper streets. (Public Archives of Nova Scotia)

# INTRODUCTION:
## UNDERCLASS HALIFAX

Historical studies of Halifax have not yet produced a synthesis of social life in the second half of the nineteenth century. The existing literature focuses largely on economic development, especially the impact of national policies and changes in the patterns of shipping on entrepreneurial activity and the city's role within the region.[1] Studies of political leaders tell us little about urban government and the city fathers.[2] Intellectual and cultural trends have attracted even less attention despite the importance of the city as an educational and ecclesiastical centre with its twenty-five churches by the 1860s, three dozen newspapers and periodicals by the 1870s and half a dozen colleges by the 1880s.[3] If the city's patricians and their womenfolk, have been largely neglected by historians, the lower classes have been equally so. We have some studies of working-class experiences, poverty and prostitution but many questions relating to popular culture and the social relations between the classes remain to be explored.[4]

None the less several important themes relating to the character of the city emerge when the historical studies are combined with contemporary accounts. First, nineteenth-century observers found the city to be dirty, dilapidated and dull.[5] They were most scathing about the low-life districts. Few visitors were favourably impressed with the area immediately beneath the Citadel inhabited by the flotsam and jetsam of society. Its street life of prostitutes, drunks and beggars frequently elicited comment. One traveller in 1855 was accosted by "miserably clad, half-starved looking children" who cried pathetically and perhaps artfully: "Please Sir, give me a penny to buy some bread."[6] The same year a much-travelled clergyman deplored the squalor he encountered and implied that the army and navy were responsible for "the quality of drunkenness and prostitution."[7]

This comment brings us to the second common theme in the literature: the role of the military. In descriptions of the city, analyses of marriage patterns, assessments of outcast Halifax and characterizations of leading businessmen, the pervasive influence of the British imperial presence figures prominently.[8] David Sutherland suggests that Thomas Raddall's emphasis on the military in *Warden of the North*, which stresses a "garrison identity," stands in need of revision. At the same time he ponders: "Unquestionably, the garrison contributed to economic and social development within the community after Confederation, but what was the measure and character of that contribution?"[9]

Clearly one effect of the British military presence, so overwhelming during the Crimean and American Civil Wars, and unique to Halifax after 1871 when the other imperial garrisons in Canada were withdrawn, was to reinforce the division of society into the rough and the respectable. The officers enhanced the genteel tone of the urban élite, the enlisted men contributed to the drunkenness and destitution of underclass Halifax. A city missionary in 1862 deplored "the deleterious influence of the soldiers and sailors on a certain portion of the community." The Church of England bishop went even further in 1889 with his assertion that "the military were a curse to this city and were the cause of a great deal of demoralization among our poor." Not all citizens would have agreed with this assessment. One claimed that "notwithstanding the fact of its being a military and naval station and a large seaport, there is not another town of the same population on this continent where there is less drunkenness and where habits of sobriety, industry and morality are more prevalent than in Halifax."[10]

Whatever the consequences of the military presence, it is certainly true that Halifax was not a particularly violent city compared with many of its nineteenth-century counterparts. The population avoided the persistent ethnic and political rioting that characterized other cities. And it also escaped disasters. Unlike Saint John or St. John's it did not burn down once in the nineteenth century let alone two or three times. Major fires on Granville Street in 1859, Hollis Street in 1861 and Water Street in 1891 did not spread. Occasional fires in the slums such as Barrack Street in 1867 were readily contained.[11] This impression of the orderliness of the city and concern for the quality of urban life provides the third theme.[12]

16

Since immigration from overseas had practically ceased by the second half of the nineteenth century, the superficial stability of the population probably contributed to the relatively tranquil veneer. Victorian Halifax remained a slow-growing city with a census population made up of over 70 per cent Nova Scotian-born. Approximately 5000 persons were added each decade to the 20,749 in 1851 to produce 36,100 by 1881 and then a sharp drop in the growth rate occurred, resulting in totals of only 38,495 in 1891 and 40,832 in 1901. Movement of population, especially out of the region, is another theme explored in the recent historical literature.[13] What census figures used for these studies conceal is the considerable amount of migration within the region and the presence of large numbers of unenumerated transient workers. Halifax drew people from the rural areas and from the other urban centres of the Atlantic region. At the same time hundreds of non-resident merchant sailors graced the city with their presence for stopovers of several weeks; royal naval sailors visited the port by the hundreds and sometimes thousands during the summer months; and British soldiers numbering between 2000 and 4000 were regularly stationed year-round in the garrison subject only to periodic changes of regiment which occurred in time sequences ranging from eight months to five years.[14]

The presence of non-resident workers who made up the vast majority of the men in the naval, merchant naval and army workforces considerably upset the balance in the sex ratio of the population. Sailors brought no womenfolk with them. For British soldiers stationed in Halifax there was a possibility of being accompanied by a spouse but it was slight since privates had no more than a six per cent chance of being allowed to bring their families with them or to have families they might acquire in the city added to the strength of the army establishment and even less chance of taking them with them when they left. The family life resulting from unions which occurred between the transient workers and local women was therefore far more precarious than industrial home life and much more likely to deteriorate into destitution and dependency.

The rough and transient elements of Victorian Halifax congregated in well-defined areas of the city. Particularly prominent in this regard were the streets on the hillside immediately to the east of the Citadel of Fort George and between the North and South Barracks. On the 'upper streets,' as the district was called by the 1860s, Barrack Street ran directly beneath the Citadel with buildings only on its east side. Until the last decade of the century it was considered the most notorious street in the city, infested with grog shops, brothels, boarding houses and tenement accommodation for military dependants and the civilians who preyed upon the army.

One critic noted facetiously in 1883 that it formed "the lowest street of the city instead of the best, as it is the highest."[15] The rough neighbourhood extended to Albemarle Street one block east of Barrack and to the upper portions of the intersecting streets of Sackville, Prince, George, Duke and Buckingham. The upper streets changed little between the 1830s and the 1870s.[16] After mid-century Grafton Street east of Albemarle received the overflow from some of these streets, as did City Street in the working-class north end. Upper and Lower Water Streets, the 'lower streets' on the harbour, were more mixed in character but, as the centre of sailortown, the long commercial street and its wharves contained a large number of taverns and sailors' boarding houses. There were more licensed premises on Upper and Lower Water Streets than on Barrack and Albemarle in the 1860s but the liquor shops in the upper streets were the ones associated with prostitution. For this reason, the upper streets were frequented by all categories of transient workers. These areas were also the most crowded of the city, Albemarle and Grafton, for example, being known in the 1850s as the two most populous streets in the city.[17]

Not surprisingly, therefore, whatever incidents of serious disorder occurred in Victorian Halifax were centred in these rough neighbourhoods, as were the bulk of individual offences against persons, property and public morality. According to the editor of the *Presbyterian Witness*, the military riot of 1863, the most serious of Halifax's disturbances, proved that the city had a "dangerous class," increasing daily and supplying the prisons and penitentiaries: "Squalor, misery, filth, everything that is distressing and disgusting may be witnessed by the person who has courage to go into the proper streets and houses at the proper time."[18] Here also dwelt the poor. They were best known perhaps to the physicians of the Visiting Dispensary, founded in 1827 and revamped in 1855, which, with the support of the public and the government, undertook "To supply medicines, give medical advice, perform such surgical operations as may from time to time be required; and attend at their own residences those who are unable to go to the Dispensary through illness."[19] In the autumn of 1867 over 60 per cent of the patients of the Halifax Visiting Dispensary resided on Barrack, Albemarle and Grafton Streets on the hill, Upper and Lower Water Streets on the harbour's edge, and the intersecting streets of Blowers, Sackville, George, Duke and Buckingham. Twenty years later this area still provided over 50 per cent of the Dispensary patients with another 20 per cent now to be found in the northern extension of outcast Halifax centred on City Street and vicinity.[20]

The Halifax people, who interacted socially and commercially with the transient seafaring and military workforces and made up the majority of both the poor and the casual labour force came from ethnic backgrounds similar to the slums of other east coast nineteenth-century cities. They were generally Irish or Afro-Nova Scotian. People of Irish heritage comprised almost 40 per cent of the population of Halifax in 1871; the blacks three per cent. The occupational structure of the employed members of these groups set them firmly within the working-class and petty shopkeeper categories. According to census data the Irish-born, some 10 per cent of the residents, were over-represented in the various carting activities, among coopers, stonemasons and tailors, as well as labourers, grocers and shopkeepers. Among the enumerated black workers, 47 per cent of the men were employed in labouring, service, and carting jobs, with another 27 per cent engaged in marine-related work as seamen, coopers, riggers and stevedores. Employed black women specified service, washing and cleaning to the extent of 92 per cent. None the less, greater social mobility and diversification of opportunities occurred in the last quarter of the century. Black men, engaged in thirty-three types of skilled, semi-skilled and unskilled jobs in 1871, found employment in forty-six types by 1881. There was also a qualitative change as greater opportunities opened up in port-related work and in new industrial enterprises.[21]

The poorest blacks and Irish were congregated in the upper streets and were over-represented among the underclass as well as the working class as a result of the poverty-stricken conditions in which they or their parents or grandparents had arrived, either direct from Ireland or via Newfoundland or Cape Breton in the case of the Irish; from Africa via the southern American states at the end of the War of 1812 for most of the blacks. Civilian habitués of the upper streets were also recruited from the army and therefore many parts of Britain; and enough continental names occur in the sources to reveal a degree of ethnic pluralism created by drifters ranging from circus performers to deserters from the international seafaring workforce.

For the destitute, drunken and dependent, the quality of city life improved but little in the nineteenth century. They lived, worked, socialized and consumed in crowded, unsanitary dwellings on streets rendered all the more unwholesome by the lack of municipal services. In 1842 one visitor found "the lower class of inhabitants, particularly the black population, in their appearance squalid and poverty struck."[22] R.H. Dana, the author of *Two Years Before the Mast*, investigated infamous Barrack Street that same year and found that it was "the nest of the brothels and dance-houses," in four of which every prostitute, black and white, "excited only loathing and pity" and "looked broken down by disease and strong drink." He ventured that "The chance of a man becoming diseased by connexion with them would certainly be ten to one with each of them."[23]

A newspaper report in 1847, which deplored the poverty of New York, also focused on the abodes of the underclass in Halifax and described a four-room tenement "not many yards east of the citadel hill," an allusion no doubt to Barrack Street. Each room was "in the most filthy state imaginable." One room was occupied by a family of seven, a second by two families amounting to six or seven. In the third a newly married couple shared the space with a family of four and in the fourth room lived a widowed mother and her four children. All these people lived in a "murky, chilling and death-like atmosphere, caused by dirt, cold and insufficient ventilation."[24] The crowded features of tenement life were confirmed in 1866, by city missionary John Grierson, a persistent visitor in the upper streets, where he found that three-quarters of the families who let him in had "only one room for all purposes, and in some of these, not over 14 foot square, eight, nine or ten persons of both sexes and all ages are huddled together."[25] In the northern extension of the disreputable area, City Street was described as being "in an abominably filthy condition, and that not a scavenger cart is at work in the locality."[26] The neglect of the slums by health officials was underscored by one of the Visiting Dispensary doctors in 1870. Dr. Edward Farrell blamed the cases of typhoid fever he found in a tenement house in Albemarle Street on "a cartload of rotting filth" decomposing in the backyard and predicted that only when the typhoid fever spread to "the homes of the wealthier classes" would the city attend to the matter.[27] Health inspectors, more vigilant in the 1880s, reported the living and sanitary conditions on Albemarle Street to be appalling. One household consisting of an old man and his consumptive sons slept together in their small room on "a shakedown of straw, which from long usage had become filthy. For bed clothes two old and dirty coats did duty....The condition of the room was simply terrible." In another house the inspectors found an open drain running to the street from a water closet serving the forty-two occupants.[28]

The rough neighbourhoods remained the catchment areas for the courts and jails. In the police court a very large percentage of charges were for drunkenness (See Table 1). Drink was also said to cause most of the violent crime. According to the *Novascotian* in 1864:

> The great course of evil and the primary cause of many of the stabbing and assault cases that occur is the large number of groggeries that exist in the upper streets, and various out of the way places. Police say that by far the greatest number of prisoners, that are almost nightly conveyed to the station house in a state of beastly intoxication, are picked up in the

vicinity of these low dram shops, while 75 per cent of the cases of assault, tumult and riot have their origin in this class of drinking houses.[29]

Despite dire predictions to the contrary, the number of charges in police court remained relatively stable between the 1860s and the 1890s, undermining contemporary assumptions about an increase in crime. The 1880s even saw a short-term decrease in crime as a result of improved economic conditions and the policies of a new magistrate.

The police station and court were located for most of the period in the city hall on the corner of George and Water Streets and included the overnight lock-up, a facility noted for its lack of salubrity and cleanliness, which was the scene of many attempted suicides in the nineteenth century. The trials in police court, before the mayor and aldermen until 1867 when a stipendiary magistrate from the legal profession was appointed, were summary ones and dealt with cases ranging from infringements of the licensing ordinances to mutiny on the high seas. From the police court the more serious cases, or those which in the opinion of the magistrate required a penitentiary term, were referred to the city criminal court or to the supreme court. In these courts, in which both civilians and military personnel were tried, convicted persons were fined or sent to city prison at Rockhead in the north end of the peninsula, a prison which replaced the "decayed and ruinous" bridewell on Spring Garden Road in 1860;[30] to the county jail rebuilt in 1865 on Spring Garden Road, which also accommodated those awaiting trial in the supreme court, debtors and condemned criminals; or to the penitentiary located on the Northwest Arm from 1845 to 1880 when penal facilities for the Maritime region were centralized at Dorchester. The magistrate also sent prisoners to the poorhouse if their physical or mental condition warranted it and, as they were established, to various homes and refuges. The military authorities had their own prisons in the Citadel and on Melville Island after 1856, to which both soldiers and man-of-war sailors were sent after court martial convictions.

For other offences, the military joined the civilian offenders in civilian jails, particularly Rockhead where on average one-quarter of all offenders tried in police court ended up. Rockhead's jail population, though fluctuating, did decline in the 1880s, again reflecting the greater opportunities for employment in an industrializing city whose population growth rate slowed to a very low 6.8 per cent during that decade, enabling some of its underclass inhabitants to take up the slack in the labour pool and graduate to a precarious working-class existence (See Table 2).

The transition in the economy was not the only change to affect the Victorian underclass between the 1860s and the 1890s. There were at least four others of major significance. The first was caused by the military authorities whose use of the upper streets very largely determined the char-

21

## Table 1
### Arraignments in Police Court for selected report years, 1862-1900

| Year | Drunkenness &c. | % | Larceny | Assault | Other | Total | % to Rockhead |
|------|-----------------|-----|---------|---------|-------|-------|---------------|
| 1862-3 | 1331 | 62 | 166 | 317 | 347 | 2161 | 22 |
| 1863-4 | 944 | 52 | 143 | 320 | 413 | 1820 | 24 |
| 1865-6 | 1380 | 60 | 143 | 227 | 580 | 2330 | 22 |
| 1872-3 | no report | | | | | | |
| 1874-5 | 1049 | 49 | 126 | 238 | 743 | 2156 | 25 |
| 1876-7 | 981 | 51 | 163 | 193 | 595 | 1932 | 29 |
| 1878-9 | 887 | 42 | 167 | 232 | 816 | 2102 | 25 |
| 1883-4 | 627 | 47 | 170 | 164 | 369 | 1330 | 27 |
| 1886-7 | 472 | 36 | 95 | 165 | 597 | 1329 | 19 |
| 1887-8 | 514 | 42 | 48 | 168 | 518 | 1218 | 15 |
| 1888-9 | 509 | 41 | 83 | 151 | 501 | 1244 | 16 |
| 1892-3 | 634 | 41 | 128 | 196 | 595 | 1553 | 15 |
| 1893-4 | 928 | 46 | 98 | 146 | 845 | 2017 | 20 |
| 1895-6 | 1228 | 58 | 85 | 136 | 673 | 2122 | 34 |
| 1899-00 | 875 | 38 | 212 | 249 | 973 | 2309 | 16 |

Source: City Marshal's Reports (latterly Reports of Chief of Police) in the *Annual Reports* of the City of Halifax.

acter of 'soldiertown,' coterminous as it was with the low-life district. It was the military authorities who chose the streets on the hill adjacent to the Citadel for the leasing of houses for married quarters in the period before sufficient barracks were provided for married soldiers. Similarly, soldiers who married without permission also settled their wives and children in the upper streets close to the North and South Barracks where they could take full advantage of their passes to visit their families. The city missionary lamented the fact in 1862 that clean and pious soldiers' wives were forced by circumstances "to live in disreputable parts of the city" where they were likely to be contaminated.[31] The military authorities also dictated the bounds of off-duty activity by proscribing certain areas of the city. Upper and Lower Water Streets, the focus of Halifax's sailortown, were always out of bounds because of the opportunities they provided for desertion on vessels bound for the United States. In addition, riots, epidemics and brothel excesses led to numerous declarations of out-of-bound areas, most commonly individual houses, in the garrison orders of the second half of the century. In the 1860s, the interdict applied to the

Table 2
Committals to City Prison for selected report years, 1862-1900

| Year (Total) | | Dr. | Lar. | Ass. | Vag. | Dis. | Lewd | Dis. House | Other | Total |
|---|---|---|---|---|---|---|---|---|---|---|
| 1862-3 | m | 124 | 68 | 29 | 23 | 34 | 9 | 5 | 24 | 316+ |
| (469) | f | 52 | 19 | 12 | 33 | 13 | 16 | 3 | 0 | 153 |
| 1863-4 | m | 107 | 78 | 27 | 25 | 11 | — | 2 | 17 | 267 |
| (431) | f | 66 | 12 | 1 | 65 | 2 | 11 | 4 | 3 | 164 |
| 1865-6 | m | 152 | 51 | 27 | 24 | 8 | 6 | — | 13 | 281+ |
| (502) | f | 109 | 16 | 1 | 50 | 8 | 24 | 7 | 6 | 221* |
| 1872-3 | m | 205 | 45 | 24 | 32 | 25 | 10 | 9 | 24 | 374+ |
| (520) | f | 58 | 16 | 2 | 27 | 4 | 10 | 29 | — | 146 |
| 1874-5 | m | 254 | 52 | 35 | 35 | 22 | — | 1 | 1 | 400 |
| (528) | f | 61 | 24 | 6 | 15 | 6 | 10 | 3 | 3 | 128 |
| 1876-7 | m | 248 | 59 | 32 | 19 | 22 | 4 | 2 | 29 | 415 |
| (551) | f | 75 | 13 | 7 | 15 | 2 | 7 | 16 | 1 | 136 |
| 1878-9 | m | 199 | 50 | 48 | 52 | 47 | — | 1 | 20 | 417+ |
| (534) | f | 42 | 8 | 5 | 33 | 6 | 10 | 5 | 8 | 117 |
| 1883-4 | m | 130 | 41 | 16 | 8 | 17 | 4 | 4 | 13 | 233 |
| (360) | f | 78 | 5 | 7 | 9 | 11 | 9 | 7 | 1 | 127 |
| 1886-7 | m | 96 | 29 | 21 | 5 | 2 | — | — | 20 | 173 |
| (254) | f | 44 | 4 | 6 | 6 | 2 | 4 | 11 | 4 | 81 |
| 1887-8 | m | 60 | 17 | 17 | 15 | 7 | 6 | 1 | 5 | 128** |
| (181)*** | f | 32 | 2 | 5 | 4 | 4 | 2 | 3 | 1 | 53$_{xx}$ |
| 1888-9 | m | 87 | 9 | 14 | 9 | 6 | 1 | 1 | 14 | 141 |
| (201) | f | 31 | 2 | 5 | 11 | — | 1 | 7 | 3 | 60 |
| 1892-3 | m | 100 | 23 | 25 | 11 | 10 | 2 | 2 | 6 | 179 |
| (233) | f | 31 | 2 | 4 | 6 | 3 | 1 | 5 | 2 | 54 |
| 1893-4 | m | 208 | 13 | 13 | 28 | 1 | — | 1 | 33 | 297 |
| (399) | f | 52 | 3 | 5 | 13 | — | 5 | 9 | 15 | 102 |
| 1895-6 | m | 336 | 19 | 24 | 9 | 93 | 2 | 1 | 90 | 574$_{xxx}$ |
| (724!) | f | 58 | 8 | 7 | 1 | 34 | — | — | 42 | 150 |
| 1899-00 | m | 225 | 14 | 20 | — | — | — | 1 | 17 | 277 |
| (375) | f | 80 | 1 | 5 | — | 2 | — | — | 10 | 98 |

Key: Dr. = Drunkenness; Lar. = Larceny; Ass. = Assault; Vag. = Vagrancy; Dis. = Disorderly conduct; Lewd = Lewd conduct; Dis. House =Keeping a disorderly, bawdy or "bad" house or house of "ill fame"; *Highest female total (l865-6); $_{xx}$ Lowest female total (1888-9); $_{xxx}$ Highest male total (1895-6); **Lowest male total (1888-9); ***Lowest total (1888-9); !Highest total (1895-6); + Differs from printed report because of incorrect 19th century addition. This also alters the totals.

Source: Reports of City Prison in the *Annual Reports* of the City of Halifax.

notorious Blue Bell tavern on the corner of Barrack and George Streets; in the 1870s it was the turn of the Daring Brig, the Royal Oak, the Emerald Hall, the Cellar and Malta House; in the 1880s soldiers were warned to avoid May's Yard, the Bowery, the Woolwich Arms, the Alder Beer Saloon, and the so-called Reform Club.[32]

Unlike civic attempts to clean up the taverns and brothels, the army's efforts to discipline its privates and NCOs were effective. As a result, military interdicts, enforced by military pickets, also profoundly affected shopkeepers, landlords and soldiers' families. The impact on the traditional soldiertown of the upper streets was decisively felt in the 1870s when interdicts of whole streets for years at a time led to the dispersal of the various disreputable services which depended on soldiers' custom and scattered the suppliers over a wider section of the city. After Barrack Street was closed to the military in 1870, for example, its liquor dealers fled, leaving one newspaper to comment: "The improvement that has taken place in the character of Barrack Street is indicated by the fact, that there is now but one licensed tavern in it."[33] But the proscriptions did not last indefinitely and newly arriving regiments were allowed to see if they could do any better. One soldier claimed in 1880, in defence of his mates against accusations of exerting corrupting influences on the youth of the city:

> The closing of the most notorious of your streets is a wise act and will produce salutary effects. It is not much to the credit of your city to possess such a street. A depraved soldiery is the natural result of unbridled licence. The habitual encouragement and flaunting of vice, the sale of vile drinks, and scanty or no police restrictions. As long as the temptations of drink and sensuality continue to be held out to the soldier by the harpies of these dens of infamy, so long will he foolishly continue to be attracted thereby...[34]

Given the intermittent nature of the interdicts, underclass culture persisted or re-emerged in its accustomed locations whenever the opportunities arose.

During the lulls in low-life commercial activities, precipitated by the military edicts, Halifax's civic reformers, constituting the second agency of change, moved in to try to hasten the transformation of the upper streets from rough to respectable. The transformation of Barrack Street owed as much to private development as to specific measures endorsed by the city fathers. Indeed, the grand jury refused to take effective measures to reform the street in 1883 when encouraged by the presiding judge.[35] Between the 1870s and 1890s, however, the street acquired a quite different flavour as a result of the erection of several substantial brick edifices: the Halifax Academy, the Visiting Dispensary, the Fire Engine House, the Jost Mission, the Salvation Army Barracks and Robert Taylor's shoe factory. Undoubtedly public feeling against underclass Barrack Street facilitated its transformation. By late century, with the problem in Barrack Street in check, attention centred on Albemarle, Grafton and City Streets.

The campaign to clean up the upper streets was encouraged by various reform-minded mayors and aldermen. It was spearheaded by the police force which underwent reorganization in 1864, when the separate day and night watches were united under the direction of the city marshal. This position was held for over thirty years (1861-1893) by Garret Cotter, an Irish immigrant who joined the police force in 1841, the year of the city's incorporation. With his deputy, detective, six sergeants and between thirty and forty dollar-a-day constables, Cotter maintained order in the city, subject only to the oversight of the police committee of city council. Whereas Irish Catholics were well represented on the force, blacks were not eligible for police jobs.[36]

The assault on the upper streets did not stop with the revamping of the police force. Part of the attack on the subculture of the area was to rename the streets as though doing so would magically reform them. Barrack was officially proclaimed the southern extension of Brunswick Street in 1872, though the names Barrack and South Brunswick also continued for many years to be used to distinguish the blocks opposite the Citadel from Brunswick Street proper to the north of Jacob Street. City Street was renamed Maynard about the same time. In the early twentieth century Albemarle Street became Market Street. Unsuccessful though it was in changing the character of 'slumdom,' the renaming marked a significant symbolic break with the past.

The moral crusaders who attacked the upper streets with some success were the temperance folk, the third force for change in the period. They were organized by 1885 into at least twenty-one temperance societies in the Halifax-Dartmouth area.[37] The high proportion of drunkenness cases in police court and the degree to which liquor sales and consumption were demonstrably associated with prostitution, destitution and family violence justified their campaign to interfere with the drinking habits of the lower classes. They also deplored the effect of the rum shops of Barrack and Albemarle Streets on the welfare of the soldiery when Crimean heroes were to be seen staggering along the streets or "laying full length in gutters or on the muddy street."[38] When the garrison swelled to 5000 during the American Civil War, the extent of street drunkenness shocked the temperance advocates, as did the number of deaths among soldiers ascribed to the imbibing of poisonous liquor.[39] The city did not seem to have changed much from the 1790s when the Reverend James MacGregor of Pictou observed that the business of one half of the town of Halifax was to sell rum and the other half to drink it. Another commentator claimed in 1862 that: "So abundant is liquor sold in various forms of strong drink in Halifax, that the City is nothing less than a great big Rum shop. Rum on the right and rum on the left; rum before you, rum behind you, and rum all round you!"[40] City missionary Archibald Morton counted sixty liquor shops in Albemarle Street in 1859, which had increased to seventy-three by 1863, most of which he said were frequented by people of "ill fame."[41]

The temperance campaign tried to stop publicans from obtaining licences by raising the cost and subjecting each licence to a plebiscite. The teetotallers also agitated to improve the enforcement of the city by-laws relating to licensing hours and other regulations and lobbied to put a stop to the illegal sale of liquor. As a result, by the mid-sixties, applications for licences required endorsement by neighbours, a measure which was made to conform to the wider provincial pattern in 1874 when a two-thirds majority was necessary in the relevant polling district. The provincial act of 1864 concerning Halifax was designed to facilitate the prosecution of unlicensed premises but the cases were difficult to prove unless the police caught the illicit vendors in the act. The prosecution had to prove "that bottles, or decanters, or tumblers, or glasses, or other vessels, which are usually employed for holding and using liquor, were found in and upon the premises of such accused party, and had been recently used." It was not really until liquor licence inspectors set out to frame people in the 1880s that such legislation was given any teeth.[42]

Another object of the temperance campaign was to strip the tavern of its attraction as a social amenity and thus discourage lower-class customers. Residents of tenements, barracks or vessels sought out the tavern for its warmth and conviviality and as the setting for their plebian pastimes. There was no scope in their own humble abodes or pinched pocket books for such a luxury. The tavern was as important to them as the rich man's drawing room, well stocked with cut glass decanters, was to him. Temperance advocates did not see it that way though one leading evangelical, the Reverend Foster Almon, curate of St. George's Anglican Church, admitted in 1868 that "he found that young men did not frequent dram shops for the love of liquor only," but also for "the love of sociability that gathered around it."[43] Legislators attempted to prevent publicans from providing forms of entertainment in their drinking shops. Gambling had been made illegal as early as the 1830s. In 1865 skittles and other pub games, music and dancing were added to the list of prohibitions. None of the restrictions was effective for long. All of the dance halls in Grafton Street, for example, were closed in the summer of 1883 after an agreement among the tavernkeepers was encouraged by the city authorities. But they soon reopened.[44] The results of the destruction of the Victorian tavern in the liquor legislation of 1886, which allowed drinking only in bona fide hotels by hotel residents, or in people's private dwellings, were the proliferation of bootleggers and increased solitary drinking by outcasts in the streets, alleyways, wharves, yards and cemeteries.

Last but not least, another force for change in the upper streets was provided by the churches. In common with their counterparts elsewhere, the major Protestant churches set out in the wake of the bible and missionary society impulses of the early nineteenth century to save souls, including those of the locally benighted. In Halifax the mission to the unchurched did not get under way until the middle of the century when the strengthening of the evangelical wing of the Church of England, a denomination which commanded the adherence of one-quarter of the resident population, to say nothing of the military, facilitated the full co-operation of Anglican clergymen with the ministers of the Presbyterian, Methodist and Baptist churches. Drawing on their experience of working together in such city-based, anti-Catholic organizations as the Nova Scotia Bible Society, the Micmac Missionary Society, and the Protestant Alliance, as well as in more secular organizations like the temperance societies, they established interdenominational and later denominational city missions. Designed to tackle the spiritual destitution, the missions inevitably confronted the poverty, illiteracy and immorality of the denizens of the upper streets. To the evangelicals Barrack Street was "one of the darkest spots in Halifax."[45] The missionaries, aided by numerous men from the sponsoring churches, invaded "the very worst and most destitute localities of the city."[46] Street preaching in Albemarle Street took Christian gentlemen into "the centre of one of the worst regions, morally, in the town."[47] The missions also advanced the cause of temperance, especially after mission houses had been erected on Barrack and City Streets in 1869 in which temperance meetings could be held and pledges taken.[48]

Halifax was, however, also a Catholic city, Catholics comprising not less than 40 per cent of the population for most of the second half of the nineteenth century. For social activists the underlying division of the city between Catholics and Protestants posed a problem. As in so many cities in the English-speaking world, Protestant missionaries in Halifax found themselves confronted not just by beggars, prostitutes, vagrants, paupers, widows, juvenile delinquents and the destitute jobless, but also by the fact that all of them were overwhelmingly Catholic. While Protestants could argue with some justification that most underclass Catholics, like simi-

27

larly placed Protestants, were sectarian only in name, the evangelical bias of many rescue projects filled the Catholic élite with unease and encouraged the development of parallel organizations. For example, by mid-century Catholics had their own temperance societies, the archbishop of Halifax claiming in 1868 that "temperance institutions ought to be considered the handmaid of religion."[49] The presence in the city after 1849 of Sisters of Charity and Sisters of the Sacred Heart provided the woman-power for establishing Catholic orphanages, refuges and hospitals. Some Protestant-Catholic co-operation was possible in a city where the public school system had accommodated separate schools within one common administrative structure. There was also the example of united efforts to help the poor through the Visiting Dispensary which managed to follow a non-denominational approach on the ground that "diseases and calamities of life are not sectarian, but the common lot of our fallen humanity."[50] But sectarianism, like racism, was always close to the surface in middle-class Halifax.

With the activist churches, temperance advocates, civic reformers and military authorities ranged against the underclass, its members frequently found themselves arraigned in the dock on charges of drunkenness, liquor licence violation, prostitution or vagrancy. As the court reporters attested:

> Day after day they have before them the same scenes of wretchedness and woe, the fruits of vice and intemperance,—and are enabled to perceive that the occupants of the prison dock are but types of the previous occupants and of those who will succeed them as surely as the sun rises. It is impossible for a correct mind to gaze on the prisoners as with dishevelled hair, bruised faces, and the tattered garments, they are crowded into the box, without feeling astonished at the depth to which human degradation attains; and how fearfully men and women can fall from the estate in which they are created. It is no unfrequent sight to see huddled together at one time both sexes and all ages and colors—first the grey-headed old man who has been so long accustomed to alcoholic stimulant as to have become a debased victim to its power,—then the elderly woman who has lost all sense of shame and descended to the lowest existence, while beside her sits a young girl not yet out of her teens who has become hardened in lewdness and dissipation, and is totally irreclaimable. Indeed it is these latter who receive their sentences most unmurmeringly, as if it were immaterial to them where they should spend their days.[51]

And it is to the frequenters of the court and the jail we now turn our attention.

# PART I

## RAISED IN ROCKHEAD.

## DIED IN THE POORHOUSE.

North End City Mission *Report*, 1896-7. (J.J. Stewart Collection, Dalhousie University)

Rockhead Prison. (Public Archives of Nova Scotia)

# 1
# RAISED IN ROCKHEAD: DIED IN THE POORHOUSE

The Wickedest Woman in Halifax: Her name is Margaret Howard. Her history is known to every policeman. Time and again has she been before the Police Court for drunkenness, fighting, and general misdemeanors. Time and again has she attempted to end her miserable existence by committing suicide in the cells. Time and again she has been sent to Rockhead prison. Time and again has the Court given her "a chance" by allowing her to go free on her promising to reform. All in vain. On Friday last she indulged in a drunken fight, for which she was taken to the Police Station. During the night she tied a piece of her dress around her neck, and this time almost accomplished her object of destroying herself. A policeman discovered her when her dirty face was blacker than usual, and it seemed that in a few minutes she would have ceased to live. She was arraigned at the Police Court on Saturday. Once more she received "a chance," and was discharged, on this condition—that if again brought up she would be sent to prison for one year. Doubtless you think, gentle reader, that this warning had the desired effect, and that she went forth resolved to do better in the future. You are mistaken. On Saturday night she again fell into the hands of the police, and to-day she will, according to the condition of the last discharge, be sentenced to serve one year in the city prison.[1]

This journalist's account of Margaret Howard's delinquency is an accurate, if disparaging, one. A native of St. John's, Newfoundland, Howard first appeared in Halifax police court in June 1863 at the age of twenty charged with drunkenness and went to Rockhead Prison for thirty days instead of paying the optional $2 fine. She served three more sentences of ten, fifteen and thirty days in 1863 for the same offence. Between 1864 and 1873 Howard was committed to city prison thirty-five more times. Thereafter her jail record continues until 1879 and includes thirteen additional committals. She served a total of fifty-two sentences in city prison. Among the literate population of the city who read the daily press and the illiterate down-and-outs and prurient spectators who thronged the daily police court, Howard had a reputation for being "a notorious member of the demi-monde." As early as 1866 she was described as "an old offender." She was also called an "unfortunate" and in 1869 her alleged wickedness was bemoaned in the Victorian cliché that she was "young in years but old in crime."[2]

Like the overwhelming majority of repeat prisoners, over half of her committals were for drunkenness and drinking-related offences. She shared with many of the other drunks what might be considered the ultimate indignity of being arrested while lying drunk in the street. Given her apparent coarseness—she was imprisoned at least four times for drunkenness combined with profane or obscene language—she was probably not particularly ashamed or embarrassed about her street drunkenness and alley prostitution; but she did revolt when she was incarcerated overnight in the filthy, verminous police cells beneath the city court. One form of protest was attempted suicide—twice in 1869, twice in 1872, once more in 1874 and again in 1879. She came close to achieving her object a couple of times but she also succeeded on three of the six occasions in eliciting enough sympathy from the magistrate to secure her discharge in court.

The other form of protest in which she indulged, regularly favoured by outcasts, was window smashing. Her arraignment on one such charge was immortalized in court reporter's doggerel:

Stipendiary Magistrate: "What did she do?"
Samuel Young: (singing)
    "The wind was blowing in the evening
    The snow was falling o'er the town,
    The drinkers o'er their pots were adrowsing
    T'was then Mag broke my windows in."

Mag:
> "His daughter threw water on my face
> She called me too a Rockhead Bird
> I raised my hand to break her nose
> T'was thus the crash of glass occurred."

Stipendiary Magistrate:
> "You often drink and break the laws
> You give the bobbies trouble too
> Thus you will see that with good cause
> I fine you $2 or 20 days."[3]

Unlike many of her contemporary recidivists, Howard appears not to have deliberately sought out the prison as a refuge. In court she "begged to be allowed to go free and promised to reform."[4] Police court reports indicate that the magistrate was not unwilling to give her a chance to mend her ways, at least from time to time. Four days after her release in August 1864, having served a thirty-day sentence for drunkenness, she was again arraigned in court on a similar charge. She was given a conditional discharge, but it took the form of banishment. The condition was that she get out of town within twenty-four hours or face a ninety-day sentence. Perhaps she did leave town temporarily on this occasion because she was not in jail again until October of the following year. By contrast, in 1868, she ignored her conditional discharge within the space of two days. Arraigned for drunkenness, disorderliness and fighting in the street on 11 April, she was threatened with twelve months in Rockhead when she next fell into the hands of the police. On the 13th, the magistrate kept his word and imprisoned her on a vagrancy charge after she was picked up for wandering drunk in the street. On another occasion, after one of her suicide attempts in 1872, Howard obtained her release (at least for a week) on the ground that she had made an engagement to go into domestic service.

The one sure way to avoid imprisonment in the mid-nineteenth century was to pay a fine. Apparently Howard was able to pay a dollar fine in court in May 1866 after she had been arrested in a yard in the company of marines. Early releases from jail could also be purchased even if no optional fine had been specified in court. Howard served slightly over three months of a twelve-month vagrancy sentence in 1873 when somebody settled her account and she went free. In the context of her jail career as a whole, the flexibility Howard enjoyed as a result of optional fines was very limited indeed. Slightly more latitude was provided by the custom of reducing sentences. It was normal practice to remit portions of sentences, even without official pardons. Indeed it appears that every pretext was used in Halifax to put prisoners back into circulation as soon as possible.

Howard was released on an official order only eleven days into a ninety-day sentence in May 1866. She also escaped the full brunt of most of her twelve-month sentences for vagrancy even without such intervention. She served less than three months on two occasions in 1867 and 1869, only four months on three other occasions—in 1875, 1878 and 1879, less than six in 1870 and terms of six months in 1872 and nine in 1873. Only two twelve-month sentences were served to the extent of eleven months, which was the normal duration of twelve-month sentences. One of the early releases, that in 1879, was not an unconditional one. She was sent to nurse smallpox patients at the contagious diseases hospital, a form of employment given to a number of female repeat offenders during the 1860s and 1870s.

In a period before there was any organized attention to the welfare of ex-prisoners, incorrigibles like Howard could not expect much improvement in their prospects on their release. All we know about Howard is that she had a brother and that his willingness to take charge of her was deemed sufficient to secure her release from prison. The jail registers occasionally specify the disposition of the releasee. On one occasion in 1866, for example, Howard was given over to a member of the Cogswell family as a servant. This may have been Isabella Binney Cogswell, one of the city's leading social activists. On another occasion, in 1867, Howard left jail to go to Boston. Since she remained at large only one day, the travel plans obviously went awry.

Margaret Howard had somewhat limited experience of two other forms of release from custody. One was prison escape. Rockhead could be described as a minimum security prison. For most inmates pursuing work on the grounds, absconding was easy. When in 1869 Howard ran away from the pond to which she had been sent to fetch water with fellow prisoner Hannah Baker (1864-73:32)*, she was soon arrested and sent back to complete her term. The other possible route to freedom was through illness. Afflicted prisoners were dispatched to the poorhouse, and, for many, the cycle of prison to poorhouse, poorhouse to prison was inexorable and ended ultimately in death in the poorhouse. Howard was referred to the poorhouse a couple of times by the authorities, at least once because they thought sending her to prison did no good, but she appears not to have spent any significant amount of time there. She thoroughly detested Rockhead but the poorhouse may have been just as unattractive to her. She declared in 1872 that she "would sooner be dead than always going to prison."[5] Yet to jail she went on average three times a year for seventeen years until she disappears from the extant records. Her case was considered

*Number of incarcerations in Rockhead Prison between 1864 and 1873.

"a very melancholy one, illustrating the depths of female degradation."[6]

With the exception of frequent offenders like Margaret Howard, petty criminals appear only fleetingly in the mid-Victorian historical record. In Halifax, certainly, the vast majority of imprisoned individuals went to jail only once, whether they were local residents or transients such as sailors, prospectors, Indians and military personnel. Between 1 January 1864 and 31 December 1873, 1200 or 65 per cent of the 1840 prisoners were one-time visitors to Rockhead, accounting for one-quarter of the 4749 committals. In contrast, Margaret Howard and the other 91 of her ilk, with their 1506 committals amounting to almost one-third of the total, constituted five per cent of the prison population. Accordingly the repeat offenders must have exerted a disproportionate influence on the formation of popular attitudes and public policy.[7] They were drawn from the ranks of the permanent civilian population, especially from those who made their homes and livings in the disreputable upper streets of the city. While it would be unwarranted to assume that an analysis of 92 repeat offenders would inform us about petty offenders in general, we can use this specialized population to gain insights into nasty, brutish and often short lives and into attitudes towards what were considered to be the 'dangerous classes.' This analysis is designed to give individual human experience a chance to predominate over the aggregate statistics favoured by those social historians who have included minor offenders in the broad sweep of their pen.[8]

The social history of crime and criminal justice has recently tended to emphasize two themes: first, attitudes towards crime and punishment and the administrative reforms of institutions which grew out of those attitudes; second, the nature of criminality, particularly of serious crime and long-term trends as revealed in case studies of offences in particular localities, including computer-based, statistical profiles of criminal populations. Both these approaches have their strengths but it must be recognized that they are heavily weighted in favour of the theoretical, the institutional and the statistical; they are also predominantly concerned with the view from the top down. Little is revealed about the criminals themselves. Among offenders, only the 'social' criminals, bent on resisting authority or protecting customary rights, have attracted historical inquiry. Yet to study popular resistance and civil strife at the neglect of more prosaic 'common' offences is to overlook the delinquents who kept the criminal courts and the prisons in business.[9]

A compilation which begins from the bottom up with a file of biographies of individual offenders raises important questions about gender, race, age and neighbourhood in addition to providing relatively predictable data on ethnicity, religion and occupation. As Table 3 indicates, the recidivist population was made up of 66 per cent natives of the Atlantic region, over 35 per cent of the 92 claiming to be Halifax-born.[10] Another 26 per cent came from Ireland. Twice as many repeat offenders were Catholic as Protestant but the erratic way in which they reported their religious affiliation casts doubt on its significance for them. The over-representation of Catholics is not surprising in a city where the most recent immigrants and a large proportion of the military, with whom the locals interacted, were Catholics of Irish origin. Whereas not all those claiming to have come from Ireland gave their denomination as Catholic, the religion of the blacks was, with one exception, Protestant and all of them expressed loyalty to the Baptist Church, at least on the majority of occasions.

Occupational identifications are loose and inconsistent. Only occasionally did the frequent residents of Rockhead Prison have jobs of any kind. When they did report jobs, the designations were often more descriptive than real. Two of the men, Patrick Cody (1864-73:28) and John Noonan (1864-73:14), for example, were described as fishermen but this categorizing was more a function of their places of origin in the Halifax County outports of Herring Cove and Prospect than an accurate indication of gainful employment. Others appear to have tried their hands at just about anything. Andrew Doyle, who went to city prison twenty-nine times between 1863 and 1874, made an occasional living from at least six different types of skilled, semi-skilled, and unskilled jobs as well as from self-employment. He was also described on other occasions as a pauper or as having "no trade."[11] The same woman was sometimes identified as a servant, sometimes as a prostitute, sometimes as "no trade," categories which reflect the combination of women's restricted opportunities. Others like William Drummond (1867-73:18) and Thomas Norbury (Norberry) (1868-73:9) were listed as British soldiers but the army was their former employer. In Halifax, ex-soldiers may have been the most difficult group to absorb into regular employment, as Gareth Stedman Jones has suggested for veterans in industrial London.[12] As we shall see, people who were frequently institutionalized were on the fringes of the casual labour market and seldom able to cope with its demands.

Data on gender, race, age and neighbourhood are more revealing. Forty-three of the 92 were women, a large proportion given conventional wisdom concerning the numerical insignificance of the female prison population. To explain their high representation we have to understand that relatively they were poorer than male offenders and therefore usually unable to pay the optional fine awarded in court. We need to realize too that many of them were prostitutes in a period when prostitution was very

## Table 3
## Profile of 92 repeat offenders

| | | Males 49 | | Females 43 | |
|---|---|---|---|---|---|
| Age on first committal to jail | | | | | |
| | under 19 | 7 | | 10 | |
| | 20-29 | 20 | | 19 | |
| | 30-39 | 12 | | 7 | |
| | 40-49 | 3 | | 2 | |
| | 50-59 | 4 | | 1 | |
| | 60-69 | 3 | | 1 | |
| | unknown | - | | 3 | |
| Literacy | yes | 9 | | 3 | |
| | no | 6 | | 7 | |
| | unknown | 34 | | 33 | |
| Race | | 46W | 3B | 34W | 9B |
| Place of origin | Halifax city | 20 | 2 | 7 | 4 |
| | Halifax Co. | 2 | 1 | 1 | 4 |
| | Sydney | 1 | | 3 | |
| | rural NS | 3 | | 2 | 1 |
| | Saint John | 2 | | 4 | |
| | St. John's | 1 | | 2 | |
| | PEI | 1 | | 1 | |
| | Ireland | 13 | | 11 | |
| | England | 2 | | 2 | |
| | USA | 1 | | 1 | |
| Religion | Catholic | 33 | - | 27 | 1 |
| | Protestant | 13 | 3 | 7 | 8 |

Source: Rockhead City Prison Registers and poor house, hospital, stipendiary magistrate's records, censuses etc.
Note: No information on literacy is available until the stipendiary magistrate's records begin in 1880. Much of the other information is reported erratically by the defendants. At least ten claimed to have been both Protestant and Catholic at various times and when Protestant denominations are reported, a similar inconsistency occurs.

openly practised and routinely prosecuted. Women comprised 46.5 per cent of the recidivist population compared with 36 per cent of the total jail population, striking evidence of the fact that women in trouble with the law had fewer options and less mobility than men.

Twelve of the 92 had black skin. Since blacks are recorded as three per cent of the city's civilian population, they are over-represented among repeat prisoners at 13 per cent. Unlike the women, their rate of recidivism coincides with their general rate of imprisonment, 12.5 per cent. However, 58 per cent of the black jail population were women, as compared to 24.5 per cent of the white. This reflects the considerable over-representation of black female prisoners. While this may suggest racial discrimination by the police, the subculture of the upper streets itself was an inter-racial one involving more co-operative than hostile interaction between blacks and whites. Black and white women had particularly close ties as prostitutes and heterosexual living arrangements were often miscegenous. Catherine Shea, who went to jail twenty-six times between 1864 and 1871, provides an example of a white woman who married a black man, William Valentine, a wood sawyer. Her marriage in 1872 appears to have ended her jail career but not her drunkenness. White repeat offenders continued late into the century to demonstrate inter-racial solidarity in court. In 1889 Thomas Norbury testified in favour of a "coloured man" charged with selling liquor without a licence.[13] In contrast, the response of the authorities to blacks was expressed in overtly racist terms though the descriptions which embellished unofficial court reports were only marginally more offensive than they were for whites. When William Dixon (Dickson) (1865-9:12) was arraigned in court in September 1868, the reporter described the scene after the defendant's name was called:

> The top of a woolly head appeared above the bar, followed soon by a black face, a pair of shoulders and a dirty-looking jacket. Out of this combination the word "here" proceeded, and William Dickson was charged with stealing a pair of boots. Produced. William said at once "Yes dem's dem, I took dem." The case being thus clear, although decidedly dark, William was informed that the city would require his assistance in the financial way to the extent of $4 or his services in the stone mansion at Rockhead for 40 days.[14]

Both black and white defendants, ridiculed before the world for appearance and manners, lied when they were asked their age in court. Some of them reported their ages with an erraticism to be expected of people without a modern respect for time and with little in the way of formal education. Others may have been expressing their resistance to authority through their contempt for the court. Jane Fuller (1864-73:11) claimed in 1868 that she did not know how old she was but that she thought she was over eighteen. The clerk reported her age as forty. Elizabeth Johnston (1864-73:43) said she was "sweet sixteen," some twenty years into her court appearances while Mary Slattery (1864-73:28) adopted the opposite approach and gave her age as eighty when she was no more than twenty-three.[15] Despite the attempted deceptions, repeat prisoners were mostly young like the detected criminal population as a whole. For the decade under consideration here, over one-half of the 92 were in their teens and twenties when they first went to jail. They were not therefore primarily old men and women worn out by depravity. They were young people in the prime of life. Years earlier the older ones in this group, like Patrick Cody and Julia Kelly (1864-72:12), had begun the same way. For them life was characterized by an inability to shake off the delinquency of their youth.

With respect to neighbourhood, the offences tended to occur in four major types of locality. First, and by far the most prominent, were the tavern and brothel streets of Barrack, Albemarle and City. These were the residential areas for drifters, outcasts and the bulk of the disrespectable poor. While many of the offences committed here took place on the street, others occurred in unoccupied houses, the use of which underscores the poverty of people desperate to secure shelter against the cold. Some of the occupied buildings in which arrests occurred are identified by name. The Blue Bell tavern on the corner of Barrack and George Streets, prominent in the annals of the city as a scene of rowdiness and demi-monde activity was, not surprisingly, a well-frequented local dive. Ellen Shefrow (Shaffro(w)) (1864-66:6) and Ann Strong (1864-68:9) testified in court in 1863 against a band of thieves operating from the Blue Bell. In 1866 Ann Strong's association with the Blue Bell again brought her before the court, this time as the complainant in a successful case against John Baker who assaulted her in the tavern. Josephine Buskins (1865-73:12), a black woman, was found guilty in 1865 along with two of her black associates of keeping a disorderly house and house of ill-fame in the Blue Bell. Catherine Dixon (1864-66:7), another black, was convicted for being drunk in the Blue Bell in 1866. Margaret Howard, too, frequented the Blue Bell and was also brought up in 1866 for being drunk and fighting in the infamous establishment.[16]

Second, the police rounded up offenders, especially in gangs, in the common land around the residential areas of the city. Tower Woods and the North and South Commons were particularly popular locations. Point Pleasant Woods and the slopes of Citadel Hill were also prominent. Homeless people often lived rough in these open spaces. In the spring of 1875, the police arrested in the Public Gardens on the South Common a group consisting of soldiers and four women. Three of these—Hannah Baker, Bridget McNamara (1865-73:21), and Julia Martin (1864-73:30)—were recidivists. They were discovered at night in "an encampment or 'shake-down,' " consisting of "quilts, mattresses, etc., in the winding recesses of the tangled labyrinth."[17]

The third major locality consisted of the commercial areas of the city—the wharves, vessels and markets. The wharves of this major port attracted men looking for legitimate work as labourers and scavengers who lived off the refuse of the docks. John Dunn(e), for example, who went to jail forty-one times in the ten-year period, was arrested in 1865 on Stayner's Wharf and on another occasion on the Commercial Wharf. When arrested in the dockside area in 1866, he was described variously as a labourer and beggar about the wharves. In November 1868 John Green (1864-69:13) made his sixth court appearance in fourteen months, this time to answer to a charge of stealing clothing from the brigantine *Eclipse*.[18] Not surprisingly, the markets were a prime target for petty larceny, especially the meat market located in the Colonial Market building on Argyle Street. John Ryno (Reyno) (1866-73:18) pleaded guilty to stealing a pig from that emporium in March 1865.[19]

The fourth location in which arrests frequently occurred was in the military installations used by the British garrison in Halifax. Here women of the streets fraternized with soldiers engaged in guard or sentry duty, much to the displeasure of the military authorities who routinely gave the women in charge to the civilian authorities. What they called "annoying" the guard probably meant dallying in the cases of Catherine Dryden (1864-73:21), Mary Simons (Symons, Symonds) (1864-72:35), Mary Slattery and Johanna Power (1864-73:35). Some of the women were actually turfed out of the barracks, including Catherine Shea in 1865, Catherine Stephens (Stevens) (1864-73:21) in 1867 and Elizabeth Masters (1869-72:9) in 1869.[20]

For the most part, then, the locations were highly visible ones in very central areas. A combination of offences committed in public and a general lack of privacy in the lives of the underclass would tend to suggest that detection, that hoary old chestnut of historians of crime, occurred at a high rate for the prison repeaters. These general characteristics serve as a background to a discussion of three aspects of the careers of the 92: the nature of their crimes and criminality; the characteristics of prosecution and punishment; and the features of life inside prison compared with that outside.

I

To appreciate the human frailties of the period, it is important to relate the nature of the offence to the life of the offender. Consequently, an analysis of people as numbers without names is almost certain to distort the evidence. To know the offenders, individual biographies are essential, and while such personal histories are impossible to compile for a statistically random sample of the general jail population, they are available for the highly visible, widely publicized recidivist population. In this respect, the information available for Margaret Howard with which we began is average. Fortunately there are other offenders whom we can place within the context of their families or other close associates and follow, like detectives, to their sometimes brutal, always ignominious ends.[21] The collective portrait attempted here allows for a description of individual behaviour while at the same time illustrating the general patterns which emerge.

Using the jail record as the base, our most comprehensive knowledge relates to the total number of sentences. While the ten-year snapshot used as the special focus for this study means that some served as few as five terms and others as many as thirty, the average number of jail terms between 1 January 1864 and 31 December 1873 for the twenty-seven of the 92 who were active through the whole decade was twenty-six.* Given the frequency with which the 92 went to jail—and even more frequently appeared in court—many of them acquired, like Margaret Howard, contemporary reputations preserved in the literary sources of the day which help us to capture their personalities. At least fifty-four of them were noted in the historical record for the quantity and quality of their criminality. The most common and neutral epithets were "frequent" or "old offender." Others were "hardened," "notorious," "abandoned," "dangerous," "rough," "bad," "brutal." Contemporaries thought that Robert Joint (1864-70:15) was "probably not surpassed in rowdyism by any other rough in the city." Eliza Munroe (Monrow, Monro) (1864-66:12) was described as "one of the worst prostitutes on the hill." James Prendergast (Pendergast, Pendergrast) (1869-73:13) graduated from being a "notorious rowdy" in 1872 to "a notorious Rockhead bird" in 1885. Andrew Doyle had become "a beastly incorrigible" by 1882. Some of them were also well known by their nicknames: Curly (Cornelius) Ford (1866-73:20) and Succeed (Elizabeth) Johnston, for example. Still others collected occasional colourful expletives from their associates. In 1865 Ellen Bond (1864-73:14) successfully prosecuted two women for calling her a "dirty, drunken strumpet and a drunken bitch," as they passed her door. Bridget McNamara

*Most available sources have been canvassed for the years 1854-1884, and in some selected cases longer, for additional biographical information when dealing with individuals, while maintaining the decadal focus for the group.

took a female "friend" to court for assault in 1867 after she allegedly called her a "rotten whore" and struck her in the face.[22]

Sixty-two of the infamous 92 went to jail 50 per cent or more of the time in the decade for drunkenness and drinking-related offences. Four of them—Thomas Drew (1868-73:12), Eliza Freeman (1864-66:7), James Hogan (1867-73:12) and John Rannage (1872-73:5)—went to jail for no other cause. In 1864, at least fifteen of the repeat offenders were, like Margaret Howard, picked up on the street in a comatose state. In addition, Andrew Doyle, James Kennedy (1864-70:11), Michael Kelly (1864-68:10), Charles McInnis (McEnnis, MacGuinnes) (1868-73: 12) and Ann Wilson (Wilsonhome) (1865-70:11) were each reported from time to time to be suffering from *delirium tremens*.[23] Chronic alcoholism took several of them to the hospital: Doyle and McInnis, as well as Robert Hamilton (1870-73:10), Thomas Kenney (1867-73:12), Henrietta McKegney (McKeagney) (1864-70:19), Patrick Magher (Meagher) (1865-73:15) and John Rannage.[24] Except for the establishment of various short-lived refuges, down-and-out alcoholics were not given much special care in nineteenth-century Halifax. Not surprisingly, the combination of drink, despair and disease drove a number of them, like Margaret Howard, to attempt suicide in jail. Henrietta McKegney in 1868, Mary Ford (1864-73:25) in 1869, Ann Wilson in 1870, Bridget McNamara in 1873 and Robert Hamilton in 1873 and again in 1875 all attempted to strangle themselves.[25] Bridget McNamara, who, in addition to her 1873 attempt, tried to kill herself on the street in 1874 by smothering herself in a snow bank, was treated in hospital in those same two years, not coincidentally perhaps, for venereal disease.[26] Described in the hospital records as a prostitute, Bridget McNamara began her jail career in 1863 at the age of twelve. At the age of fourteen she was sentenced to one year in the newly established juvenile reformatory wing of the city prison.

While Bridget McNamara's first two adolescent misdemeanours involved larceny, her frequent incarcerations after 1870 were mostly for prostitution under the charges of lewd conduct, common vagrancy and living in a house of ill-fame. She was described as spending "half her time in Rockhead, half 'camping out' with soldiers." Prostitution was a prominent offence in this period. At least thirty-eight of the forty-three women were imprisoned for prostitution-related offences but they were not primarily in jail for such transgressions. Indeed, we must place prostitution within the wider context of disrespectable behaviour that occurred in the rough neighbourhoods. It was one of the illicit business activities for which the upper streets were noted but, unlike the drinking establishments, the sale of sexual services was unregulated by licence and therefore liable to entirely capricious prosecution. Whether they were arrested individually or in groups after brothel raids, prostitutes were treated in the court very much like drunks and vagrants. But it was as prostitutes that female offenders became the target of moral reformers who established a number of refuges for "fallen" women which are described in Chapter Six. Whatever success rates such institutions claimed, we can be fairly certain that hardened offenders sent to them like Eliza Cahill (1867-73:13), Mary Clifford (1864-67:6), Catherine Dryden, Mary Ford, Eliza Freeman, Ann Mahoney (1864-73:27), Henrietta McKegney, Catherine Shea and Ellen Shefrow were among those reported in anonymous rescue statistics as having returned to their former way of life.

Prostitutes are the most readily identifiable members of the subculture of the upper streets. The amount of interaction within the prostitute-recidivist group itself is significant. At least thirty-five of the women, sometimes only once, but, for a significant majority, on many occasions, went to court in the company with one another. With few options in life and much privation, deviant women could at least rely on a degree of companionship, arising from their work and neighbourhood solidarity, which seems to have thrived as much inside the jail as it did on the outside. The network was inter-racial and inter-generational; it included sisters and room-mates who were often also cell-mates.

Apart from drunkenness and prostitution-related offences, the other charges for which the 92 frequently went to jail were petty larceny and various forms of assault and fighting. Since these were crimes which did harm to others, they were more directly threatening to local society. Only twenty-one of the 92 failed to become involved in one or both of these more aggressive types of offences during the decade. Fifty-two were in court for larcenies, fifty-three for assaults.

Most of the police court cases for stealing by recidivists pertained to items of food or clothing which suggests that need often determined the larcenies. Since we are not dealing with professional burglars, but rather, 'sneak' thieves, much of the activity was confined to the upper streets where there was only a limited scope for stealing. A few larcenies involved small amounts of money and bottles of liquor. Most frequent were the watch-and-chain robberies, a timepiece being a valuable plebian possession. The motives for most of the seemingly trivial larcenies can only be surmised. Julia Kelly stole papers from the mayor's office, which may have been sheer perversity on her part. Others could not resist temptation. James Riely (Reily, Riley) (1866-73:23), for example, took three pairs of cricket boots from the Common in 1871. Others stole to resolve differences with cell-mates. David Fowler (1869-73:13), "an old and notorious thief," took a rubber coat from fellow recidivist James Smith (1864-68:8). Julia Kelly purloined Mary Patterson's (1864-71:10) cap and handkerchief. Apart from Kelly, who received a sentence with hard labour for her lack of deference to the mayor, we have only a few cases of people stealing from their social superiors. Elizabeth Masters stole $18 from her employer in 1869; Michael McGrath (1864-70:12) tried to keep his advance wages without doing the required work in George Lang's brickyard in 1865.[27] Several of the men, such as James Riely in 1866, were charged with robberies serious enough to be transferred to the city criminal court or the supreme court. James Smith was sent to the supreme court after examination in police court in 1864 on a charge of stealing two watches. Denis Hurly (1864-73:12), a man distinguished by a hare-lip, was sent after a jury trial to the provincial penitentiary for two years in 1865 for burglary. In 1866 Michael Kelly spent more than two months in the county jail before being acquitted in a supreme court trial for burglary.[28] On the whole, however, the evidence both in respect to crimes against property and other offences would tend to support the view of historians that petty offenders did not generally graduate to committing indictable offences.

This is not to say that recidivists did not commit serious offences; certainly they were serious for their victims. While more through luck than judgment none of the 92 ended up as murderers, some became more violent over the years. They assaulted the authority figures they regularly encountered in the streets and other public places. Most frequent were their disputes with the police. Cornelius Ford, a regular bobby-basher, was sentenced to six months in the penitentiary in 1867 for attempting to stab a policeman. Violence against British soldiers and Royal Navy sailors pitted the highly visible members of the military against the equally identifiable repeat offenders. In 1869 Johanna Linehan (Linnehan) (1865-70:11) badly beat a soldier of the 16th regiment with a bottle in a bawdy house in City Street. Elizabeth Johnston had several assaults in her record, one of which consisted of a blow to a soldier which resulted in his death in the same street. She was acquitted in 1872 after a supreme court trial. Catherine Shea, Catherine Stephens, George Deminas (1869-73:7) and Mary Simons were each arrested on various occasions for assaulting soldiers.[29]

Other serious assaults were attacks by men against women and children. Andrew Doyle beat up his sister, sister-in-law and mother before he criminally assaulted a little girl in 1882, a crime for which a Society for the Prevention of Cruelty prosecution, detailed in Chapter Eight, sent him to the county jail for a year and awarded him twenty lashes with a cat o'nine tails. James Riely was convicted in the supreme court for an assault "with criminal intent" on a woman in 1876; James Prendergast went to the supreme court for an assault on a female shopkeeper in 1880. The vulnerability of children to attack was demonstrated again in 1868 when Thomas Woodlin (Woodling) (1867-73:15) assaulted a boy with a stone. John Hamilton (1866-73:12) assaulted two little girls in 1877, for which he was imprisoned for vagrancy, a good example of the catch-all nature of that category of crime. Prendergast, who was notorious for beating up his mother and father, also attacked fellow jailbird Mary Ford after their marriage in 1872, an assault with a knife that was only the first of many during their life together.[30] It was the family, gender and class contexts of these offences, not the degree of violence, that determined the relatively light sentences. Short of murder, the assaults were as violent as any. When it came to murder, however, it was the petty offenders who were on the receiving end of the assaults, as we shall see.

## II

How then did the 92 offenders fare in court? Charged either by the police or their relatives or close associates in the upper streets, they shared Margaret Howard's experiences. They did not always go to jail. Discharge was a common feature of the court appearances of repeat offenders. At least seventy-five of the 92 were let go in court on one pretext or another, some many times. In the sample year 1868, for instance, we find twenty-two of them escaping conviction. In a number of cases this occurred because the accuser failed to appear. For this reason, John Kane (Cain) (1867-72:9) avoided a trial for trespass, Mary Ford for disorderly behaviour, Robert Joint for assault on one occasion and fighting on another, Johanna Linehan for assault, Henrietta McKegney for stealing, Ann Mahoney for breaking windows, Thomas Norbury for assaulting his common-law wife, Johanna Power for drunkenness and Mary Slattery for annoying a military guard. This seems to suggest that many of the underclass complainants were satisfied with arrest and did not require conviction to settle their scores.

On other occasions that year, several well-known repeat offenders were admonished and dismissed. This happened to Henrietta McKegney after she had attempted suicide while locked up for drunkenness. Mary Simons received a similar magisterial rebuke after being brought up for annoying the soldiers performing guard duty at the military hospital. In still other instances, there was insufficient evidence or compelling reason to convict and the magistrate dismissed the case. This occurred to Bridget McNamara in a drunkenness case, to Thomas Norbury in one assault and two larceny cases, to Mary Slattery when she came to the police station for protection and to Eliza Walsh (1866-73: 23) when she was suspected of larceny. Undoubtedly those represented by counsel, the number of whom we have no way of knowing, benefited from professional advice, the court being, according to one newspaper, "harassed a good deal by lawyers who are ready to defend everything and everybody."[31]

The greatest number of discharges however were, like that of Margaret Howard's in 1868, chances to avoid incarceration by meeting conditions specified by the magistrate. Catherine Dryden was discharged after being charged with vagrancy on condition that she leave the city, as were Julia Martin, John Noonan, Catherine Shea and Mary Slattery. Judge Henry Pryor sometimes displayed a good-natured sense of humour when dealing with the more spirited repeat offenders. Julia Martin got off because she treated him to a joke. She asked for a chance on the ground that she had been away from the city for ten months. " 'Where,' asked the Stipendiary. 'Out in Rockhead,' answered Julia."[32] The magistrate also looked favourably on even the slimmest evidence of reformation. Mary Barry (1864-73:23), up for drunkenness in May, had actually been out of the city at service for nine months and was able to produce a favourable character reference from her employer. As it was also the Queen's birthday, Pryor exercised the royal prerogative and let her go. When Mary Slattery was intercepted in the street in December 1868 she was not only sober for a change but also possessed of a "sit" for the winter. The chance she extracted from Pryor was designed to see if her new situation at service would work out. In other cases that year again involving Julia Martin, Ann Joseph (1864-73:16), Elizabeth Johnston, Henrietta McKegney, Johanna Power, Margaret Howard and others, the penalty for failing to take advantage of the chance was spelled out, usually a twelve-month sentence, a procedure that was not questioned by legal counsel until 1881. Like Margaret Howard, most of the dischargees in 1868 were soon picked up again and given twelve-month sentences.[33]

The tendency of the court to deal leniently with inmates of Rockhead was reinforced by the attitude of the aldermanic prison committee, the members of which seem to have released prisoners at every opportunity. Even the press, which was often critical of early releases, favoured discharging vagrants as soon as some means for their support became available.[34] Since this was a period before tickets-of-leave or parole, entirely *ad hoc* remission procedures prevailed. It was always possible to secure release from Rockhead on payment of a fine, the least controversial form of commmutation. The jail registers indicate that eight women and fourteen men secured early release by this means during the 1860s and early 1870s. Thomas Drew and Patrick Scully (1864-73:10), both of whom were thereby released several times, may have been able to pay their fines because of the nature of their occasional employment, the former as a barber, the latter as a cooper.

To cover other cases both senior government officials and the press agitated from time to time for a more systematic policy on remission, one which would remove all suspicion of bribery or favouritism. When it was revealed that, in the year ending 1 July 1868, only four of the eighty-three Rockhead prisoners discharged before their terms had expired had been released on the authority of the lieutenant-governor, his excellency publicly proclaimed that he alone could release prisoners charged with criminal offences. His protest appears to have had no effect on the activities of the city prison committee.[35] The jail registers give very little indication of the specific reasons for the reduction of sentences. Early release was universal with a slight bias in favour of discharging men and whites, and, in so far as we can tell, it occurred whenever a prisoner could convince a prison officer or alderman that the release would correspond with the public good. Early release to enable the offender to leave the city fell under this rubric. Twenty-three of the 92 were released during their jail careers to leave town, some more than once. For Mary Barry, destinations included Antigonish and Saint John; Ann Burke (1867-73:16) was released twice to go to Truro and three times to go to Saint John.

Despite the difficulty that the authorities encountered in making banishment work, they met with some success. The jail careers of three women ended when their last entry in the jail register recorded their departure from the city. Ellen Hawke, an English woman who went to jail eighteen times between 1860 and 1867, was sentenced to Rockhead for twelve months in August 1867 as a common vagrant. Towards the end of September she was released to be sent to England after which she does not reappear in the Halifax records. Henrietta McKegney, a Sydney, Cape Breton woman whose jail career covers the period 1857 to 1871, was released for the thirty-third and last time in June 1871 after serving eight and one-half months of a twelve-month sentence for vagrancy and was sent by steamer to New York. Similarly, the Halifax woman, Bridget McNamara, left Rockhead, also for the thirty-third and last time in November 1877, to facilitate her banishment to New York. These cases stand, then, as the prison authorities' vindication of early release.

Early releases also occurred in the case of illness because the city prison did not contain an infirmary. Mary Butler (1864-68:10), for example, became ill and was sent to the poorhouse in 1865 and again in 1868. Altogether twenty-six of the 92 were sent to the poorhouse from city prison, but we know that on many other occasions repeat offenders were sent to the poorhouse by the police instead of being charged in court or, like Thomas Woodlin and Ellen Hawke in the winter of 1867, were sent there by the court.[36] This resort to the poorhouse indicates their poverty as much as their incorrigibility. Halifax had no public system of outdoor relief: institutionalization was the only alternative. It is also evidence of the obvious: young prostitutes had to cope with pregnancies; outcasts were marked with debilitating conditions which plagued them from birth or childhood to death; people on the precarious margin of existence aged rapidly. In a city without a maternity home, homeless women found refuge during their confinements in the poorhouse. Mary Cahill (1867-73:9), who was in and out of jail between 1867 and 1876, was sent to the poorhouse from Rockhead in September 1869 and remained there until June 1870. The poorhouse registers record the birth of William Cahill in November 1869. Catherine Dixon was sent from Rockhead to the poorhouse with "sore feet" after serving one month of a twelve-month sentence in 1866. Rebecca Leonard (1865-68:9), an Irish woman in her early forties, went to the poorhouse two months after the commencement of a twelve-month sentence in 1868 on the ground that she was nearly blind, a move which appears to have provided her with a residence for the rest of her life.[37] As the city authorities grew accustomed to their new public hospital, established in 1865, repeat offenders were also sent there when they were diagnosed as having curable illnesses.

Referrals of this nature were, however, hit and miss affairs, and certainly the entries in the registers of the hospital and poorhouse do not altogether account for the large number of unexplained early releases from prison. One suspects that offenders were readily released to members of their families who were willing to have them or at the request of their victims, who they usually knew and with whom peace must eventually be restored. Critics of prison discipline complained that inmates released themselves. Twenty-three of the 92 escaped during the decade. In 1869 Robert Joint left the prison on the sly to attend the civic Natal Day festivities, voluntarily returning to his cell the next morning after the holiday was over. Escape continued to be a common occurrence. James Prendergast, the most infamous of the escapees, was described in 1880 as "a veritable Jack Sheppard in his ability to set locks and bars at defiance."[38]

The only other readily identifiable cause for early release was the employment of the prisoner. The jobs were often those that no one else wanted; in other cases they were ones for which the demand for labour was high. Then again, employers were sometimes willing to take on convict labour because it came cheap. The range of jobs was not very extensive: for men there was seafaring. Cornelius Ford and his brother-in-law James Prendergast were members of the casual sailor labour market in the port city and were released to go to sea. A number of the men—William Burke (1867-73:16), George Deminas, John Kellum (Killum) (1865-73:17), James Prendergast and Edward Sheehan (1864-73:28)—were given over to private employers in the early 1870s sometimes as prisoners, sometimes as freed men. During the city's building boom property developers were willing to use whatever labour was available. Seasonal unemployment considerably influenced the incarceration patterns of some recidivists. John Kellum and George Deminas, well-known local whitewashers, frequently spent their winters in Rockhead. The city got its whitewashing done both at Rockhead and other civic property in return for the black prisoners' room and board. In 1880 after Deminas had secured his seasonal imprisonment by stealing a quilt from a clothes line, he was released to work in the stone-shed maintained that winter by the Association for Improving the Condition of the Poor, the subject of Chapter Seven.[39]

The work arranged for women on release was confined to service but domestic employment of an institutional rather than a private nature. They came to the jail from the semi-public establishments of the upper streets: bars, boarding houses and hotels. They left to staff the public institutions no other woman would consider. Johanna Power was sent to bleak Sable Island as a government servant in 1872. Along with Margaret Howard, several women, including Henrietta McKegney, Ann Mahoney and Elizabeth Johnston went to work as 'nurses' in the city's smallpox hospital, which was for most of the period maintained in the prison grounds. Hannah Baker ended up in the quarantine station established on Lawlor's Island in 1885 at the request of the Salvation Army to which she was one of Halifax's first and least satisfactory converts. These engagements cannot be described as voluntary: they were more akin to a Hobson's choice. Yet the general willingness of repeat offenders to undertake employment in the prison itself at the expiry of their sentences suggests that jobs were scarce and sought with desperation by delinquents. Several preferred to accept duties as members of the prison staff to the prospect of returning to the upper streets of the city and the attendant temptations and problems. One or more spells of employment in prison were undertaken by Cornelius Breslow (1864-72:39), John Dunn, Robert Hilton (1865-69:8), Michael Kelly, Julia Martin, Ann Pritchard (Prichard) (1864-73: 18), George Small (1864-71:18) and Ann Wilson.[40]

# III

This reluctance to leave the confines of the prison brings us to a discussion of the last topic. To what extent was prison preferred by its frequent inmates to the rough existence in the streets? We know that Margaret Howard hated prison and tried to avoid it by attempting suicide several times. But it seems that she was atypical in this regard. However we explain her outlook, most of the evidence suggests that the prison was an important resource for alcoholics, the chronically unemployed and prostitutes. Today we would have difficulty sustaining the argument that prison is safer than the street. Mid-Victorians, however, used it as a refuge, a use well documented both by their contemporaries and in recent historical writings on nineteenth-century crime.[41] The plebian use of the prison corresponds to the plebian use of litigation, as the lower classes turned from informal to formal ways of satisfying their grievances and solving their problems. Nowhere is the popular resort to formal justice better illustrated than by the 92 themselves. They frequently appeared in police court as complainants as well as defendants. Between 1864 and 1873 at least fourteen of them initiated prosecutions for assault with varying degrees of success. Often the assailants were kinfolk or neighbours. In 1871, for example, Julia Martin prosecuted Catherine Shea for assault. Informing against associates sometimes gave female servants and lodgers their revenge against liquor sellers and brothel-keepers who forced them into prostitution. Turning Queen's evidence was not unusual for the jailbirds. Despite the unpopularity this might have caused, the same network of acquaintances was expected to help with the prosecutions as witnesses or money lenders. Bridget McNamara borrowed money from a friend in 1864 to pay for the warrant to arrest a man she unsuccessfully charged with assault.[42]

A similar proprietary interest occurred in respect to the jail. As we have seen in the case of the team of Kellum and Deminas, they sometimes asked to be placed in prison or committed offences specifically to secure a sentence. The former practice, which we can call self-sentencing, affected the careers of at least seventeen of the 92. If we add those who went to the police station for protection, knowing full well that they were likely to be sentenced on drunkenness or vagrancy charges, the number increases to thirty. The latter practice is illustrated not only by the whitewashers but also by James Smith who stole a sheep from the Colonial Market in 1867 explicitly for the purpose of being sent to Rockhead for the winter. Seven others were sent to jail because they were judged to be incapable of taking care of themselves, an involuntary form of self-sentencing. Old Patrick

Cody remarked on being given one year for drunkenness in 1868 that "he was satisfied; it was better to live somewhere than nowhere." They did however expect proper treatment in prison. When Edward Sheehan, described in 1881 as an old tramp of fifty-six who had been "living in the streets, in prison, or the Poor house for many years," was told that "he was too feeble to be any use" at Rockhead, he took the first opportunity to escape. He claimed in court that he was too proud to stay where he was not wanted.[43]

Usually, then, Rockhead Prison was not sufficiently unpleasant to act as a deterrent for the incorrigibles of the upper streets of Halifax. Described as "a palace of luxury and idleness," the prison was, during the mid 1860s, crowded with inmates well in excess of the 120 it was designed to hold, some of whom had been turned away from the even more crowded poorhouse. Contemporary comments indicate that the discipline was lax and that the prisoners were "permitted to revel in comparative idleness." Whatever labour was pursued at this period was clearly not enough to satisfy the "hard labour" sentences offenders sometimes collected, and the number of return visits was interpreted by critics as a sure sign that life was too easy at Rockhead. Various suggestions regarding ball-and-chain labour on public works and the desirability of a treadmill do not appear to have been pursued by the prison committee. The inadequacy of prison farm labour was obvious by 1866. Stone-breaking was the standard employment but it was not regularly pursued until 1868. In the meantime the prison was reported to be "but little more than a house of refuge for indolent and depraved persons." In 1868 a stone-crusher was finally put into operation and some of the prisoners were also employed in the winter of 1868-9 removing snow from the city streets. Blacksmith, carpenter and cooper workshops were opened but they were maintained for the occasional skilled prisoner and not used to train unemployables. The articles produced—buckets, tubs, wheelbarrows, children's sleighs—were sold each spring at a moderate profit. Observers claimed that the conditions of work were not imposed with noticeable harshness. For example, in cold weather the stone-breakers were given ample opportunity to move around during working hours and when they exceeded their quotas they were individually rewarded with an extra "inch and a quarter of tobacco." The women did the domestic chores and made all the clothing required by the prison community. While the silent system was reportedly in full force in the workrooms during the day, the prisoners were left unguarded in their locked cells at night, which presumably provided the men in the east wing and the women in the west wing with ample opportunity to catch up on their conversation. In any case, the prison population was frequently too large for separate accommodation and the doubling up served to undermine whatever penal discipline there was, particularly solitary confinement as the chief mode of punishment.[44]

Not only was the work exacted without ball and chain and with rewards for merit, but prisoners, often homeless in the streets before going to jail, enjoyed heated wards, clean bedding and nourishing food. They saw visitors on Fridays, were entertained to a lavish spread at Christmas by the prison committee and successfully refused in most cases to attend the weekly religious services at the prison. The severest punishment seems to have been a certain amount of physical restraint at least for the more belligerent residents. Cornelius Ford, John Green and Robert Joint were put in irons, for example. The whipping of juveniles was advocated in 1868 but there is no mention in the records of corporal punishment or bread and water diets. To the contrary, frequent allusions occur in the public press before 1880 to the humane approach of Governor Matthew Campbell to "the pets of society." Even the more severe Governor William Murray mellowed with the years. He stopped using shackles in the 1880s and reintroduced them only when ordered to in 1897 to prevent violence between prisoners and keepers. When prisoners complained, they referred usually to the lack of medical attention at Rockhead. If the environment of the prison was not particularly repressive, it was also far more secure than that prevailing in underclass Halifax.[45] Nourishment, protection, survival itself mattered more to outcasts than liberty. For people who spent most of their lives in prison, half a life was better than the half-life of the streets. How can we illustrate this?

One measure is the quality of family life. Since quite a few of the recidivists began their jail careers as juveniles, we can assume that all was not well at home. The Cahill sisters, Mary and Eliza, the Ford siblings, Cornelius and Mary, and the McNamara sisters, Bridget and Catherine (1864-69:16), as well as Hannah Baker, Catherine Dryden, Andrew Doyle, Robert Joint, Michael Kelly and 'city arab' James Walsh (1869-73:6) were all native Haligonians who first appeared in court as children. Andrew Doyle's initiation to the judicial system arose from his problems as helper to his elder brother Joseph, a butcher. Hannah Baker was reputed to have been sent out to beg by her parents who thereby launched her upon her life of crime. Mary Cahill, Bridget McNamara and Catherine McNamara appeared in court as errant daughters, being pursued by their fathers for leaving home.[46] The family context of the problems persisted in some of these cases long beyond the juvenile stage. Catherine McNamara was discharged for assaulting her mother in 1864. Andrew Doyle repeatedly assaulted his parents, siblings and other kin during his long criminal career. Cornelius Ford assaulted his father in 1866. In 1864 four of his sister Mary's first five court appearances were with members of the Ford family: her mother, father and sisters with whom she drank, whored and behaved in a disorderly manner. Her activities continued to involve her family for the rest of her life. In 1872 she charged her father with assault; in 1881 he charged her with being drunk, disorderly and breaking his furniture. She committed offences with Cornelius and also with her husband James Prendergast, an inveterate wife-beater. Other family members who broke the law together were William Drummond and his wife Mary (1867-73:20) who shared drinking bouts and court appearances. Patrick Scully and Kate Dryden had their plans to marry interrupted by a term in Rockhead for drunkenness.[47]

Actionable offences against family members were frequent. James Prendergast, like Catherine McNamara and Andrew Doyle, assaulted his parents and was joined in family violence by others for whom home was a centre of conflict. David Boyce (1865-69:9) threatened to stab his mother, John Green beat his mother, Edward Sheehan battered both his mother and his father and William Eaton (1864-73:18), his father. We know about these assaults because the parents did not hesitate to use the formal process of litigation to punish their grown children. Parents like Michael Ford charged children for less violent offences too including drunkenness, abusive language, disorderliness, annoyance and stealing. Such offences also sent the parents of Catherine Dixon, John Hamilton, Charles McInnis, John Noonan and James Riely scurrying to the magistrate. The unhappy relationships that prosecution between blood relations reveal were complemented, as in the case of Mary Ford, by conflict between husbands and wives. Besides James Prendergast, we find Cornelius Ford (his brother-in-law), John Kellum, John McDonald (1864-73:30), Michael McGrath and Thomas Norbury in court for assaulting their wives and John Kane for being disorderly towards his wife. Ellen Shefrow was battered by the man with whom she lived in 1866. Husbands also charged their wives. Julia Kelly was arraigned in court by her husband for drunkenness and selling his property. Similarly, Mary Slattery was given in charge by her husband for drunkenness.[48]

The lives of the next generation were indelibly marked by their parents' misdeeds and inadequacies. Elizabeth Johnston had her child taken from her in 1875, Emma Lee (1867-72:10) escaped an indictment for child murder in 1869 when the coroner's jury, after hearing evidence that she was "awfully fond of the child," concluded that she had accidentally overlaid it during the night. Elizabeth Masters was imprisoned at hard labour for abandoning her child and Mary Patterson for neglecting her children. When John McDonald went to the bridewell for neglecting to support his family in 1856, he was required "to be employed at his Trade [of shoemaker] and after paying for his maintenance, the balance to be given for the support of his family." Thomas Norbury was convicted of failing to support his wife and two children after a prosecution by the Society for the Prevention of Cruelty. Curly Ford's wife tried unsuccessfully in 1880 to strangle, drown and smash out the brains of their baby. Recidivist Mary Barry mothered recidivist Mary Slattery. Ann Wilson, a soldier's drunken widow, took her daughter to live with her in the poorhouse; her lame son expressed his disgust by refusing to have anything to do with her.[49]

For Ann Wilson and others the poorhouse acted as an alternative to the prison and as a place of final resort. When one of the Halifax city missionaries coined the motto, "Raised in Rockhead: Died in the Poorhouse," he could well have been thinking of thirteen of the 92 who most certainly died in that institution. Final references to another twelve, can be found in the poorhouse registers, though without definitive dates of death. Since about one-quarter of the twenty-five were those who had terrorized their families, we can conclude that we have been examining some pathological cases who needed constant care and restraint. Any one of them might have ended up in the insane asylum, though only John McDonald did so briefly after he assaulted his wife. John Hamilton was said to indulge in "shamming idiocy" in order to secure more lenient treatment. Unable often to coexist with the more normal street people, repeat offenders frequently withdrew to the poorhouse.

In many respects the poorhouse (or poors' asylum as it was usually called in this period) was similar to the prison. Discipline, work and regular meals were part of the regimen in the four consecutive facilities which housed the inmates during the Victorian period. The erstwhile criminals shared the poorhouse space with a much older collection of humanity than they encountered in Rockhead. The elderly and the mentally and physically handicapped, ranging in age from infancy to old age, joined the seasonally unemployed and unwed mothers, amounting altogether to several hundred. Most of the work of running the institution was done by the inmates, including such tasks as nursing the sick and stoking the furnaces. Other forms of labour provided in a stone-shed or wood-yard were also promoted to discourage "idleness" among those men who entered the poorhouse for unemployment relief.[50] Many of the social problems of nineteenth-century Halifax were reflected in microcosm in the poorhouse where drunkenness often prevailed and blacks were usually segregated. There was however a greater chance for sociability in accommodation based on dormitories instead of cells.

With the passage of time, more and more of our mid-Victorian repeat offenders became known to the police as residents of the poorhouse. When they were "out for an airing" they often got hold of a bottle and ended up in court. Old Ann Pritchard, attired in her night-cap in 1880, and William Drummond, the lame ex-soldier at large in 1889, were both returned to the poorhouse after their drunken sprees. By 1889, Elizabeth Masters, in court for the same reason, had been an inmate of the poorhouse for many years. Once she had been the handsome young wife of a shipmaster; now she was decayed: "her beauty faded; a broken nose disfigures her face; the marks of dissipation are on it and her hair is sprinkled with grey." While we do not know which institution the repeat offenders preferred, one reporter claiming in 1884 that "life at Rockhead seems infinitely preferable to life in the asylum for the poor," the inside of the poorhouse was as well known to Halifax's dependent population as was that of the jail.[51]

The centrality of the poorhouse—the institution reputedly feared and shunned by the honest working poor—to the experience of the 92 is even more graphically illustrated when we consider their lives as well as their deaths. Sixty-one of them are recorded in the poorhouse registers with varying degrees of frequency. Since the registers are unfortunately missing for 1871-75, years central to this analysis, it seems likely that the number who depended on the poorhouse for at least part of their life outside the prison were well in excess of the two-thirds positively identified as inmates.[52]

A third and final illustration of the problems of life outside the prison is provided by the obituaries of eight of the 92 who died either violently or in abject circumstances and ended up on the coroner's slab. In three cases the verdict was death from exposure. Ann Wilson strayed from the poorhouse in November 1871 and was found dead on the Halifax Common. Described as "a hard drinker" who "spent most of her time in Rockhead and the poor house," Wilson's death was ascribed to "exposure to cold probably while under the influence of liquor."[53] John McDonald, the shoemaker, died in June 1874 shortly after he was found in Sackville, on the road from Halifax to Windsor. "The evidence adduced proved that he died from exposure; that he was a hard drinker; that he belonged to Halifax; that liquor crazed him while under its influence; and that he had spent the better part of the past ten years in the Rockhead prison, to which place he had been from time to time adjudged for his habits."[54] Johanna Power's death in 1879 was not dissimilar. She sought refuge one rainy summer evening in a house occupied by fellow jailbird Mary (Ford) Prendergast in

Albemarle Street. Shortly after being admitted she dropped dead. Mary Prendergast testified at the coroner's inquest that Power was "a hard drinker and vagrant, spending most of her time in jail." The jury concluded that Power had died from "cardiac disease hastened by exposure to the weather."[55]

Two others drowned, either accidentally or suicidally. Alice Donnelly (1871-73:10), the wife of a labourer and discharged soldier, Michael Crowe, disappeared from her home on Albemarle Street one snowy spring night in 1880. Her body was found several days later in the harbour at O'Connor's Wharf. Described as a cheery little Irish street seller of about forty-five, she was reported by her husband to have "had a touch of the horrors," evidence which encouraged the jury to conclude that she had drowned accidentally "while suffering from an attack of Delirium Tremens."[56] Old Patrick Cody met his end on the other side of the harbour when he fell off the ferry steamer *Sir Charles Ogle* as it was docking in Dartmouth on 11 September 1882. Despite attempts to revive him, he expired at the Dartmouth police station, apparently sober but completely penniless.[57] The other accidental death was part of a much wider tragedy in the city. Although Ann Pritchard died in her bed, she was one of eighteen women in the hospital ward of the poorhouse who died when it was gutted by fire in November 1882. She had reached the venerable age of seventy-eight in spite of her record of dissipation. A military daughter and wife, she sought her solace in the bottle after her husband's death "and sank to the lowest depths, being frequently confined in the city prison, and, in the usual order of things, went to the poor-house in her old age."[58]

The three remaining women died violently. Six weeks after her final release from jail, Eliza Munroe died naked, plying her trade underneath a drunken soldier on 1 March 1867 in a backyard in Albemarle Street. The soldier was allowed to escape and the coroner's inquest failed to cite assault as a cause of death. Instead it was ascribed to "the effects of alcohol and a depraved life."[59] Mary Slattery and one of her cell-mates, Ann Mahoney, came out of jail on 31 March 1874 in company with John Keily, a somewhat less frequent resident of Rockhead whose record included convictions for exposing his person and assaulting women in the street, one incident of which had been "grievous." The trio made their way to Annie Foster's house in City Street where Slattery took a room and, according to her own deathbed deposition, Keily "attempted to take liberties with me when I resisted and he set me on fire with a lighted match by putting it to my skirt. I rushed into the room of Annie Foster when some soldiers of the 87th [regiment] who were there put it out. I believe said John Keily set on fire my clothes with intent to do me some serious bodily injury." He was reported to have concluded their fatal argument by telling Mary: "I have burned my mother and I'll burn you, you bloody whore.'' Mary died of burns and shock in the hospital on 2 April 1874, aged twenty-nine. Keily spent two years in the penitentiary.[60] Julia Martin, a Prince Edward Islander who had recently spurned the city's attempt to repatriate her, also gave a deposition before she died after being taken to the poorhouse with serious injuries in 1881. She claimed that she had been kicked and beaten in Jeremiah O'Brien's public house in Albemarle Street by two men, one of whom was the tavernkeeper himself. Although the evidence emphasized her three-week drunken binge, the coroner's jury concluded that she had died from "inflammation of the bowels, brought on by injuries received from a person or persons unknown.'' No charges were laid.[61]

********

Given the desperate and often violent lives that the repeat offenders lived outside the prison, Rockhead was undeniably better for many of them than the street and incarceration contributed to their survival. In the mid-nineteenth century, therefore, the prison was an essential institution of social welfare without which the levels of alcoholism, family violence and assault against women would have been worse and the fragile lives of society's helpless outcasts even more desperate and uncertain.

The 1869 poorhouse after the fire of 1882. (Public Archives of Nova Scotia)

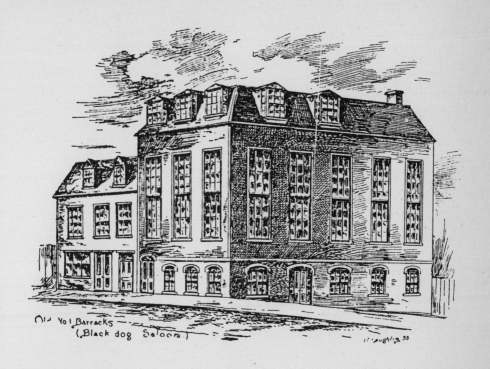

The Black Dog Saloon (part of the Waterloo Tavern). (*War Cry*, 23 January 1893)

# 2
# FROM ROUGH TO RESPECTABLE: ISAAC SALLIS OF BARRACK STREET

In June 1859 the budding delinquent, Henrietta McKegney, was sufficiently aggrieved with her employer, Isaac Sallis, to initiate a prosecution against him for keeping a disorderly house. Her evidence suggested that Sallis and his wife Mary had actively connived in her sexual transactions with soldiers and sailors. The court sympathized with the young servant girl and convicted Sallis, whose earlier appearances in court, like those of McKegney herself, had begun in 1857. Other mid-Victorian jailbirds who interacted with the Sallises included Ellen Shefrow, prostitute and friend of McKegney, whom Mary Sallis assaulted in 1863, and Eliza Munroe, whose street prostitution offended Isaac Sallis so much that he gave her and her customer in charge for lewd conduct, also in 1863.[1] None of these women—McKegney, Shefrow, Munroe, or Mary Sallis—was alive and in Halifax in 1904 when the following obituary appeared in the press of 20 August.

The death occurred this morning at his residence, 137 Cunard Street, of Isaac Sallis, a gallant old soldier, who fought many a well-contested field for the honor of the British flag. Mr. Sallis, who was a native of Gloucestershire, England, was seventy-one years of age. He was formerly a sergeant in the Sixty-third Manchester regiment and served throughout the

61

Crimean campaign with distinction, being awarded the four bars—Alma, Inkerman, Balaclava and Sebastopol—the Turkish medal, and the medal for "Distinguished conduct in the field."[2]

To judge from the solicitous comments about his recent illness and the favourable references to his role in the Royal British Veterans' Society of Halifax, turn-of-the-century readers had every reason to regard Sallis' life as a respectable one and, on the basis of the $7500 estate he left to his only child and married daughter, Jane Murphy, a successful one in material terms.[3]

Yet between 1857 and 1880 Sallis faced at least thirty-three charges in the Halifax police court, three trials in the city criminal court and three criminal trials in the supreme court.* He appeared in the dock very frequently between 1859 and 1866: certainly often enough for him to qualify as a repeat offender by any social investigator's criteria.

Given the ignominious careers of Halifax's mid-Victorian jailbirds, Sallis' ability to prosper in spite of his legal problems provides an interesting and instructive contrast. The most striking difference between him and the 92 characters we met in Chapter One was that he served only one term in the bridewell (the pre-1860 city prison) in 1858 and only one in the county jail in 1879. Otherwise, when convicted, he paid his fine; when remanded for trial in a higher court, he posted his bail. Unlike the McKegneys and Munroes of the city, he did not need the prison as a refuge. He was not a derelict, sinking under the combined weight of disease and drink, gyrating between prison and poorhouse. On the other hand, like other habitués of the upper streets he used the police court to settle personal scores, appearing there as complainant and witness as well as defendant. His language, pastimes and employment also belonged to the disrespectable society of that rough neighbourhood.

Rather than languishing as a victim of circumstances, he emerged as a consummate opportunist. Unlike other army veterans of the Drummond and Norbury variety—enlisted men who were not successfully absorbed into civilian life—Sallis was able to triumph over somewhat similar adversities and become an underclass boss. Although he was not as successful as Charles McKiernan, proprietor of Joe Beef's Canteen in Montreal, the two men shared one major similarity. As ex-soldiers they entered the drink trade where they served the needs of both the permanent and transient lower classes of their respective cities at the same time as they aroused the hostility of the middle class. Peter DeLottinville portrays

---

*Court papers are too incomplete to ascertain an accurate total. This is undoubtedly an underestimate.

McKiernan as a folk hero; Sallis on the other hand was neither as prominent nor as decent.[4] But then Sallis was chosen for inclusion here because of his encounters with the law and interaction with some of our 92 outcasts, not because of his popularity. His career illustrates that low-life, petty entrepreneurs were sometimes able to secure enough economic independence to manipulate a hostile environment to their own advantage. His life may also confirm Peter Bailey's assertion that "it is from studies of the individual that we may best discern the pattern of movement in and out of respectability and thus illuminate the broad territory that lies between its two idealised poles."[5]

Sergeant Sallis purchased his discharge from the 63rd regiment ten months after its arrival in Halifax in June 1856, fresh from the Crimea. As a new settler he had youth (he was only twenty-three) and literacy on his side. A further advantage was his honourable veteran status in a society dependent on the British forces for a considerable portion of its livelihood and a military command reliant on the private sector for the organization of the social life of its soldiery. The military ambience both of the city and of his experience was particularly important for the first years of Sallis' settlement in Halifax. He took up his residence in the upper streets reviled by respectable society. But the upper streets, especially Barrack and Albemarle, formed not just a neighbourhood distinguished by poverty and crime. This was also the unofficial military district of the city. Sallis lived and worked first on Barrack, then on Albemarle Street. The military connection was especially intimate for the first five years of his twenty-year establishment in that neighbourhood because his former regiment remained in the Halifax garrison until 1862.[6] When he began to use his lodgings in Barrack Street as a place of business, he was assured of the clientele of his former military associates. In the short term such support was necessary for survival in the highly competitive, cut-throat trade of catering to the social life of the army rank and file and other waged workers on the loose.

Since Sallis probably began his civilian career as a tenant in Barrack Street, he would have commenced his business activities as a side-line to his initial labouring jobs, with only a room or two for this purpose. Within this limited space, the first opportunity to secure ready cash was to provide lodgings for the married soldiers whom the barrack-master could not accommodate, often soldiers with unofficial or common-law wives. During 1857 Sallis lodged both soldiers and women and made the transition very quickly from managing a small establishment to renting a house or a considerable portion of a building.[7]

Like the female servants he employed, it was Sallis' other method of securing a livelihood in his lodgings which brought him into conflict with the law. The servants resorted to prostitution; Sallis, like most entrepreneurs in the upper streets, sold liquor. Since Sallis appears not to have been prosecuted for selling liquor without a licence, he must have secured the official status of a licensed tavernkeeper soon after his settlement on Barrack Street where his sitting room doubled as a saloon. His former good character in his regiment was an important factor in securing the licence. As early as June 1857, however, his licence was placed in jeopardy when he was charged in police court with selling liquor on Sunday. He conducted his own defence, confidently attired in "respectable" dress and his Crimean medals. He cited chapter and verse of the statutes to establish his right to supply liquor to persons boarding or lodging in his premises. But the court contended that the Lorings, who had informed on him, were his tenants, not his lodgers and the mayor was unwilling to allow Sallis off in view of his recent solemn promise to keep an "orderly" house. The fine was accompanied by a warning: next time he would be imprisoned and lose his licence. The following May Sallis went to jail for keeping a disorderly house, perhaps a fulfilment of the warning though the court seldom displayed such a keen memory of its pronouncements. He soon regained his status as a publican. In September 1859 he was again fined, this time for keeping his tavern open after 11 p.m.[8] Sallis also maintained a tobacco shop. His first known appearance in police court as a complainant was in 1857 after twelve pounds of tobacco valued at twelve shillings, one box of cigars valued at seven shillings, and sundry small change were stolen from his shop by two Royal Marines in the early hours of 17 October.[9]

Accumulation of stock by the shopkeepers of the rough neighbourhood was an important step in the capital formation necessary to the success of a business in an uncertain and often hostile environment. We do not know what methods Sallis used to acquire his property. Illicit liquor sales was probably one. Other illegal methods were available to those who were willing to use them. The shopkeepers of the upper streets were the logical receivers of goods stolen by local thieves and stores and cargo broached by soldiers and sailors. The marines who stole Sallis' tobacco in 1857 sold some of it to neighbouring shopkeepers; Sallis himself went to trial in the supreme court for receiving silver plate and other goods stolen from the residence of gentryman Henry Albro in 1865 by a soldier who implicated him in the disposal of the booty. His acquittal on that charge is not necessarily evidence of his innocence. Rather this acquittal, along with the other major discharges he secured, including an implication in the disappearance of a gold watch in the late 1860s, are evidence of his rising status in society.[10] A property owner and voter always enjoyed the benefit of the doubt in court over the transient or unenfranchised contestant. And, by fair means or foul, Sallis had become a not inconsiderable property owner. By the time his former regiment left Halifax in 1862, Sallis had secured an interest in the real estate of the upper streets. He had bought his own house which was valued at $600. With total rateable property of $800 in 1862, he enjoyed the distinction of being one of the most substantial resident taxpayers of Barrack Street.[11]

His marriage to a Nova Scotian, Mary Frost, in May 1857, soon after his discharge from the army may have contributed to his initial establishment in the neighbourhood though we have no way of knowing. Undoubtedly it contributed to his success as a shopkeeper. Mary Sallis would have functioned as a lodging-house keeper and mistress to the servants who served in the tavern. Fourteen months after their marriage, two of their female lodgers, Jane Ross and Mary Ann Little, were sent to the bridewell on the complaint of another resident, Margaret Donovan, that they were making their living in the Sallis house by prostitution. Whether or not Mary Sallis herself was selling her sexual services when she met Sallis (one of the witnesses to their marriage was a prostitute), she was soon aiding and abetting her servant Henrietta McKegney's prostitution. On two occasions in 1859, according to McKegney's testimony, Mrs. Sallis took from her five shillings or a dollar as "bed money," apparently "the usual charge" in these matters. On the distaff-side therefore, Mary Sallis, contributed to the earnings of the business and the facility with which Sallis could pay his court fines while still accumulating the capital to achieve a secure position in the upper streets.[12] The Sallis household during the 1860s, the years crucial to the establishment of the family's well being, began the decade with an enumerated population of nine. It probably included McKegney who, despite differences with the Sallises in 1859, was still a resident of their tavern in 1863 where she was taken after being assaulted in the street.[13]

A family man, a trader and employer, a property owner and elector, an honourable veteran, Sallis had many of the social characteristics but none of the social graces of the respectable middle class. What he did have were the distinctive social values of plebian culture. He followed the morality, business practices and justice of the streets, a code of standards that contributed to the self-regulation of his rough neighbourhood. In order to enforce that code, he used whatever means were available: fists, litigation, threats, petition, bribery—a flexible combination of formal and informal, open and clandestine methods.

Sallis' sense of morality was first demonstrated in 1857 when he resisted the entreaties of a fellow shopkeeper to partake of the pleasures of her house.[14] This is not to suggest that he was squeamish about fornication. The casual resort to brothels was appropriate for male transients and off-duty soldiers but not for aspiring businessmen like himself. He had a lady friend in 1861, a Mrs. Sarah Inglis, whom he visited frequently.[15] His permanence in the neighbourhood discouraged him from indulging in the fly-by-night arrangements that went on around him. He prosecuted two men and one woman in 1867 for being lewd characters and "keeping a disorderly room in his house." While this court case, which resulted in their conviction, may have been evidence of his notion of growing respectability (it being eight years since he had been convicted of a like offence), it could also indicate his intolerance of business transactions occurring in his establishment without his knowledge and without a cut of the earnings. Whatever his motivation, he was by this date dutifully protecting the women in his house from the "skylarking" of drunken male customers.[16]

We do know that he considered street prostitution to be a blight on the neighbourhood; otherwise he would not have taken Eliza Munroe to court for lewd behaviour in 1863. His concern for the proper use of the streets was demonstrated also in 1860 when he and a soldier-customer met William Smith urinating against a wall in Albemarle Street, twenty-eight years before the first public urinal was opened in the city. Since women were in the vicinity, Sallis and his associate objected to Smith exposing himself and claimed that "it was no place to commit a nuisance while females were passing." A fight ensued for which Sallis may have been responsible since it was alleged that he gave the soldier a shilling to thrash Smith. Sallis also appears to have discriminated in his tavern between the honest workingman and the layabout. He was in court in 1862 for assaulting Richard Hodgins by setting his dog on him. William Evans, an entertainer who was singing in Sallis' tavern at the time, testified that Sallis, who described Hodgins as a loafer, had loaned Hodgins $6 for which the latter thanked him by drinking himself under the table. In his disapproval of indecent behaviour and excessive dissipation, Sallis won the approval of the magistrates who exonerated him in both the Smith and Hodgins prosecutions.[17] In addition, even though he was a liquor seller and not entirely unblemished himself in the city's annals of drunken and disorderly behaviour, he was quite willing to lay charges against others for drunkenness. Nor, perhaps, was he unwilling to adulterate his wares. In November 1867 a group of naval sailors belonging to HMS *Sphinx* claimed that one of their mates had died as a result of imbibing "poisonous" liquor at Isaac Sallis' tavern. They would have gutted the building

66

had not the police, led by Garret Cotter, come to Sallis' rescue. This event became known in the city's lore as the "sailors' riot."[18]

Sallis' lack of scruples was more decisively revealed in his relations with the opposite sex. He was in court at least five times for abusing women. In 1861 Jane Brennan, a seamstress attending Sallis' friend Jane Inglis, alleged that he kicked her in the hip, knocked her on the floor, and told her she was "a damned old bitch who should go and calve." Like other rough and ready men, he did not hesitate to assault his wife. In 1864 he failed to convince the court that he was justified in disciplining Mary for her interference in his public house. She testified that he said "he would break the bloody stick over my bloody back and struck me across the back twice, and made me black and blue." One of the other assaults was against a black woman, a common enough occurrence in the inter-racial neighbourhood of the upper streets and not necessarily racist. In support of this contention we know that a black man, Henry Russell, perhaps the man of that name who later became a leader in the black community, was a tenant in Sallis' house in 1863. But Sallis' conviction for abusive language towards Amelia Reynolds, another black, in 1866 probably did contain a special significance because Reynolds was a rival tavern and brothel-keeper.[19]

Fighting with competitors was one of the common business tactics of the day. Sallis' most serious rivalries as a Barrack Street proprietor were with his fellow publicans John Smith and Michael Hines. They both appear to have exceeded him in the lengths to which they were willing to go in their vengefulness. The problems with Smith began innocently enough in 1862 when Sallis appeared as a prosecution witness on behalf of Thomas Leary, a customer who charged Smith with assault. Sallis testified that he saw Leary thrown out of Smith's door and given a running kick in the head by Smith. When Smith took Sallis to court the following January for assault on New Year's Eve, Sallis convinced the court that he was no more at fault than Smith and both men were ordered to give $50 in securities to keep the peace for six months. Before the six months had elapsed, Sallis successfully charged Smith with using abusive language. The uneasy peace which ensued between the two was broken in February 1866 when Sallis was remanded for trial in the city criminal court charged with assaulting Smith and threatening to shoot him with a pistol. The dispute was said to be "the result of a long-standing grudge." When the case came to trial in March, Smith failed to appear and Sallis was discharged. All this unfavourable publicity came at a bad time for Sallis who was, during the fortnight between his arraignment and the meeting of the court, fined in the lower court on another charge, that of assaulting several seamen. At the same time he was awaiting the outcome of his implication in the Albro robbery for which he was indicted in May in the supreme court for receiving stolen property. Whereas the grand jury reported a true bill against Sallis in the robbery case, they decided to support Sallis in his feud with John Smith by indicting the latter for perjury on the ground that he had earlier lied when he claimed that Sallis had threatened him with a pistol. A large number of supporters of both men appeared as witnesses, totally confusing the petty jury which then failed to agree on a verdict.[20]

Smith's discharge may have settled that score but only in time to allow the other rivalry between Sallis and Michael Hines, erstwhile proprietor of the infamous Blue Bell tavern to send Sallis to the autumn 1866 sittings of the supreme court for arson while the charge of receiving stolen goods was already pending. In the early hours of 1 August two persons were observed kindling a fire against the wall of the Blue Bell. After examination in the police court, Isaac Sallis, described by the chief justice as a man who "had hitherto evaded justice," and one of his cronies, Gordon Thom, were committed for trial charged with attempting to set the tavern on fire. Hines was the key witness for the prosecution but the tables were turned on him in November when the jury found Sallis and Thom not guilty and indicted the accuser instead.[21]

All of Sallis' appearances as a defendant in the supreme court arose out of his occupation as a tavernkeeper. On his part he tended to protect his business interests in informal ways rather than through the formal mechanism of litigation. This preference is confirmed by some of his everyday practices. He preferred to escort tipsy soldiers back to the barracks rather than turn them over to the military police. He avoided involving the civilian police who interfered with the free enterprise of the public house, nosing around to make sure the licensing hours were kept and order maintained. When serious disorder occurred, Sallis used strong-arm tactics. In 1863 he intervened in a row in his tavern between two sailors for which he was rewarded by being pushed through his own window and then charged with assault by one of the belligerents. Violence in the drinking dens was endemic. The following year a knifing by a naval sailor in Sallis' tavern resulted in a penitentiary term for the assailant.[22]

It was indeed Sallis' attempts to conduct his business in an orderly manner that led to a dozen or more assault charges being preferred against him by individual men during the first decade or so of his residence in Halifax. The few cases for which details are available are suggestive of the informal methods he used to settle his scores. The charge of assaulting John Woods in 1863 was dismissed on the evidence that Woods had gone

68

into Sallis' house "for the purpose of having a row." In 1865 the court allowed Sallis the right to hit a naval sailor with a stick in self-defence. The magistrate was generally unsympathetic, however, to Sallis' attempts to collect his debts through physical persuasion. He was fined for assaulting John Mann, a truckman, in his tavern on Christmas night, 1860, after he resorted to fisticuffs to force Mann to pay his bill. The court might have been better disposed towards Sallis in this case had not the evidence referred to card-playing in the house. In July 1861 Sallis incurred a hefty fine of $20 after putting James Phillips out of his tavern for refusing to pay for his ale. Besides acting as his own bouncer, Sallis did not hesitate to set his dog on recalcitrant patrons. His tavern at the corner of Barrack and Prince Streets was not known as the "Black Dog" without good reason. The disciplining of debtors was a state responsibility which Sallis infringed every time he mistreated a difficult customer. Only over the longer term did he learn to use the civil litigation demanded by the state.[23]

If Sallis' moral standards and business practices were overwhelmingly self-serving, his notions of justice reveal a certain degree of class solidarity. They owe something to his army experience. In August 1856 he joined his fellow NCOs of the 63rd regiment in a protest to their commanding officer about one of their rank, Sergeant H.C. Elliott, who "chose in a most unsoldierlike and officious manner to volunteer with the town police, to inform against certain inhabitants of Halifax for selling liquor without license." Since the liquor sellers were three poor widows, one with seven small children, the men felt Elliott's "peaching" and acceptance of a share of the fines for the purpose of securing his discharge had brought great "disgrace" and "odium" upon the corps. They requested that the offending sergeant should no longer be allowed to mess with them.[24]

As a civilian, Sallis was not unwilling to provide alibis for neighbours in trouble with the law. He would also go to some lengths to defend the weaker members involved in the trade of the upper streets. A case in 1865 will serve to illustrate this. Julia Donovan was convicted of keeping a bawdy house and sentenced to six months at hard labour. Because of the unusual severity of her sentence she appears to have been victimized, perhaps as an example, perhaps because she was a woman conducting business on her own in a rough neighbourhood. She had already been in court several times during the previous couple of years, both as a complainant and defendant. While at the time of her imprisonment, she had supporters in the upper streets, including two married sisters, she was without her husband who had gone to the United States three years earlier. She was only twenty-four, with three small children to support. Sallis attended her trial with one or two other tavernkeepers to see what could be done for her. In the end he was able to have her sentence commuted to a staggering $100 fine by petitioning the lieutenant-governor. The case became a civic cause célèbre.

The trial occurred shortly before a municipal election in which alderman James Tobin was a mayoralty candidate. Sallis' attempts to do something for Julia Donovan met with Tobin's assurances that he could get her off if Sallis delivered the vote of the upper-street tavernkeepers in his favour. This Sallis was apparently prepared to do. Another alderman, J.D. Nash, with an eye to re-election, explained to Sallis that Tobin had no authority to secure Donovan's release and persuaded Sallis to pursue his original plan of helping the illiterate Julia draw up a petition begging for her release. The petition, which according to one newspaper was "of such a nature as to convey a wrong impression," asked for clemency on the ground of her need to support her children. The subsequent commutation of her sentence involved not only the unusually large fine but also the requirement that she remove immediately from the upper streets. A cynic might argue that by this decision Sallis and his associates, described in the press as "a few of the lowest liquor dealers on Barrack and Albemarle Streets," were rid of one of their competitors but that motive seems misplaced here. Poor Julia was dead within two years; her fellow liquor sellers, licensed and unlicensed, still had another three years to enjoy the bounty of the upper streets.[25] During these years there is no evidence to suggest that Sallis followed up on his intervention in the Donovan case by becoming a nice man. He joined forces with Terrence Healey in 1868 to pour petroleum oil in the eyes of a little black whitewasher, John Harris, for no apparent reason. Harris effectively undermined his case in court by accepting a $5 out-of-court settlement from his assailants. In Sallis' favour also was his retention of the services of one of the city's smartest criminal lawyers, Robert Motton, and the erraticism of the city's first stipendiary magistrate, Henry Pryor.[26] The wheels of justice were beginning to move in Sallis' favour.

Sallis' court appearances became less frequent in the late 1860s. In 1866 he moved from 59 to 35 Barrack Street and then in 1868 gave up the liquor business briefly to become (according to the City Directory) a music teacher at 145 Albemarle Street. Back in the liquor trade in 1869, at 147 Albemarle Street, he found he had left Barrack Street at just the right time. In April 1870 a military order placed Barrack Street out of bounds to soldiers because of a smallpox epidemic. Although the proscription included Albemarle Street for four months, it remained in force in Barrack Street for four years initially, long enough to precipitate the social transformation of what soon became known as South Brunswick Street.[27] The census of 1871 identifies the relocated Sallis as the proprietor of a liquor store, residing with his wife, their four-year old daughter and three female servants.[28] Despite Sallis' continuance in the rough neighbourhood, the 1870s marked an important transitional period in his progress towards a respectable status. By 1871 when his vote was being eagerly sought by candidates in the provincial election, the *Acadian Recorder* proudly portrayed him as a loyal and courageous soldier who had bayonetted six Russians at the Battle of Inkerman.[29] In court he was now more often sinned against than sinning. In 1871 the prosecution of a man for assaulting the police was combined with a charge of breaking Sallis' windows. In 1872 Sallis clamped down harder than ever on the transactions being negotiated in his tavern when he gave one of his customers, Thomas Carroll, in charge for enticing a naval sailor to desert his vessel. In 1873 Sallis himself was charged with a military offence but he succeeded in gaining an acquittal for "unlawfully having a pair of soldier's shoes in his possession," at a time when the civilian authorities were actively co-operating with the military authorities to punish aiders and abettors of soldiers' misbehaviour.[30]

But the military authorities would not be appeased when it came to the continued use of the upper streets by rank-and-file soldiers. In June 1874 after conflicts between soldiers and sailors, Barrack and Albemarle Streets were again declared unequivocally out of bounds to military personnel. This time Albemarle Street suffered a four-year interdict with drastic effects on soldiertown traders.[31] Quite simply, Sallis and his associates had to move. Hard times having hit Halifax, military customers were more important than ever. At first Sallis did not go very far. While optimistically retaining his properties on Albemarle and Barrack Streets he transferred his liquor store in 1874 to 52 Duke Street. Other dealers moved to Sackville and George which ran parallel to Duke or to Grafton immediately below Albemarle which rapidly became the new centre of disreputable activities. With businessmen like Sallis in mind, a civic official emphasized the results of placing Albemarle Street out of bounds some sixteen months after the restriction took effect.

> The owners of property suffered, and have continued to suffer severely, owing to the difficulty in finding tenants to replace the married soldiers, and to the decline of trade. The shopkeepers saw their business dwindle down so low that they could hardly pay rents and taxes, and it was clear that to exist they must migrate; unless indeed the military were readmitted. There were no advantages to counterbalance these evils...[32]

While Sallis continued to maintain a bar-room at least until 1879, his years on Duke Street were ones which must have been marked by uncertainty about his future prospects. With the clientele necessarily dispersed, it became more difficult to rely on the military for his livelihood. At the same time the city's licensing laws were becoming more restrictive under the increasing influence of the moral campaign against drink. There is no evidence however that Sallis was suffering financially. His real estate holdings increased.[33] He lent his aid to associates in the trade, serving as late as 1877 as a bondsman for a fellow licensee.[34] Yet he does appear to have diversified his business activities during his Duke Street years. Since tavernkeeping was never a one-faceted activity, being combined with shopkeeping, landlordism, brothel-keeping and a range of other illicit activities, it is not surprising that an enterprising publican and property owner would venture into other fields. Sallis always had an eye to new opportunities. In the mid-sixties he had joined the local gold rush either as a prospector or illicit liquor seller at Halifax County gold mines. One of his pastimes was horse-racing: his association with horses had not only recreational but also business dimensions. In the late seventies he appears to have branched into the city trucking business. We know this from accounts of runaway carts and horse-stealing.[35]

Ironically, this new venture, removed though it was from the shady world of drinking, brawling and prostitution, also led to the court room. The interventionist tendencies of voluntarist reform left no aspect of life of the humbler orders untouched. At about the same time as Sallis was adding trucking to his employments, the Society for the Prevention of Cruelty to Animals was established in 1876. Its members proceeded to ferret out all the instances of maltreatment of animals that could be found both in the city and beyond. Sallis' carting business made him vulnerable. So did his past reputation as a not-very-respectable resident of the city's roughest neighbourhood. Accordingly in October 1879 he was charged in the supreme court, along with two others—possibly his employees—with malicious mischief, that is cutting and wounding a horse or horses on the Citadel. With Robert Motton again defending him (in one of his last major trials before he changed sides and became the leading prosecuting attorney for the anti-cruelty society) and the attorney-general prosecuting, the jury failed to reach a verdict and was discharged. Faced with a six-month remand until the next sitting of the court, Sallis balked at the idea of spending the winter in the county jail. Motton applied for bail for his client "on an affidavit that Sallis is possessed of considerable real and personal property in the city, of which he has no intention of disposing and is ready for a second trial whenever it is ordered." After a rancorous debate, Sallis was released on an enormous bond of between $2000 and $4000 plus two sureties of $1000 each.[36]

Sallis was accustomed to waiting for supreme court trials but this one wounded his sensibilities far more than his earlier indictments. His past reputation had obviously come back to haunt him despite his acquisition of property and his middle-class aspirations. Not surprisingly he reacted strongly when his daughter of thirteen, a pupil in the old Acadian school, traditionally the nursery of the middle class, now a girls' slum-district school, was exposed to Prevention of Cruelty propaganda vilifying her father's unproven misdeeds. When Sallis' lawyers complained that Jane Sallis had been subjected to taunts suggesting that her father was a jailbird, the school board admitted that anti-cruelty literature had been circulated in the classroom contrary to rules and that Sallis had just grounds for demanding reparation.[37]

While he waited in early 1880 for the second trial to begin, Sallis found himself hauled into magistrate's court yet again for cruelty to animals after a bizarre incident in which he threw two live ducks on to a hot stove in a house on South Brunswick Street. The evidence revealed that he and his friends had also "knocked over the stoves, broken the furniture and generally wrecked everything...," not the first time he had created havoc in this fashion. Since he apparently had a quarrel with the residents, it is conceivable that the strong-arm tactics were those of a landlord disciplining his tenants, Sallis, as we know, being a property owner on that street.[38] After this debacle he was fortunate to secure an acquittal in the supreme court when the horse-maiming trial occurred two weeks later.[39]

His acquittal coincided with his flight from the disreputable neighbourhood and the ignominy of the liquor trade to a more genteel living on semi-rural Cunard Street on the edge of the city's North Common, where at the time of the 1881 census his household included only his small family. Listed thereafter in the city directories variously as gardener, contractor, and gardener and florist, in the 1891 census (by which time he was a widower) as a government contract drayman, and on the forty-third anniversary of the Battle of Inkerman, as a florist with a large business, his activities on Cunard Street preoccupied him in one way or another for the last quarter century of his life.[40]

Now his life was very different. Tending his interests on Cunard Street, where he purchased property in 1885, he passed over the great divide from rough to respectable, from lumpen to petty bourgeois. He appeared in court exclusively as a litigant, in civil cases pressing small claims against his debtors; in criminal court the last mention of him is in 1884 when he successfully charged a man with assault. But we do not know what use he made of his properties on the infamous upper streets. Was his property on Brunswick (Barrack) Street tenanted by the same Frederick Allen with

73

whom he had mortgage dealings in the late 1880s? If so, was this the Fred Allen prosecuted by the city in 1887 for keeping a house for the resort of prostitutes? Was Sallis' property on Albemarle Street similar to the hovels and tenements described as "Scenes of Squalor" by a visiting committee of prominent citizens in 1888? Only one thing is certain. If his properties were disreputable, he was able to distance himself sufficiently to avoid any of the opprobrium which characterized his active years on those streets.[41]

Having achieved a respectable status in life, he could now indulge his fraternal propensities. The opportunity came in 1884 with the formation of the Royal British Veterans' Society of Halifax. Conceived as a benefit society commemorating the thirtieth anniversary of the battle of Sebastopol, it began with fifty or sixty members and the prestigious presidency of Major-General J.W. Laurie. Sallis' fine sense of protocol almost destroyed his participation since he refused to accept the vice-presidency of a society to which he had been elected without his consent and in his absence.[42] Sallis' pique was overcome in due course. By the time of the second annual general meeting of the society in September 1886, Sallis was firmly ensconced as first vice-president of the 150-member organization. In an expansive mood, Sallis relished his new role by donating a marshal's baton to the society and proposed a toast to Queen Victoria at the annual dinner following the procession of 200 veterans through the streets.[43] Filling various positions over the years, he rose eventually to the presidency. He subsequently celebrated the Boer War with a distinctive blend of Canadian pride, imperialist fervour and British chauvinism.[44]

Sallis' twilight years contrast markedly with those of the most unfortunate of the city's petty offenders with whom he had interacted in the upper streets in the 1850s and 1860s. The chances of independence, let alone prosperity, in the environment of a rough neighbourhood were very slim for people who started off without property and connections. Yet Sallis managed through pragmatic and probably illicit means to carve out for himself a life marked first by relative material prosperity and latterly by respectability. Despite his affinity with those who spent most of their lives in Rockhead and the poorhouse, his good luck, relative temperance, sharp business intelligence and male gender enabled him to succeed where others failed. Ultimately, in order to transcend the infamy of the upper streets he had to change his residence, change his visible means of livelihood and associate with honest workingmen—the labourers, servants, artisans and small businessmen who comprised the Royal British Veterans' Society and accompanied Sallis' cortege to his final resting place in the summer of 1904.

Royal British Veterans host their American counterparts in 1900. Sallis and his colleagues are wearing union jack badges. (The Army Museum, Halifax Citadel)

Post office on market morning, 1894. Painting by Ozias Dodge. (Slater Memorial Museum, Norwich, Connecticut)

# 3
# BIRDS OF A FEATHER:
# THE FAMILY CONTEXT
# OF DISREPUTABLE
# BEHAVIOUR

When Isaac Sallis, for reasons unknown to us, assaulted the young whitewasher, John Harris, in 1868, one of the witnesses, who was subsequently also an assaulter of Harris, was the 'master' whitewasher John Kellum. Kellum went to jail about one hundred times between his first appearance in police court in 1857 at the age of eighteen and his last incarceration in city prison in 1903, two years before his death in the poorhouse at the age of sixty-six. His criminal record exceeded that of his kith and kin only in degree because many of his committals were in company with his siblings and in-laws and, later, his relatives of the next generation.[1] The family context of deviant behaviour is one of the most marked features of the Kellums' confrontations with authority. Nor were the Kellums exceptional. Slightly less extended in kinship patterns but every bit as frequent in criminal activities was the Ford/Prendergast clan, the two principals of which terrorized underclass Halifax in the last third or so of the nineteenth century.[2] An examination of the features of petty crime in the Kellum and Ford families illustrates also their poverty, underemployment and violence.

These two families shared with others, from which our group of 92 are drawn, the importance of class inheritance and family pathology as

77

determinants of their marginal lives. Because we are concerned with illiterate people whose experience cannot be captured through oral evidence, the reconstruction of their lives is fraught with problems and can never be complete. Jerry White's analysis of family and adolescence in his study of a lumpen street in north London in the twentieth century reveals the kind of family violence, poverty, lovelessness, interdependence, persistence and state intervention that affected our group in the previous century.[3] And yet family biographies like those of the Fords and Kellums exhibit as many differences as similarities. For the Kellums and their associates 'crime' was a rational strategy for survival in a society where blacks were not accorded equal opportunity. For the Ford/Prendergast fraternity it represented a deep-seated maladjustment which defies economic explanations and is perhaps to be explained partly by first-generation reaction against immigrant parents, born in this case in Ireland. While both families, therefore, appear to have been characterized by pathological disorders, the former's were sociopathological, the latter's psychopathological.

The main actors in these family dramas of the Victorian era figured among the 92 repeat offenders introduced in Chapter One. The supporting roles in the cast of Kellums were played by people who went to jail less frequently or were to become jailbirds of later decades. The incarceration in prison of adolescent Kellums long after the establishment of juvenile industrial schools tends to suggest that the family's colour precluded its access to the new private institutions. Members of both families demonstrated an uncanny talent for attracting like-minded companions. We cannot know, given the nature of the sources, whether as many family members married out, moved out or rose above lumpen activities as those who perpetuated them. But we are dealing with patterns of behaviour which reinforced family problems and family strife.

The wonderfully vivacious, defiantly carefree Kellums and associates turned the police lock-up into a music hall, the police court into a theatre, the city prison into a winter home and the poorhouse into a final sanctuary. Shut out from opportunities for employment and improvement to which their white counterparts had access, the Kellums used the public institutions as their own. The sire of the family appears to have been Charles Kellum who figures briefly in the criminal record,[4] but whose main significance for us was his fathering of John, Charles, Henry, Martha and Mary. The biography of the oldest son, John, indicates the general outline of family activities.[5] Between 1864 and 1873, the years which provide the focus in Chapter One, his record included petty larceny (the standard watch-and-chain robbery, for example), gambling, drunk-

78

enness, disorderly conduct, common assault, assaulting the police, throwing stones, soliciting charity under false pretences and vagrancy. The conviction for obtaining money under false pretences reveals that the illiterate Kellum had somehow contrived to draw up a deceitful petition in which he and his accomplice, John Willis, solicited aid from benevolent citizens to bury Kellum's mother, lately departed. Brought before the presiding alderman in the police court, Kellum was described as "a notorious character," and given ninety days at hard labour, while his chum was dismissed and told to keep better company.[6] The jail register indicates that despite his 'notoriety' Kellum was released by the mayor twelve days later.

During that decade Kellum usually went to jail for periods of twenty to ninety days (with one twelve-month conviction) between two and four times a year. Sometimes he pleaded not guilty. In October 1872, for example, he was tried for stealing several bottles of liquor from a dealer named Patrick Meagher. Kellum's friends provided him with an alibi. Unfortunately for his defence, he had acted in concert with Richard Hobin, a sometime resident of Rockhead over the previous five years, who had just up and died. When the police claimed that on his deathbed Hobin had named Kellum as the thief and also that several bottles of Meagher's booze had been found in Kellum's possession, the alibi was blown. As Kellum left the dock to go to Rockhead for forty days, he protested his innocence and declared that "when he got out of prison he would sue Meagher for his character."[7] Just imprisonment was one thing; unjust imprisonment called for a resort to the law to protect his honour.

By the late 1870s, though only in his thirties, Kellum's ability to survive in the hostile environment waned and he frequently sought out the prison as a refuge. Sometimes he was awarded short sentences at his own request. He also became belligerent. In the early 1880s the magistrate court records indicate that members of the Kellum family were charging John with assault, though not very successfully since his discharges from court were more frequent than his committals to prison. John Kellum also brought his own prosecutions in the police court, charging a female family member with assault in 1889 and another woman with a similar offence in 1899. He was not fabricating this violence. In 1895 he showed signs of madness shortly after going to Rockhead, a condition brought on by a severe beating he had received from his family. Having spent considerable stretches of his youth in jail, by the 1880s he was also beginning to go to the poorhouse. In 1884 at the age of forty he visited that institution for the destitute aged and helpless seven times. By the turn of the century he had become a semi-permanent resident of the poorhouse as well as the jail.

When in 1903 the governor of the city prison referred to the solid worth and unrealized potential of many of the well-known prisoners, he singled out for praise John Kellum, by then known to be failing in health. Governor Murray described Kellum as "one of the most widely known characters in Halifax. Everybody gave John a bad reputation, but said the governor, he is one of the most trustworthy men that has ever been at the prison. He never will attempt to escape and has frequently been given charge of one of the teams. He was a good worker, an artist with the white wash brush."[8]

Since escape from prison was relatively easy, the fact that John Kellum never fled is some indication of his preference for the prison over the hostile world outside. In fact the Kellums appear to have developed what might be described as a pact with the prison authorities whereby prison room and board were provided in exchange for the whitewashing services frequently required in the city's public buildings. Given the eagerness with which the authorities welcomed the whitewashing done by the Kellums, we might conclude that the labour of the blacks was handily exploited. In May 1883 the *Morning Chronicle* reported that George Deminas (whose jail record contains about half the number of incarcerations of his kinsman John Kellum) was sentenced to thirty days of whitewashing.[9] But John and his associates did not see it this way. Described as "the well-known Anglo-African whitewashing firm...to whose indefatigable efforts the success of the city whitewashing is largely due," Kellum and Deminas turned up at the police station in late November 1878,

> out at the elbows and knees, and asked to be sent home. They explained "dat dere wasn't no white-washing; dey couldn't get nuffin to do, and couldn't get paid for it." If the Stipendiary would send them up for six months, they would feel obliged. By way of inducement they said, "Bine by dey might be 'cused of stealin,' and den dere would be a big fuss in dĕ papers 'bout Kellum and DeMinas." Their request was granted, and they joyfully went up to their usual winter home. [10]

Here surely is an eloquent acknowledgement of poverty as the cause of crime.

The next year George Deminas stole a quilt from a clothes line in the north end to secure his winter in jail.[11] In January 1882 he was sent up at his own request "as he could find neither bread nor work in this cold, unfeeling, protected world."[12] When both Kellum and Deminas were discharged from court in March 1883 after the manager of the Church of England coffee-house turned them in for not paying their bill only to withdraw the charge, they soon returned to the lock-up to beg for further lodging. This time Jack "Nuckshaw" Kellum claimed that his homeless predicament was caused by his hard-hearted family. Sent out on 17 March to secure a contribution for the family board, he returned home empty-handed, for which his sister-in-law turned him out. John blamed his lack of success on the St. Patrick's Day festivities.[13] The employment options for blacks were few enough. John's whitewashing jobs were at best intermittent. Some forms of alternative work were horribly degrading. The press carried a ludicrous and pathetic description of John's role at the Washburn Circus in 1897. In a side-show his head served as the target at three shots for five cents and one of the many balls injured, and perhaps fractured, his collar bone. To dull his memory as well as the pain, he decided to drink the wages he received for his dangerous work.[14]

In exchange for the easy access they had to the city's penal accommodations, the Kellum crowd performed a number of useful public services. They aided the police. For this reason the press always had a soft spot for John Kellum. On one occasion in 1878 when Kellum might have escaped a charge of throwing a brick at a military policeman had not a civil policeman attested to his guilt, the *Morning Chronicle* reported that: "He is a harmless fellow whose principal offence has been getting into family brawls, and he has always been a willing assistant to the police."[15] In August 1883 John Kellum and George Deminas were witnesses for the prosecution of a court case concerning a liquor licence offence and John and his brother Henry again cheerfully betrayed a bootlegger in 1889.[16] Street life provided regular residents of the slum areas with various opportunities to interfere with their fellow unfortunates. Later in 1889 John Kellum and an associate discovered Joseph "Tug" Wilson attempting to hang himself in a barn north of Maynard Street and cut him down.[17]

In return for the labour they performed for the city and their good citizenship in public places, the Kellums believed they deserved a standard of incarceration which lived up to their modest expectations. In the winter of 1877 their expectations were not met: they were troubled by rats. Accordingly in October 1878 John Kellum and George Deminas "expecting to winter there as usual...prepared by taking up a detachment of cats—about ten and deposited them in the yard of the prison. They 'low dey isn't gwine to be clawed up by no rats dis wintah."[18] The change of administration at the prison in 1880 presented a new problem for the jail habitués. Considered an enemy of Rockhead's dependants in his early years, Governor Murray deliberately set out to make the prison less attractive to the regulars. Henry Kellum, who had been an occasional inmate since 1871, and who, like Deminas, went to jail some fifty times during his life, made his escape in October 1881 because "times ain't as good as dey used to be, dar" and he "wasn't goin' to stay whar dey starves niggahs."[19]

On another occasion when he was sent to Rockhead in September 1885 he was perturbed to discover "afterwards that the sentence would not carry him long enough for a Christmas dinner as he had hoped."[20]

The Kellums' court, jail and poorhouse statistics take on a compelling human dimension when embellished by descriptive reports of the personalities involved. Henry emerges from the court reports and other occasional accounts as "effervescent," eloquent, earnest, gullible, opinionated. In February 1884 he was one of the audience at the "Huckleberry" when his sister Martha, "the celebrated Little Buttercup" and her friend Andy Fletcher were in the dock.

> Martha was charged with being drunk and disorderly, and making a disturbance in a house of mourning on Duke Street in the presence of a corpse; also assaulting several policemen who kindly tendered her their assistance on the way to the station. She said she had been invited to the wake, and the mourners insisted on her joining them in drowning inconsolable grief in the flowing bowl, so if she got drunk it wasn't her fault. At this stage Henry edged to the front, backed up by several admiring friends of his own color, to offer a few remarks as to the views "ob de whitewashin' club" on the new Dominion Liquor License Act [McCarthy Act] and other affairs, including the prisoners, of present interest; but he was ignobly snubbed and silenced by an officer of justice.[21]

Henry's intercession on Martha's behalf was a suitable testament to their close association in disreputable activities. Many of his convictions were with his sister. In February 1883 Martha appeared in court to ask permission to go to Rockhead in company with Henry and his white female companion who had been sentenced for vagrancy until "the warm weather would give a boom to the whitewashing business."[22] In June the "wildly drunk" Henry and Martha, described as "two of the most notorious of their notorious family" were taken to the lock-up in a coal cart after they had been found on Gottingen Street creating a riotous disturbance. Martha proceeded to make "the night hideous with declamations of horrible profanity" which prompted the news writer to conclude that the whole family should be transported.[23] Two months later the drunken Henry joined the drunk, disorderly and profane Martha and her "sweetheart" Andy Fletcher in durance vile after they had all found themselves in the lock-up together.[24]

Next to John and Henry, the irascible, highly strung, equally opinionated Martha was the most colourful of the clan. Her jail career spanned the last quarter of the nineteenth century. Given the sexual division of labour, Martha did not join her brothers and in-laws in the whitewashing trade.

82

But there is no doubt that she had to contribute to her keep during the spells between her jail sentences. She is described in the 1880 records of the magistrate's court as a berry picker, an indication of rural origins, but blueberrying in August can have offered only limited seasonal sustenance. The hospital records, which record her treatment for secondary syphilis in 1879 and again in 1881, identify her occupation as prostitute. But, with one exception, none of the convictions she received in court were prostitution-related. It is possible therefore that her colour and her condition rather than her occupation determined the job description entered by the clerk. This is not to suggest that she did not join other poor young black women of the city in prostitution. But venereal disease was also in the family. Her brother Henry received treatment for it in hospital in 1875 and the opportunities for infection were rife.[25] Sister Mary, a fellow berry picker, who married William Maxwell, was convicted of keeping a house of ill-repute.[26]

Martha's earliest sojourn in jail resulted from a conviction in conjunction with Henry and Mary Kellum in 1876 when she was fifteen. Until 1885 she was repeatedly in jail, about thirty times in fact, frequently for drunkenness, though assault, larceny and vagrancy were also prominent among her offences. From 1886 until 1897 her jail sentences decreased to about a dozen, women being incarcerated less frequently by this period. She was also out of town occasionally. In 1889, for example, she returned from several months' residence in Falmouth with money in her pocket, only to be robbed by her sister and thrown out into Grafton Street after which she broke fifteen panes of glass in the house in a fit of drunken profanity. That summer she attempted suicide one night by jumping off the harbour ferry as it approached the Dartmouth dock.[27]

Martha bore the brunt of judicial disapproval of her incorrigible family in the summer of 1897 when she and her white friend Mary Crowe were sentenced in the county court for "murderously assaulting" Annie Maxwell by biting off the top of her ear outside their current abode on Maynard Street. All three were members of the Kellum's extended family network. Judge James W. Johnston concluded that they belonged to "a notorious crowd that need breaking up." While Martha's elder brothers John, Henry and Charles languished in the poorhouse, Martha went off to Dorchester Penitentiary where she served three and one-half years of her six-year sentence as punishment for her "heinous" crime.[28] An inmate of a bawdy house in 1904, she appears to have married at the age of fifty-four in 1914, probably not for the first time since she was described as a widow. Marital arrangements in the family as a whole are confused partly because in that "family like some of higher degree, the brides retain their maiden name."[29]

What made the Kellums prominent in contemporary annals was not their crimes but their solidarity and their unabashedly flamboyant style. As a family, they had their noisy quarrels which got them into trouble as much as did their petty crime but they stuck together through thick and thin.[30] Henry's loyalty to Martha, which was fully reciprocated, is a case in point. His concern for John reduced him to tears in 1895 when some one told him that his brother had been murdered in jail. Henry "rushed into the sergeants' room and shouted 'Let me see the body of my poor dear brother John who was killed at the city prison last night,' " an event which the officers had great difficulty persuading him was entirely imagined.[31] Mary Crowe who accompanied Martha to penitentiary in 1897 had been inseparable from her for several years. In May 1895, for example, when the police ordered Martha "to leave a field where she was picking dandelions," her conviction for drunkenness, profanity and obscenity brought Mary scurrying into court to ask to be sentenced with her friend "as she could not part with Martha."[32]

Both their togetherness and the local perception of their incorrigibility meant that the Kellums were often found guilty not because of what they did but by association. Sarah Kellum was fined in 1874 for profanity mainly because she was, like other family members, "a denizen of the notorious 'Shin-bone alley' " off Maynard Street.[33] "Nearly all the tribe" was in the dock in August 1880, charged with stealing rice and meat from a shopkeeper's cart. Despite the fact that they vociferously denied the charge and the complainant did not appear to prosecute, they were all sent up for thirty days because "they were a common nuisance."[34]

What they lacked in respectability they made up for in ebullience. In the institutions of law and order they were known for their entertaining performances, which were neither deferential nor dignified. In June 1885 when Martha asked "with a twinkle in her eye if she couldn't get a chance to go home" to Rockhead, the magistrate engaged in a haggling session with her, telling her "yes, she might go up to the old [prison] farm a little while if she'd be good; 'how many days do you want' he asked, 'well say twenty, please' replied Martha. 'All right,' responded the magistrate, 'forty days—who's next '..."[35] When Martha appeared in police court in September 1893 with her brother Henry's white wife, "her responses and antics caused much merriment." She failed to convince the judge that she should return to the poorhouse from which she had been recently released and made a great hullabaloo when she was instead locked up to await transport to Rockhead.[36]

Behind bars the family was famous for its song and dance routines. When Martha and Henry were locked up in September 1884 they "gave a concert—the programme included: 'I've been redeemed,'—'Don't be weary children'—and 'It's up to Rockhead boys, we're bound to go,' for which they had 'quite an audience.' "[37] They also sang 'Sweet Bye & Bye' and 'Pick up the young lambs and tole 'em in your bozerum.' Overnight in the lock-up in July 1885, Henry and John along with George Deminas contemplated "with songs and jest" the prospect of joining Martha and Charlie at Rockhead, and "made a particularly merry night of it behind the bars."[38] Henry and Charles and George Deminas "made the air sweet with melody and gay with dancing" in the police station on a September evening in 1885 and on a January night in 1886 Henry and John again with George Deminas "made the police station lively" with their popular renditions of old favourites.[39]

The resignation, if not eager anticipation, with which they accepted their frequent sentences suggests that they were often homeless between their spells of residence in the substandard housing of Albemarle, Grafton, Maynard and Creighton Streets and their back lanes. In 1889 the police claimed that Henry and John Kellum and Andy Fletcher, were "continually coming to the police station at a late hour for protection." They drew on the city's welfare services for the sustenance, accommodation and clothing essential to their existence. In November of that same year Henry Kellum and Fletcher sought admission to the poorhouse explicitly for the purpose of securing suits of clothing after which they scaled the fence and ran away, only to be picked up and sentenced to six months for vagrancy and theft.[40]

As far as we know, the Kellums never interacted with the Fords and Prendergasts who inhabited the same streets in underclass Halifax at the same period and were in and out of the prison and poorhouse with the same regularity. But, unlike the Kellums, they were not sources of amusement or cheap labour to the city. To observers, the members of these two families exhibited instead the worst features of the Dickensian underworld. The vital link between the Fords and the Prendergasts was Mary who was born into delinquency as a Ford and married into it as a Prendergast. She was a young girl when she first went to jail in 1864—allegedly sixteen, possibly as young as twelve. Her jail career stretched from 1864 to 1883. She died in 1885. Mary's life outside the prison appears to have been one long drunken debauch, characterized by family violence and family crime.[41]

Altogether Mary Ford went to city prison twenty-five times between the focal years 1864 and 1873. The first year of her jail career includes four sojourns in Rockhead and one in the county jail. Four of the five court cases involved other members of her family. Her first conviction in June for being drunk and disorderly was with her mother, Honora (Nora) Ford and the ill-fated Mary Slattery. Nora Ford had been imprisoned several times since 1860, on one occasion for ill-treating her child, possibly Mary.[42] Mary Ford's second conviction in July involved getting drunk with her sister Margaret. They were imprisoned under the vagrancy act. The third conviction in November was for keeping a disorderly house with her father, Michael Ford who, like Nora, was familiar with the jails of Halifax. The fourth court appearance in mid-December, for which she was held in county jail, did not result in a conviction. She appeared in the dock with her mother Nora and her sisters Ellen and Johanna charged with keeping a common bawdy and disorderly house in Albemarle Street. Her mother went to prison, sister Ellen was discharged and Mary and Johanna were sent to the poorhouse. Poorhouse destination notwithstanding, a couple of days later Mary was found drunk and sent to Rockhead for ninety days as a common vagrant.

When she next appeared in police court in July 1865, she was described as "young in years but old in crime."[43] By now she had extricated herself, at least temporarily, from her family and was working as an independent prostitute in the red light district. John O'Brien, a tavernkeeper of doubtful respectability in Barrack Street, gave her in charge for assaulting him and his wife Catherine. Unwilling to languish in Rockhead for ninety days, Mary tried to take her revenge on the O'Briens by charging them with keeping a brothel. Her evidence tells us something about her working life. Claiming to be eighteen, Mary testified that she frequented the O'Brien establishment where she secured rooms for her liaisons with sailors. For the room she paid Catherine O'Brien bed money—two shillings and ninepence on one occasion, five shillings on another. Her resort to the court to settle her score with the O'Briens proved unsuccessful: they were acquitted and she continued on the road to ruin. In June 1869, her unhappy state led to a suicide attempt in the verminous police cells below the court room where she was being held overnight for arraignment on one of her frequent drinking violations.[44] The magistrate took pity on her and allowed her to choose between banishment from the city and imprisonment. She could leave town immediately or go to jail for twelve months.

By the early 1870s other forms of violence had become a feature of Mary Ford's life. In 1872, when she went to jail five times, she also charged two men with assault on different occasions. One was her father, Michael, the other was her n'er-do-well husband, James Prendergast, whom she had married that very year. In May her father claimed that her injuries had been sustained by falling down the stairs and Mary failed to carry through with the prosecution.[45] There were witnesses, however, to the other assault in August. James Prendergast, described as usual as "a notorious rough," celebrated one of his frequent releases from prison by quarrelling with Mary in an Albemarle Street tavern and stabbing her twice in the head with a knife. The law scarcely noticed such plebian family violence at this period, sentencing Prendergast to a mere forty days in prison.[46] In 1874 Mary was subjected to more physical abuse and stabbing for which she gave James in charge in August and had the satisfaction of seeing him receive and actually serve a ninety-day sentence. Between her own terms and during James' terms in jail and absences from the city, either as an escaped convict or a sailor, Mary continued to support herself by prostitution. In 1875 while the escaped convict-husband was out of town, Mary encountered a brutal client in a house in North Street who beat her on the head with a poker and left her badly cut and bleeding in the street to be rescued by the police.[47] In 1880 she was thought to be a fit object for reformation in the house for "fallen" women but expressed her lack of gratitude by escaping and securing admission once more to Rockhead. Undaunted by the experience of middle-class rescue efforts, one of her last periods of incarceration was for being an inmate of a house of "ill-fame" in 1883. In the meantime James continued to batter her. Recorded assaults occurred in 1878, 1879, 1881 and 1882. Even her not very loving father and her brother, Cornelius Ford, began to intercede on her behalf, resulting in their own violent confrontations with James. When she again fell out with her father, he took her to court in 1881 for breaking his furniture. On this occasion Mary was described as "a scarred, ugly looking caricature of what she was ten years ago."[48]

In 1884, her jail career over, Mary graduated to the poorhouse. But she was at service in January 1885 when James descended upon her, demanding money and assaulting her for the last time. On this occasion the Society for the Prevention of Cruelty, the new protector of abused wives, prosecuted James. He went to prison for a year but the intervention of the SPC came too late to save Mary. Five months later she was considered a fit object for that more modern institution, the hospital. Described as a domestic servant, married and thirty-three years of age, she entered the Victoria General Hospital in July in severe pain with frequent vaginal bleeding. The physicians looked in vain for evidence of venereal disease. In contrast, her childlessness, her intemperance, her criminal record and her destitution were not in doubt. Discharged in late August, she returned a month later after "a prolonged debauch" which ended in paralysis. Entered in the record this time as "a rather stout fat woman," a hard drinker like her brother and sisters, with irregular habits, and the wife of "a notorious 'Rockhead bird,' " Mary died on 18 October 1885 and was given a Catholic burial in Holy Cross Cemetery.[49] Mary left her brother Cornelius and her husband James to carry on the family traditions of drunkenness, violence and frequent incarceration.

While Mary's female vulnerability brought her briefly and belatedly into contact with the reformist opponents of both prostitution and wife-battering, no reformers were interested in rescuing her menfolk. They were left to be chained in prison or banished to sea. Curly Ford, her brother, survived his sister by almost twenty years, dying in the poorhouse in 1903. His criminal record spanned nearly half a century. He served over eighty sentences in Rockhead prison plus a few in the county jail and at least one in the provincial penitentiary. His appearances in the poorhouse began in 1884. As a young offender he was often turbulent, spending long stretches of his time in irons at Rockhead in the early 1860s. His confrontations with the police, symbolizing a resistance to authority which was in itself almost pathological, led to frequent assault charges. Unlike the Kellums, he seems never to have been a willing prisoner. He escaped from prison as often as the authorities banished him from the city. Much of his violence was dealt out indiscriminately, but the police assaults, even if exaggerated by the police themselves, were notably specific, as were the attacks on family members.[50] In 1880 his assault on his wife of some two years occurred about a week before she made a desperate public statement by attempting to murder their child.[51] His general bellicosity was demonstrated in 1884 when shortly after being released from Rockhead, he was found on Lower Water Street offering a challenge to fight "anybody in the crowd."[52] His resistance to arrest for creating a disturbance in Albemarle Street in 1877 demonstrated that even a man of his notoriety could command the benign indifference, if not the support, of the public:

> Curly who is a powerful man and has spent the greater part of the winter in Rockhead, being fed and kept at the expense of the city, was in good fighting trim and gave the policeman much trouble. A crowd gathered round, and although called on to do so, not one of them lifted a hand to assist the policeman. [53]

Cornelius Ford's problems were greatly aggravated by his drinking habits. He appears to have been incapable of quiet intoxication. When he surreptiously acquired rum at the police station in 1876, he attacked the policeman who came between him and his bottle. A promise of good conduct which secured his early release in September of the same year was broken when he became besotted and disorderly. When he got drunk in July 1878, he decided his great desire was "to clean out the city." He started and ended with the police.[54]

When he was not in jail he often shipped as a sailor, casual employment he shared with his brother-in-law James Prendergast. In the summer of 1867, he went to sea after his fine was paid, possibly by a none-too-particular shipmaster. At the time of his marriage in 1878, he described himself as a seaman.[55] He also worked at labouring jobs, some of which were on the waterfront where he was frequently arrested. Given his strength and energy, we can speculate that he may have been a casual cargo-handler. By the time he was in his fifties in the 1890s, he had become a local tramp. In this capacity he teamed up with fellow down-and-outs to congregate on street corners by day and "nightly repair to the wharves." He became known as a member of the 'chain gang,' not a reference to prison labour but possibly an allusion to jailbird status.[56]

In his youth Curly had sometimes joined forces with Prendergast before the latter married his sister Mary. Police court observers were unable to decide which of the two was more notorious. They were described as "the pride and flower of Halifax ruffianism."[57] James' thirty-year criminal career was distinguished by two major features: his violence towards all members of his family—blood relatives and in-laws—and his prison escapes, which were almost as numerous as his prison terms. As we have seen, Prendergast's assaults upon his wife were so excessive that the SPC intervened. Local opinion foresaw a Dickensian finale. Though Mary died in hospital with paralysis, not in the gutter with a stab wound, the brutality of her husband, who was described, in this connection as a "veritable Bill Sykes," contributed to her early demise. A couple of years before her death the *Morning Chronicle* had predicted that "the tragic end of Nancy Sykes would be hers."[58]

James' violence was by no means confined to his wife. He beat up his father many times. As often, his father complained to the police but family feuding did not dissuade James from returning to his father's home again and again. It was a useful halfway house for him, half way between prison and freedom. In 1872 police were called to the house after Prendergast threatened its occupants. When they arrived, he extended his anti-social behaviour to them as "he seized a carpenter's goudge or some similar weapon and threatened to kill the first one who approached him." In 1875 he resorted to his father's house after escaping from Rockhead. He exchanged his prison garb for his father's clothes and made for Four Mile House to catch the morning train inland. Whenever he went away as an escaped prisoner or a merchant seaman, Prendergast soon returned to the city and his old haunts. It was a perversity which defies explanation. On several occasions he gave the impression that he was trying to reform. When he got the opportunity, renewed misbehaviour or past misdeeds soon thwarted his better intentions. In 1872, for example, he went to sea after one of his regular escapes from prison. Some weeks later he was arrested on board the *MA Starr* on her arrival in Halifax from Yarmouth. "He had been down the western shore and thinking that the police had forgotten all about him ventured a return to the city." Two years later, he begged to be let go during one of his equally regular appearances in police court, "stating that he would leave the city, and not come back again for two years." Although his discharge was given on condition that he would go to prison for a year if caught, Prendergast relapsed two weeks later and went to prison as a punishment for breaking his promise after he had been found drunk on the street.[59]

The frequency of his prison escapes meant that Prendergast could never shake himself free of the police. It was noted in 1880 that he seldom served a sentence without escaping once or twice. When he escaped in 1882, the press reported that it was "for about the seventieth time."[60] Governor Murray provided a detailed description of "a plausible plan" James had for an escape from Rockhead in 1885.

> The governor found that he had succeeded in removing the fastenings of the bolt which secures his cell door, and carefully plastered up the traces with bread, to resemble the mortar. Suspecting something further, the prisoner's leg shackles were examined, when it was found that the bottom of the rivet in one had been neatly filed off, so that it could readily be pulled out, and as the rivet of the other could not be reached the whole shackle had been filed through transversely so that it could be sprung off at any time after the fashion of a patent key-ring. All this had been done with a piece of razor made into a saw and carefully concealed. The detection was probably just in time, and the prisoner was just waiting a good chance to mature his little scheme and jump. [61]

By the late 1880s, after the death of his equally notorious wife, Prendergast appeared less frequently in court and, unfortunately for his biographer, his name disappears from the record without a trace by the late 1890s.

The saga of the Fords and Prendergasts provides none of the situation comedy that was associated with the escapades of the Kellum clan. The contrast can be explained partly by the racism of the police court reports and partly by the greater violence in the white family. Respective family prospects were also different and helped shape society's perceptions. While we know little about the parents of either family, it seems likely that the delinquent generation represented by Mary and Cornelius Ford and James Prendergast marked a decline in status. The Kellums, on the other hand, may have perceived their combination of whitewashing and prison as an improvement over the rural destitution which had characterized their lives in Halifax County.

In both instances temperament and personality have to be taken into account as well as race and ethnicity, but there must also have been something amiss in the relationship between parents and children particularly to have produced Cornelius, Mary and James. Their two fathers, Michael Ford and John Prendergast, may have had difficulty adjusting as immigrants but they appear to have been more successful in life than their unruly children whose crucial formative years coincided with the period in which their parents established themselves in the city. Michael Ford was himself in police court several times in the 1860s; by the 1880s his public image was untarnished. He was described in 1881 as

> ...a very respectable little Irishman whose family have unfortunately turned out bad. His son is a hard working, decent fellow when he is sober, but that is not often, and when he is drunk he is admittedly the hardest rough in town. The daughter [Mary]...was a comely looking girl, but she became addicted to drinking, and soon, from associating with bad company, took to other species of vice. She had made frequent attempts to reform, going off to the country....A few years ago she was married to a scoundrel who was one of her amiable brother's drinking companions and combines the business of sneak-thieving to that of general rough.[62]

Perhaps the weak link was the mother. Nora Ford disappears from the record in the 1860s. Another wife to Michael, Mary, had replaced her by the time daughter Mary married James. When Cornelius married six years later, an Ann was named as Michael's wife. Perhaps she was a successor to Nora and Mary or perhaps a predecessor; we have no way of knowing whether children tended to report, when asked for information, the name of their natural mother or current stepmother. Maternity in the Kellum family is even more difficult to unravel. The names which appear in formal marriage records indicate a surfeit of mothers. No two siblings reported the same parents. Despite the discontinuity the siblings or half-siblings were very much attached to each other. Conceivably that attachment was a substitute for parental concern and affection. While the whole matter of mother identity is highly speculative, it none the less warrants closer attention. Unfortunately, given the nature of the sources, more detailed family biography for the nineteenth-century underclass is impossible.

The Fords and Kellums were members of the two major ethnic groups in lower-class Halifax: Irish and African. Disadvantaged by their wretched origins and harsh settlement experiences, the blacks and Irish devised various ways of coping with the alien environment. For the very poor and most misfitted among them, like these families, the opportunities were few and the discouragements many. They tried the strategies that

91

appeared to work for others: the Kellums made deals with the authorities, married whites, specialized in particular labouring activities. The Fords left town when the pressure was too great and allowed interventionist organizations like prostitute rescuers and the Society for the Prevention of Cruelty to interfere in their lives. Despite the prominence of family in their activities, it proved to be an inadequate protection either against trouble from without or disorder from within. Perhaps the objective failure of family was attributable to the instability of the maternal element, perhaps the family as a whole exhibited an alien and suspicious culture. Could it have been the exuberant boisterousness of the Kellums which attracted Halifax's white, Anglo-Celtic policemen and caused the arrests for rowdiness and riotousness? Other strategies like drinking and stealing were so regularly indulged in that they were clearly means to some other end rather than ends in themselves. The object, openly espoused in the case of the Kellums, no more than subconsciously exhibited in the case of the Fords, was to be locked up. Only in the prison or the poorhouse could members of these families achieve order in their otherwise chaotic lives. Where their families failed them, the institutions of 'social control' did not. It seems the wrong way round therefore to suggest that incarceration was a form of social control imposed by the powerful upon the ne'er-do-wells. In the case of these disreputable families, the control was a self-generated form of protection in an environment as inimical to survival at the family level as it was in the streets.[63]

The police patrol wagon. (Halifax Police Museum)

The old City Hall which housed the police court, police station and lock-up until the 1890s. (Nova Scotia Museum)

# 4
# WOMEN WITHOUT CHOICES: PUBLIC PROSTITUTES IN A GARRISON-PORT

It is not surprising that underclass women in trouble with the law like Mary Ford and Martha Kellum should have been identified from time to time as prostitutes. Women, without prospects and often destitute, resorted to prostitution as naturally as their brothers turned to stealing. They did not enjoy the luxury of many choices in a city that remained largely non-industrial in its orientation and, in its few industrial establishments, as exploitative of women as other forms of employment. Although we have no nineteenth-century surveys of prostitution in Halifax or controversial issues like the British campaign against the Contagious Diseases Acts on which to draw, enough court cases, city missionary reports and press accounts exist to provide some evidence for assessing the world of prostitution known to those women whose names frequently appeared in the jail registers.

Recent historical interest in prostitution has focused on four overlapping themes. One is an attempt to understand changes in attitudes towards sexuality, especially, though not exclusively, women's. Feminist historians have been particularly concerned to explore the double standard which united women, both "the pure and the impure," against the profligacies of men who indulged their sexual appetites with impunity.[1]

A second concern centres on the employment options and survival strategies of the labouring poor in which prostitution is viewed as work which women chose within the circumscribed limits of available options. In terms of income, prostitution was an attractive alternative to the drudgery of household service. For some women it was an occupation which led to capital accumulation and upward mobility.[2] Another issue relates to the policies affecting prostitution. Here the interest focuses on the stages in the criminalization of prostitution and the role of the state in shaping regulations through legislation and enforcement.[3] A fourth historical preoccupation has been to understand where the anti-prostitution campaigns fit within the wider framework of social movements, especially during the periods of moral reform in the nineteenth century and social purity reform of the early twentieth-century progressive era.[4] Without denying the validity of any of these approaches, in fact quite the reverse, there is also room in this field of inquiry in Canada for the regional historian, someone who asks what was unique about the features of prostitution in a given geographical setting.

Halifax was unique in this regard in two respects. First, it was an imperial city dominated by the British military presence throughout the Victorian era. Second, local efforts at the reform of prostitutes, the regulation of commercialized sex and the abolition of the 'social evil' were minimal despite the fact that Halifax's military character led nineteenth-century moralists to deplore the degree of depravity and suggest that the city had the worst prostitution problem for its size in Canada.[5] Obviously there was a close connection between the military clientage of prostitutes and the civilian failure to interfere with the trade. Prostitution was part of the service sector on which the economy of the city and its women depended. For Halifax residents to attack prostitution was for them to cut off their noses to spite their faces.

Still, given the widespread contemporary knowledge of moral and social reform movements, the existence in Halifax of a wealthy and leisured middle class and the customary practice of copying British and American fashions, it does seem strange that a sustained attack on prostitution did not characterize Halifax society. Besides the "garrison identity," two other explanations can be suggested. In its public manifestations, the occurrence of prostitution was confined to soldiertown and sailortown, areas coterminous with underclass life. Most of the male customers who were caught in compromising situations or otherwise found in the company of known or suspected prostitutes were soldiers and sailors. Visible prostitution did not therefore seem to infringe on local middle-class and upper-class families: it was not their fathers, husbands and sons who frequented the low dives. Secondly, the lack of concern in these circles had something to do with the large proportion of black prostitutes. Although they never expressed it publicly, the guardians of virtue in Halifax may have felt relieved that the supply of prostitutes for the empire's soldiers and sailors, men often considered in any case to be the dregs of society, was drawn from the black underclass. This chapter deals with four questions relating to prostitution in Halifax: the nature of the demand for commercial sex, the sources of supply, the control of prostitution and the culture of prostitution.

The demand for prostitutes came from the military establishment, the lower ranks of which interacted with the damsels of the upper streets. The demand was, however, part of a larger need for women generally by Her Majesty's forces overseas. The British garrison in Victorian Halifax in the second half of the nineteenth century represented only about one per cent of the regular forces of Great Britain but the enlisted men in the infantry regiments, artillery, engineers and service corps, who rotated through Halifax on overseas service, comprised close to 25 per cent of the adult male population of the city. Since they were predominantly without wives, their impact on the balance in the sex ratio of the population was considerable. Unlike their seafaring counterparts, soldiers were often stationed in the city for years at a time and they tended to establish regular monogamous relationships which frequently resulted in marriage. Marriage, however, was actively discouraged in the Victorian army. It was not conducive to the maintenance of a highly mobile, single-minded fighting force which could be easily transported from one part of the far-flung empire to another. It detracted from the rakish cult of masculinity romantically associated with soldiering. It interfered with the undivided allegiance to regiment required of the soldier. As a result, only six per cent of the private soldiers were allowed to be officially married— that is, to marry with the permission of the commanding officer and secure recognition for their wives and children in the form of rations, living quarters and the right of transport from station to station. Beginning in 1867 the men also had to have seven years' service to their credit. Sergeants were allowed greater latitude but they comprised less than ten per cent of a regiment. These rules did not stop the other 94 per cent of the rank-and-file soldiers from establishing conjugal relationships. Indeed, army marriages in Halifax were a demographic factor of considerable significance. One study of marriage patterns indicates that 16 per cent of all marriages contracted in Halifax from 1871 to 1881 were between rank-and-file soldiers of the British army and local women. The 8th regiment—the King's Liverpool—on service in Halifax in the mid 1890s produced one hundred marriages in eighteen months, which involved about one-eighth of the men. The army disapproved but what could the officers do? Marriages were at least less likely to spread venereal disease than was prostitution. To the extent that the military authorities and civilian critics complained at all, it was to blame local clergymen, the resident upholders of middle-class values. They persisted in performing marriages without securing military approval whereas the garrison chaplains were required to ensure that the marriages had the permission of the commanding officer.[6]

Most of the soldiers' wives were drawn from the ranks of the city's domestic servants, a useful preparation for the hard life that lay ahead of them. Unofficial wives enjoyed none of the advantages of being 'on the strength' and the soldier's take-home pay of considerably less than a shilling a day provided insufficient subsistence. They also lived in constant expectation of the termination of their marriages once the soldier-husbands received a new posting. Undoubtedly the optimistic aim of many marriages, and indeed the only way to explain the willingness of women to enter into such seemingly dead-end arrangements, was to secure a discharge for the husband and thereby avoid the forcible severing of the relationship. Many young couples earnestly endeavoured to raise the necessary capital to purchase the liberating discharge. This was an additional incentive to sheer economic necessity for brides to continue in domestic service. They could work as live-in servants in the shops and houses of the upper streets as long as their employers did not object to visits from their husbands who had to live in barracks.

Did the wives themselves engage in prostitution as part of their two-prong economic strategy? Moral reformers certainly thought so. John Grierson, recently appointed city missionary, wrote in 1866: "By far the greatest number of prostitutes have been the wives of private soldiers, who have not the means, many of them, nor have they the inclination to provide them with any comforts of home."[7] To the extent that this is true, we are probably dealing with the kind of part-time, short-term prostitution which Judith Walkowitz has shown to have flourished among poor women in military areas of high demand. If Grierson was correct in his analysis he was even more cogent about the fate of the unofficial wives who were inevitably left behind when soldier-husbands boarded the troop ships for their next posting in the West Indies, the Mediterranean, South Africa or Britain. He described with reprehension the serial monogamy that resulted when the wife of the departing soldier became the wife of a soldier in the replacement regiment.[8] But it does an injustice to the pragmatism of people at the bottom to interpret a series of semi-stable relationships as prostitution the way Grierson did. The anti-familial policies of the British military establishment forced army wives or ex-wives to resort to prostitution or bigamy in order to support their children much as the capitalist labour market forced servants and needle-trades workers to supplement their pitiful earnings through prostitution. Like the army elsewhere in the empire, the military establishment in Halifax depended on both wives and prostitutes. Wives were the charwomen and washerwomen of the regiment, often doing more real work than their husbands in peacetime. For their service to 'Queen and Empire' as the reproducers of soldiers' labour power, soldiers' wives, including several of the infamous 92, frequently ended up as inmates of the poorhouse in their penury either as grass-widows or real widows. Prostitutes supplied the missing companionship for those soldiers with wives at home in Britain or those men understandably reluctant to become seriously involved with a woman who could only be an unofficial wife. As Myna Trustram has argued in her study of military marriages, prostitution was essential for the maintenance of an unmarried soldiery, the military authorities preferring "clean prostitutes" to "wholesome wives" for their soldiers.[9]

In response to the demand for prostitutes sustained by male sexual habits and the demographic features of a garrison-port, a supply of women emerged to fill the requirements. We have no way of determining how many women might have engaged in prostitution. When Dinah Pickering, a black brothel-keeper was reminded in 1854 that she had a lot of girls in her employ, she responded, "not half girls enough."[10] Moral reformers in the 1860s estimated the number of prostitutes in Halifax to be between 600 and 1000.[11] About the sources of supply we are better informed. John Grierson, so knowledgeable about army wives, claimed that prostitutes were working-class women, either servants themselves or the daughters of poor workingmen.[12] Although he failed to mention the daughters of poor workingwomen, our knowledge of the nature of female poverty and the significant incidence of inter-generational prostitution would suggest that the daughters of female heads of families figured even more prominently. In 1864 sixteen-year-old dressmaker Margaret O'Brien and her sister Mary, who lived with their mother, made forays into houses of assignation with their occasional customers. Elizabeth Grant wanted to leave the dens of iniquity and return to her mother's home in Middle Musquodoboit. Nora Ford, probably separated from her husband, kept a bawdy house for soldiers and sailors in her rooms in which her daughters, including Mary, responded to the demand.[13]

Young girls also sought out brothels as refuges from the family home. While this evidence of family crisis does not invalidate Grierson's analysis, the girls were not necessarily poor. Margaret Power, a "very fine looking young woman about nineteen," left her respectable father's home of her own accord in 1862 to set herself up as a high class (or officer class) prostitute in a house maintained by John Templeman and Maria Adams. Margaret Sims was convicted in police court of leaving her home and frequenting houses of questionable character. On the pronouncement of the verdict, "she commenced crying bitterly and approached her mother and threw her arms about her neck and implored her to intercede for her, and made promises of amendment, but both the mother and magistrate were inexorable." Ellen and Kate McKenzie, aged seventeen and twenty respectively, were charged by their father in 1879 with leaving home and frequenting houses in the upper streets.[14]

As a reformer Grierson was particularly interested in ascertaining how women became degraded. Besides military marriages he identified two major routes to a life of infamy in Halifax. First, unsuspecting country girls were introduced to brothels as boarders or servants and found themselves having 'to go with men,' as they put it. Grierson said nothing about the legendary cases of the seduction of servants within middle-class households, young women who were then turned out and denied character references. Kitty Morricay, a good-looking Halifax prostitute whom R.H. Dana tried to rescue in 1842, was one of these. Her mother having died when she was fourteen and her intemperate father having spurned her, Kitty went out to service. Seduced by the young son of a baker, she was dismissed and "could not get another place as she had no certificate of character." Since her father refused to help her, she was reduced to seeking a job in "a bad house" where "she fell into a set of the lowest girls of the town, & was soon out in the streets." Dana attributed her status as a low-class prostitute rather than a courtesan to her misfortune at being ruined by "a poor lad."[15]

Second, girls who entered the few available occupations outside domestic service such as dressmaking and millinery were unable to earn sufficient wages for a satisfactory livelihood in a city where women were unprotected by legislation or unionization. They turned to prostitution as part-timers. Ex-carpenter Grierson, showing little working-class sympathy for his sisters, blamed the girls' extravagant tastes and lack of industrious habits, not their low wages, for this occasional resort to prostitution.

The empirical evidence in the police court minutes confirms that both domestic servants in licensed and unlicensed shops and girls employed in the needle trades who boarded out were inclined to enter the ranks of Halifax's prostitutes. Yet few of them lived in specialized brothels. Indeed the term 'brothel' can be used only to suggest a building in which prostitution occurred. As Grierson reported, the prostitutes, with a few exceptions, "all live in little shops or private houses where liquor is sold with or without license."[16] Many of the houses of soldiertown fulfilled a multi-purpose function which was typical of the unspecialized nature of urban buildings in a pre-industrial setting. A house was likely to be the living quarters of the lessee, it was also his or her business premises. That business usually consisted of a combination of two or more functions which might include boarding, eating, dancing and entertainment, tavern (with or without licence), retail shop selling ready-made clothing or groceries or service shop offering barbering, pawnbroking and the like. In addition such a house (or rooms) acted as a brothel either regularly or on occasional demand from customers. It was obviously to the lessee's advantage to have women on hand to act as prostitutes when needed.

A number of cases before the police court in the 1850s and 1860s, the only years for which official minutes are available, reveal that the lessees, husband and wife partnerships usually, employed legitimate servants within their establishments but that these servants doubled as prostitutes when required. Margaret Davy lived as a servant in the house of a Danish couple. Her agreement with Mrs. Peterson was that she should bring custom to the house. Peterson would board Davy and Davy give her mistress half her earnings.[17] It may well be that service-oriented Halifax was over-endowed with small shops in which case the retail establishments catering to the needs of the soldier-sailor consumer market would have been operating in cut-throat competition with each other. In order to compete, unlicensed shops certainly sold liquor under the counter. Survival may also have depended on the provision of prostitution services. In Robert Evens' house in Barrack Street, Charlotte Bainbridge was employed not as a servant but specifically "to bring custom in the house."[18]

Grierson was particularly critical of parents who used their daughters as "an attractive decoy for soldiers and sailors, to bring them to their liquor store." John and Jane Coffin kept a house in which Jane's daughter was forced to provide sexual services against her will. When Ann Dryden's daughter was found in bed with a marine in her parents' house, she said she was no worse than her mother who also went with men. John and Catherine O'Brien's daughter also prostituted herself in her parents' brothel. A former tenant of that house "saw a man in Mrs. O'Brien's daughter's room stripped to his shirt and Miss O'Brien was lying on the bed, the door was unlocked to let a man in with some brandy and water."[19]

The availability of women attracted custom for food and liquor or whatever else was normally on sale and gave a marginal shop the edge over its equally unstable neighbour without such extra services. The servants in the Scammell household were plied with drink on a summer's night in 1859 and requested to service men-of-war sailors. Mary Pennagar, a servant hired at seven shillings and six pence per month, received "a dollar" (five shillings) for sleeping with one of the sailors. When she protested against this extra duty, Jane Scammell retorted: "why not take money when you can get it." Eliza Neal, the cook, was told by her mistress that she could keep the sailor's fee as the Scammells were unable to give her much in the way of wages. Bridget Young, aged thirteen, maidservant to the Scammells' daughter, was offered to another sailor who paid her five shillings. The testimony of the two women and the girl in the court case that followed indicates that not one of them was in the habit of engaging in regular prostitution.[20] Maria Walsh, a servant at the shop of George and Amelia Reynolds in 1856, described sharing facilities with a street-walker and two marines on one occasion and being given the room of her mistress' daughter in which to fulfil her extra duties on another occasion.[21] Servants in such shops therefore functioned as reserve labour for the local prostitution market.

Similarly women in the needle trades who lived in shops that served as boarding houses often found themselves called upon by the mistress of the house to entertain men in their rooms. The woman boarder usually paid bed money to her mistress on these occasions, an amount equal to half her prostitution fee.[22] The boarder's function as a prostitute might continue to be spasmodic. She was a low-paid, legitimate wage earner, living on her own or perhaps the wife of a soldier or sailor, who was given the occasional opportunity to supplement her paltry wages. Her relationship with the mistress of the house was less exploitative than in the case of the mistress-servant relationships found in other shops or even within the same shop. Since she was not actually an employee of the house the boarder could more readily quit if the arrangements became unpalatable. Her position was also better than the relationship between mistress and boarder in the establishments where the high weekly boarding fee, usually ten shillings but in some cases as high as one pound, could have been paid only through a regular prostitute's earnings or from the purse of the client of a kept woman.[23] These hard-core operations probably used their shop function as a front for prostitution rather than occasionally offering prostitution in order to compete with other small-scale, unspecialized shops. None the less, the prevalence of competition among all the shops of underclass Halifax ensured a degree of freedom of action for those prostitutes who engaged their customers indoors rather than on the street. This freedom of action is confirmed by a high rate of change of residence. There may not have been much upward mobility for Halifax's prostitutes but there was certainly a flexibility in circumstances of under-supply that protected them from the clutches of pimps, who do not appear in the sources and who may have been as relatively unimportant to the conduct of prostitution in Halifax as they were in other nineteenth-century cities before the criminalization of the trade.[24]

Those brothel-keepers who went so far as to beat, threaten or expel their boarders could be rewarded with the vengeance of their former servants turned police informers. Aggrieved prostitutes turned against their land-lords and sometimes had the satisfaction of seeing them fined or impri-soned. In 1855 when Mary Ann Williams, who boarded as a prostitute at the licensed shop of George and Amelia (Molly) Reynolds, was kicked out for her inability to pay her weekly board of ten shillings, she informed on the proprietors. As a result the Reynoldses were find twenty pounds for keeping a house of ill-repute and deprived of their liquor licence. Eliza Pennington successfully charged brothel-keeper John Smith with molest-ing and striking her after she refused to board at his house for ten shillings a week. The women in David and Ellen Horner's establishment turned against them in 1864 after a series of incidents including outbursts of abusive language in which Ellen called one of them a "Black Whore."[25]

Other low-paid or unemployed women had to work in the streets. Their business was conducted in yards, porches, military installations or, on the payment of bed money, in the spare room available in taverns and board-ing houses. It was dangerous work as Eliza Munroe discovered.[26] Higher class clients, including military and naval officers, took their women to houses of assignation. Susanna Prowse's house was notorious for its nightly succession of visitors in cabs. Margaret O'Brien visited this estab-lishment with her sister and their two clients and received twelve shillings and six pence for her half hour's work. Mrs. Prowse was paid for the rooms by the gentlemen.[27] The youthfulness of such prostitutes was much deplored by Grierson but nothing was done before the 1890s to rehabilitate them. In 1866 the court expressed sympathy for a new street-walker, described as quite a young girl, by offering to release her from her ninety-day jail sentence if she secured a position. How she was to find one while behind bars was not explained.[28]

To summarize, then, there were four distinct forms of prostitution in mid-nineteenth century Halifax: street-walkers working in open spaces, empty buildings and military facilities; women, some of whom might be street-walkers, who accompanied their clients to houses of assignation for more leisurely sex; servants in shops of the upper streets who provided the reserve supply of prostitutes and either kept their earnings or paid half to their mistresses; and boarders in the houses of the same area who, on becoming regular prostitutes, either paid a high weekly rent to the keeper of the house or, in the more tightly controlled establishments, paid a weekly rent plus half their earnings.

Overall, John Grierson's analysis of the background of Halifax's prostitutes may be accurate as far as it goes but it ignores one vital feature that the less impressionistic data solidly underline. Beginning about mid-century, it is possible to identify the public prostitutes whose behaviour was sufficiently offensive to the middle-class forces of law and order that they were frequently before the courts and in jail. An analysis of the prostitutes in the 1860s discloses that about 40 per cent of those prosecuted in Halifax were black. This racial dimension does not invalidate Grierson's explanation: blacks too could have come to prostitution from domestic service, the needle trades or the ranks of soldiers' wives, but some refinement is necessary to explain their predominance.

Generally, blacks in Halifax were oppressed because of colour. They filled the meanest jobs in society. Racial oppression reinforced class oppression. During the middle decades of the nineteenth century there was little upward mobility for blacks. They were the poorest of the poor, the workers with the bleakest prospects. What they tended to do over time was to counteract the effects of oppression by monopolizing a number of labouring jobs and services. In the absence of any other viable way for their women to earn a living they probably secured a significant share of the prostitute market. Does their low status in the community mean that their approach to prostitution differed significantly from that of whites?

The majority of black prostitutes claimed to belong to Halifax-Dartmouth and the nearby rural black ghettos. They were therefore unlikely to have come to prostitution as unsuspecting country girls. The slim opportunities for unskilled labour for women and the lack of training schemes suggest that black women, as the most disadvantaged of local women, would have been the last to get any new jobs available through expansion and early industrialization. This undoubtedly meant that they were vastly under-represented in the legitimate female workforce. Certainly, given that the racial breakdown of the Halifax population in the censuses of 1861 and 1871 shows blacks as three per cent of the residents, they were greatly over-represented as 40 per cent of the prosecuted prostitutes. In both the 1871 and 1881 censuses black women outnumbered black men in the city to a greater extent than white women exceeded white men. If it is true that "the sexual imbalance in the black community was due to the immigration of females in their late teens and early twenties into the city," we may be dealing with prostitution as a source of family income for the nearby rural communities of Hammond's Plains and Preston.[29]

We need to look for cultural as well as economic reasons to explain the preponderance of black women as prostitutes. Middle-class sources for the Victorian period give a totally misleading view of lower-class sexual behaviour instead of enabling us to recognize that sexual mores may have varied. Attitudes and practices were conditioned amongst the working class by early exposure to the realities of life and death, unlamented loss of virginity at an early age, pre-marital sexual relations and a flexible approach to cohabitation. For the underclass, experiences were presumably even further removed from those of the middle class. The sexual characteristics of black community life are likely to have exhibited both working-class and underclass features as well as cultural characteristics unique to the historical development of that oppressed group in Nova Scotia. In Halifax, prostitution may also have appeared to be a reasonably attractive way of earning a livelihood to a black woman who could look forward only to a life of drudgery and poverty afforded her by white society. While prostitution may have attracted white women too for this reason, the relative disadvantages of blacks made it even more desirable to them. And there may have been some chances of economic betterment. A high proportion of arraigned brothel-keepers or women with premises that became the resort of prostitutes were black, reflecting a certain degree of upward mobility for black prostitutes.[30] Or perhaps this explanation of sexual behaviour misses the mark and instead we should be asking about the prosecution of a disproportionate number of black women as prostitutes. Perhaps we are witnessing racial persecution. The significance of the racial dimension of prostitution is unlikely to admit of a single explanation.

Prosecution was one of the two major types of control applied to both black and white prostitutes. The law provided many pretexts for arresting public prostitutes. Disorderly behaviour, indecency, lewd conduct and vagrancy were the most common euphemisms for prostitution. Convictions on these charges meant anything from thirty days to twelve months in prison with the option of a fine when the magistrate was so inclined. Occasionally, during stepped-up campaigns to raid brothels, prostitutes were let off if the magistrate could be sure that the establishment would be broken up or the women leave town. We cannot assume that the information gleaned from court cases alone reflects an accurate picture of prostitution in Halifax. We do not know how many prostitutes may have escaped prosecution. In Montreal during this period brothel-keepers kept the police at bay by means of bribery.[31] Halifax too may have had privileged brothel-keepers and protected courtesans. Most of the prostitutes who appeared in the Halifax police court were street-walkers or denizens of the underclass boarding-houses that catered to the 'foreign' military-naval presence. Civilian dalliance largely escaped notice.

An examination of the only well-documented prosecutions that occurred in Halifax—in the 1850s and 1860s—reveals several patterns. Firstly, women who were prosecuted for prostitution were continually before the magistrate's court and in and out of jail. As we saw in Chapter One, they included many repeaters. While most of their offences were sexual in nature, the same women were had up for a range of moral and criminal charges which were not necessarily euphemisms for prostitution: charges such as drunkenness, obscene language, fighting, assault, larceny. These 'notorious' women lived on the fringes of respectable society and as a result had either to resort to deviant behaviour in order to survive or found themselves victimized by the police and the court system for their past sins. They used the street as their forum and battleground; their visibility exposed them to repeated police harassment. Most of those who came before the police court were unable to pay a fine when that option was held out to them. They therefore became regular residents of city prison, occasionally being sent to a rescue home or reformatory or transferred to the poorhouse for treatment of their illnesses, birth of their offspring or as recognition of their incorrigibility. The prosecuted group of prostitutes was remarkably persistent through the mid-century period: jail did not deter them, occasional banishment to the country as servants did not keep them out of Halifax for long.

To illustrate the patterns we can cite a couple of examples from our 92 recidivists. Ann Mahoney, a white woman from Saint John, first came before the police court in 1861 when she was twenty.[32] She served ninety days for being a lewd character in company with four other prostitutes. For the next thirteen years she was convicted on average at least twice a year for prostitution-related offences: lewd character, vagrancy, keeping a house of ill-fame, being an inmate of a house of ill-fame. On one occasion she spent eleven months in Rockhead; her other terms were considerably shorter. Altogether, twenty-eight of her thirty-seven convictions were a direct result of her prostitution. She spent three months in the Catholic archbishop's House of Mercy in 1862 but that experience had no apparent reformist impact on her subsequent career. Her associates in the street and in the brothel were women with skins of every hue, just like the "whites, blacks and copper coloured" women described by the *Acadian Recorder* in 1855.[33] Her last visit to Rockhead was as an inmate of a house of ill-repute and it terminated with her death a day before she was due for release in April 1876.

Unlike Ann Mahoney, Eliza Munroe was a street-walker.[34] Her first appearance before the court was in 1858 when she was fifteen years old. A black girl from Halifax, Eliza spent the bulk of her life between 1860 and 1867 either locked away or drunk in the streets. The jail record reads like this: 1860, five months on three convictions; 1861, four months on two convictions; 1862, nine months on five convictions; 1863, six months on four convictions, the last of which kept her in jail into 1864 when her confinement totalled nine months on the basis of four additional convictions. In 1865 she spent half the year in jail for four convictions, the last of which, combined with four further convictions the next year, gave her nine months in jail in 1866. She was released for the last time on 17 January 1867, six weeks before her violent death described in Chapter One. Thirteen of Munroe's twenty-six convictions were for vagrancy; two for lewd conduct. Her homelessness and her wretchedness landed her in the poorhouse for six and a half months in 1864-5 and again for two and a half months in 1866. She was incarcerated, then, for forty-seven of the final eighty-four months of her life. One of the months in city prison was secured at her own request.

Eliza Munroe differed from many of the Halifax prostitutes in that she usually worked without female companions. Often she was found with her customers in street, barn, stable or yard. At the inquest which followed her death, she was described as having been "constantly intoxicated and one of the worst prostitutes on the hill." Eliza suffered a physical handicap which undoubtedly made her life even more difficult than that of other poor prostitutes: she was lame. She had apparently lost the heel of one foot and toes of the other, perhaps through the frostbite that frequently afflicted the poor in the cruel winter climate. Certainly she worked out-of-doors in all seasons. Whatever the cause of the amputations, this affliction effectively disqualified her for both domestic service and marriage and reinforced her status as an alley prostitute.

Another prominent feature of the prosecutions was the way in which the sexual double standard operated in cases where men and women were caught together in sexual acts. More often than not the men did not appear in court. In a small minority of cases their names came before the court and they were admonished or given a token fine.[35] If they went to jail they got much lighter sentences, possibly on the ground that they were first offenders, and these were likely to be speedily commuted by the authorities. John McDonald, a Pictou man, jailed for ninety days in 1867 with three women from the infamous Blue Bell tavern, was released by the lieutenant-governor after serving only thirty days. In another case involving the Blue Bell in 1865, the women got thirty days, the men ten. In 1866 four

107

well-known prostitutes found in a house in George Street were sentenced to ninety days while five male clients paid fines of one dollar each. When James Kennedy and Eliza Munroe were found together in a stable on Barrack Street, Kennedy was fined five dollars; Munroe got six months in city prison. The only men the law took serious cognizance of were the brothel-keepers.[36]

Crimes against prostitutes were not necessarily treated lightly but the women were frequently made to feel the weight of their status as low-class citizens as well as the injustice of the double standard. The outcome of the trial of petty officer Hugh Lattimore of HMS *Duncan* in August 1866 for robbing Mary Holmes was certainly determined by the victim's status. He pleaded guilty to the charge of taking the prostitute's cash box containing some forty dollars but was acquitted when he explained that he had stolen it "as a joke." Holmes presumably was not amused. That same year in circumstances where the roles were reversed, 'wicked' Margaret Howard was sent up for ninety days for stealing money from another seaman belonging to HMS *Duncan*.[37]

A final feature of the prosecutions relates to the role played by middle-class sensibilities. As we have seen the Halifax establishment was relatively indulgent with regard to barrack-side and dockside prostitution. It was not fornication itself which stirred the ire of respectable society. As long as it was contained within bounds that left respectable society unscathed, none but a handful of zealous moralists worried about it. What Halifax society would not tolerate and eagerly prosecuted were noisy, rowdy houses offensive to the ear and eye. In addition to raids, disreputable houses were kept before the public by the occurrence of crimes, fires and, in 1863, the demolition of a house by disappointed sailor-clients.[38] Society was also outraged by brothel-keeper partnerships consisting of a white man and a black woman or vice versa, such as the Pickerings, the Reynoldses and the Morrises.[39] Offensive also to middle-class notions of propriety were the liberties taken by duly licensed tavernkeepers. The publicans of licensed houses were expected to repay the city authorities by observing middle-class rules of decorum; they were not entitled to keep brothels. For doing so they lost their licences.[40] Society's new and increasing concern for the welfare of children, particularly the rescue of juvenile delinquents, meant that the exploiters of young children were beginning by the 1860s to receive an unfavourable press.[41] Offensive too were sexual perversions and outrageously lewd behaviour, the details of which occasionally became public. To middle-class sensibilities, the everyday over-crowded conditions of the slum tenements did not sufficiently explain the bed-sharing that went on in brothels. In December 1864 Mary Slattery

108

slept in a bed in the Horners' house with her customer from the slaughter-house as well as her friend Mary McKenzie.[42] By the end of the 1860s, after the appointment of a stipendiary magistrate, the court was beginning to hear the more salacious cases in camera, thereby depriving the habitués of the police court gallery and the readers of the police court columns in the newspapers of their prurient entertainment.[43]

For the hardened prostitutes, middle-class opinion revealed little sympathy. Garments in shreds, homeless, spending their summers almost entirely out-of-doors, they were described as "pitiful specimens of decrepit humanity." It is perhaps no wonder that such women sought out the jail as their refuge and made little effort to stay outside its walls for prolonged periods. As Jane Harsin discovered with respect to the most downtrodden nineteenth-century prostitutes in Paris: "Some women seemed unable to survive outside; prison represented a kind of discipline that they were unable to maintain for themselves."[44]    They also used the poorhouse and the hospital as their own welfare services.

Piecemeal prosecution of keepers of houses of prostitution, inmates and street-walkers was not the only form of attempted control of prostitution in Halifax. The military concern about maintaining order and minimizing the risk of venereal diseases led the commanders of the army and navy to press unsuccessfully for the enactment of a Nova Scotian equivalent to the controversial British Contagious Diseases Acts of the 1860s which involved the licensing and regular medical examination of prostitutes in garrison and naval towns. Although the passage of such legislation in the pre-Confederation province of Canada in the 1860s proved to be a dead letter, it is less historically significant than a jurisdication like Nova Scotia never having passed it at all, even after Halifax became the bastion of the British forces in Canada.[45] In the absence of government legislation, the commanders of the forces were left with only one weapon in their arsenal: declaring notorious houses out of bounds which they did with great regularity. Martha Norton's house, earlier used as a billet for soldiers, was declared off-limits in 1857 because of its reputation as a brothel. The house frequented by soldiers where Mary Slattery was set alight in 1874 was declared out of bounds after that prostitute's well-publicized death.[46] Sometimes fear of disease led to whole streets being proscribed. In 1889 when between forty and fifty soldiers were in hospital with venereal diseases, the military authorities declared off-limits four streets below the Citadel which ran between the North and South Barracks and six intersecting streets, an area in which they claimed 90 per cent of the dives frequented by soldiers could be found.[47] While military and naval proscriptions did not always coincide, the keepers of houses used for prostitution felt the effects of parts of the upper streets being declared out of bounds for years at a time, much as Isaac Sallis and his fellow publicans did.

The scatter syndrome effect of such regulations was emphasized when the military out-of-bounds orders of 1897 cleared the three most Dickensian streets. According to a newspaper report: "The soldiers now frequent other streets and leading thorough fares and cause disturbances."[48] Although the regulations were directed at the soldiers, the effect of the edicts on local society was the same as the brothel clearances which occurred in other cities, making work more difficult for the prostitutes as well as the police.

If a brothel had to move it usually relocated in the marginal working-class neighbourhood to the north of soldiertown proper rather than in the lower streets by the dockside because of the standing military prohibition on Upper and Lower Water Streets. The only site near the waterfront which was popular at mid-century was Artz Lane just above the dockyard gates. The preferred upper-street locations reflect the reliance on the year-round military customers as opposed to the seasonal seamen. Seamen, on the other hand, were undoubtedly the more desirable customers since they had more money in their pockets than the soldiers. When the Tars were in port, they got priority over the penniless Tommies. This helps to explain the preponderance of naval sailors in prostitution-related court cases.

The city council, for its part, was always very reluctant to indulge in rooting out the prostitutes from the upper streets. Shortly after incorporation in 1841, the location of the brothels was well enough known to serve as something of a tourist attraction. R.H. Dana on his first visit to Halifax in 1842 donned his "rough" sailor's clothes for "a cruise about the town" one July evening. He investigated the noisy and crowded houses on Barrack Street.

> Buttoning my coat & pulling my cap over my face, I went into the largest of these houses. The door was open & people passed in & out as they chose. The entry terminated in an oblong room with low & black walls, sanded floor & closely barred shutters, used as a dancing hall. At one end was a platform holding two chairs upon which the fiddle & triangle player sat. At the other end was the bar, at which the bloated, red faced master of the house sold the glasses of rum, brandy & wine to the girls & their partners. In the middle of the room, in an arm chair, sat the old harradan [sic], the "mother" of the house, with a keen wicked eye, looking sharp after the girls & seeing to it that they made all the men dance & pay the fiddler & treat them at the bar after each dance. There were about a dosen [sic] girls, nearly all of whom were dancing, & the average number of men in the room at a time was from 20 to 30....

Having staid as long as I dared to without either dancing or going to the bar, or attracting notice, I slipped out & went into the next house. This was smaller & more filthy, & there were only two or three white girls of the lowest description among half a dosen [sic] black girls or women....There was very vulgar & rough work here, two or three drunken sailors & a good deal of horse-play...[49]

Fifty years later the brothels were still "in full blast...in the heart of the city, crowding up against a church on one side, flanked by a high school in another, in the shadow of the police station, girt round with factories, professional offices, and pure homes." At their liveliest about 10 o'clock in the evening, the houses still offered such entertainment as piano playing, singing and dancing as a prelude to sexual intercourse.[50] The gradual gentrification of the upper streets meant that the council was called upon increasingly in the 1880s and 1890s "to clear out houses of questionable repute in the vicinity of the Halifax Academy" when the middle class became concerned about the effect of immoral behaviour on children as they passed through streets no longer reserved exclusively for the lower classes. The chief of police continued to drag his feet on the ground that "there was some doubt as to the legal authority to attack such places without formal complaint, and there was also doubt as to the wisdom of scattering about the city such characters as occupied those houses."[51]

The culture of prostitution which flourished despite prosecutions, grounding of soldiers and sailors and middle-class distaste included many other problems for Halifax's demi-monde. We know that it was an exceedingly dangerous occupation. In the primitive state of medical science and the absence of effective contraceptive devices, venereal disease, abortion and pregnancy made a prostitute's career a risky one. The excessive use of alcohol and drugs may have dulled the senses and helped to alienate the woman's mind from her ill-used body; but they also ate away at her vital organs. Infanticide and premature death characterized the public prostitute's outcast existence.

We know also that women whose patterns of cohabitation simply deviated from the norm were labelled as prostitutes with no regard for their special circumstances. This category included vulnerable women on the fringes of professional prostitution who were occasionally trying to make ends meet in the absence of dependable support from their menfolk. Middle-class society could not comprehend the problems of soldiers' and sailors' women any more than it was willing to understand sexual behaviour that fell within the grey area between monogamous marriages at one extreme and overt prostitution at the other. Three sailors' wives, whose husbands were at sea, were implicated in a brothel case in 1856 as boarders in a dancing house kept by a couple with an earlier brothel conviction. The women's status as sailors' wives did nothing to protect them from the magistrate's displeasure.[52] As we have seen, such women with intermediate arrangements were numerous in Halifax and their exposure to prosecution served to complicate their already precarious way of life.

Finally, we must appreciate that a woman alone in the upper streets was likely to feel the full weight of patriarchal society's prejudice against independence for women. She was almost automatically suspect. Sarah Little entered a disreputable house in 1859 to fulfil her duties as a wet-nurse only to leave it for the bridewell convicted of lewd behaviour.[53] Julia Donovan, whom we met as Sallis' associate in Chapter Two, tried to run a small shop as a legitimate business but it became the resort of doubtful characters who tried to pervert its purposes. In 1863 she turned a well-known prostitute over to the police for disorderly conduct in her house and later resisted an assault on herself and her bartender by a local intruder. Before her conviction in 1865 for keeping a bawdy house, Donovan was involved in several liquor licence cases, was herself convicted of public drunkenness and was briefly and inconclusively implicated with a married couple for keeping a bawdy house. After she went to jail the final time, she admitted that she was young and weak and had not always been able to prevent disorderly proceedings in her house. Although this confession may have been designed to elicit the sympathy of the lieutenant-governor, her subsequent release was a Pyrrhic victory. The city fathers put an end to her independent business initiatives by making the commutation of her six-month sentence conditional on her immediate removal from the upper streets and the shopkeeping opportunities that area afforded.[54]

Despite being treated like pariahs, prostitutes relied on co-operation from the justice system, their male associates and each other. They expected fair trials and, though open to victimization, they were not automatically convicted just because they were known to be prostitutes. After Henrietta McKegney was arrested for being on the street late at night in November 1868, she was able to convince the magistrate that she had been both sober and homeward bound.[55] Not surprisingly women sometimes protested noisily when they were prosecuted on the basis of previous convictions or known reputation rather than clear evidence of wrongdoing. One of the four women arrested in Ann Smithers' house in Albemarle Street, a house which was described as an eating house, complained loudly in court that she was condemned as a prostitute without any trial: that guilt by association was insufficient proof of her complicity.[56] Furthermore they argued that they were worthy of some recognition for their contribution to the public in service-oriented Halifax. A twenty-eight-year-old black circus woman named Harriet Jackson, about to be sent to jail in 1862 for repeated improper conduct on the streets, protested unsuccessfully in an especially hostile court room that she was surely entitled to her freedom because she had worked long and hard for the public.[57]

The men with whom they interacted in the upper streets helped to shape the prostitutes' work environment, with both positive and negative effects. Several prostitutes in a house in Barrack Street were defended by black repeat offender William Dixon in 1860 when John Morley, a private of the 63rd regiment, made his demands in an uncouth manner. He accosted one of the occupants with the demand: "give me a f—k, you D—D Black Bitch. I want a Woman; I want a piece of skin." Dixon jumped to the attack when Morley began to abuse the prostitute physically.[58] In another instance, when a male brothel-keeper proposed to break up his house in 1863 to go into barbering, the women protested strongly against what they considered to be a violation of trust between employer and employee.[59]

The union of the women against the would-be barber highlights prostitute solidarity in the face of external threats. Prostitutes lived together, worked together, drank together, went to court and jail together. They did not normally discriminate against each other on grounds of race, religion or ethnic origin though they occasionally fought with each other over men, reputation and betrayal, using their tongues, their fists and the courts.[60] The broader pattern remained one of co-operation as they shared their rooms and demonstrated a united front in the face of threats to their tenuous, marginal way of life. A raid on a house in City Street in 1862 described by police as "a horrid den of iniquity and a haunt of vice" sent nine women to court. They did not deny being prostitutes. Mary Young testified that all the women in the house "go with men" and claimed: "I know no other means of getting a livelihood without sleeping with men." In that establishment Mary shared a room with one of the other women, Mary Ann Goldsworthy, the mother of a babe in arms. Another mother in the house was Mary's sister Bridget, who had been prostituting herself as a servant girl of thirteen, three years earlier.[61] Dispatched variously to the poorhouse and the city prison, these women would emerge eventually to regroup with other women on the margin and pursue once again the difficult task of survival in the upper streets. Like their counterparts in Paris, "prostitution was for these women a part of the cycle of poverty, crime, and uncertainty."[62]

113

The upper streets after the construction of the high school (Halifax Academy). The long building in the left of the picture is the South Barracks. Grafton Street is in the foreground. (Public Archives of Nova Scotia)

# PART II

The North End City Mission of 1869. (J.J. Stewart Collection, Dalhousie University)

Brunswick (Barrack) Street after the construction of the Taylor shoe factory and the Jost Mission. (Public Archives of Nova Scotia)

# 5
# EVANGELIZING THE MASSES: VICTORIAN CITY MISSIONS

Cross-class contacts for the persistent victims of underclass life centred on the police, the magistracy and the keepers of the poorhouse and the prison. But they did not end there. Beginning in the 1850s and increasingly in the 1860s and 1870s, the forces of Protestant evangelicalism and Catholic social action, closely followed by more secular urban reformism, descended on the areas of the city inhabited by outcasts as part of the wider mission to convert the unchurched and spread the moral and domestic values of the 'respectable.'

Do-gooders involved in urban moral and social reform in the Victorian period have intrigued historians on both sides of the Atlantic for several decades.[1] They have been interpreted variously as forerunners of several groups—social gospellers, Christian socialists, social imperialists, feminists, environmentalists and professional social workers. To understand this diversity we must acknowledge the validity of F.K. Prochaska's assertion that in "charitable activity, no one class or denomination had a monopoly."[2] In Halifax, as in England and America, volunteers and paid agents concerned with prevention, rescue and salvation represented a broad cross-section of society from the gentry class to the working class. Among the former was Isabella Binney Cogswell, a wealthy spinster who

117

was prominent in most Protestant charitable ventures involving women and children until her death in 1875. In the middle ranks were many of the city's clergymen, businessmen and professionals and their wives, sisters and daughters who donated ideas, money and volunteer time. At the lower end of the social scale were the actual city missionaries and agents, usually laymen, who came to the work in their middle age after experience as small businessmen, artisans or soldiers. The activist lay women were usually the wives or widows of such men. Among the trained religious who devoted their efforts to the city's social problems were Catholic nuns and Salvation Army officers, people drawn normally from the lower classes. Many of the patrons, volunteers, paid agents and trained workers were British immigrants whose appreciation of social problems had been honed in the old country; a few had American experience. All of them were stalwart supporters of the temperance cause. They were also firm believers in collective efforts and structured procedures. The major vehicle for their initiatives was the voluntary association, sometimes in conjunction with an appropriate institution. Such organized undertakings depended for their survival on community support in the form of a favourable press and generous financial contributions.

Carroll Smith-Rosenberg has observed that just because "those who chose to do good seem to us moralizing and socially conservative does not invalidate the genuineness of their commitment."[3] What concerns us here is not their commitment but their impact. The denizens of the upper streets were both helped and hindered by the efforts of these Victorian moral reformers. Family bonds, however undesirable they appeared to the outsider, were loosened by their interference with traditional family life. New opportunities were offered to, or perhaps more accurately forced upon, children of parents deemed unsatisfactory by their social betters. The influence of religious control was strengthened by the constant use of clergy as informants and agents for relief and by their prominence in the various institutions, particularly those involved in child rescue. Through organizations with national and international links like the Salvation Army and the Society for the Prevention of Cruelty, wife deserters and runaway children were tracked down. Work, even if it was only gruelling physical labour at starvation wages, was provided for men who were frequently unemployed and shunned charity. The evils of drink were trumpeted far and wide until even those derelicts who drank to excess must have begun to believe that liquor, rather than the conditions which caused them to drink, was the cause of their downfall. And last, but not least, outcast people who seldom heard a kindly word were confronted with 'friendly visitors' whose interest was appreciated even if their message was not.

\* \* \* \* \* \*

The moral deficiencies of urban society were first systematically exposed to public scrutiny by the Halifax City Mission established in 1852. It was the brainchild of G.N. Gordon, a young Presbyterian theological student who became Halifax's first city missionary, nine years before his massacre in the New Hebrides as a foreign missionary. The mission was concerned primarily with spiritual destitution of which the missionaries found plenty. The second city missionary John Steele, an Anglican sent out by the London City Mission, on which the Halifax one was closely modelled, claimed that "the irreligiousness of the community surpasses in proportion anything of the kind he had witnessed in English cities." Soon, however, the missionaries were exposed to other social ills of the "heathens" of the upper streets. Their frequent visitations to the houses of the poor and outcast gave them ample opportunity to identify sickness, sloth, violence, crime and immorality, all of which they blamed on the misuse of alcohol.[4]

At the same time they recognized that some problems, even if alcohol-related, required special attention. For the twelve years these concerns centred on illiteracy, prostitution, juvenile delinquency and family squalor, prominent features of underclass life. John Grierson, the fourth missionary and a Presbyterian like Gordon, identified "abject ignorance" as the cause of "the degradation and misery" of the upper streets. While Gordon was performing what he called the disagreeable task of visiting every house in Barrack Street he found young men assembling at dusk to pay their first visits to the local prostitutes. Methodist Archibald Morton, the third and longest serving missionary attached to the City Mission, watched the number of prostitutes increase between 1856 and 1865 and ventured that even the thirteen- and fourteen-year-olds "daily use *strong drink*, to drown alike the voice of conscience and their sorrows." He also recorded "the painful fact that scores of children and youths of Halifax are growing up in idleness and ignorance, and the many vices that almost always accompany them." One of the strongest supporters of the mission among the city's evangelical clergy, P.G. MacGregor, pastor of Poplar Grove Presbyterian Church, declared with environmentalist optimism: "one fifth of our families are crammed into cellars, garrets, and single rooms, where industry, morality and respectability, are all but an impossibility. We have been accustomed to regard this perishing class as the natural and inevitable residuum of society. No such residuum, however, is to be regarded as inevitable."[5] This important shift in attitude from the acceptance of the status quo to a determination to reform the underclass encouraged cross-class interventionism.

The significance of the campaign of the interdenominational Protestant mission against the sins and omissions of the 'residuum' is threefold. First, the mission was an effective publicist of the social ills of the city's underclass neighbourhoods. Second, it pursued an important lobbying function, especially through its well-informed reports to the civic authorities about the problems of the slums. Third, the City Mission spawned, promoted or inspired a number of the specialized institutions which the missionaries recognized as necessary adjuncts to their work of saving souls.

Since the City Mission was dependent on congregational and individual contributions for its support, publicity was part of its continuous fund-raising campaigns. The missionaries' journals were widely distributed in printed annual reports. Highlights of reports and meetings were carried by the local press. Well known too was the pamphlet called *Halifax: "Its Sins and Sorrows"* issued in 1862 by a mission supporter. It was considered by some to be a grossly exaggerated and distorted account of the city's social problems but by others a fair reflection of the nature of the city's moral depravity when it came to drunkenness, prostitution and sabbath desecration.

The mission was also well known to the poor and outcast because it pioneered street preaching in "the very worst and most destitute localities of the city" and because the missionary visited the houses and institutions inhabited by the underclass.[6] For his domiciliary visits the missionary concentrated on the upper streets: Barrack, Albemarle, Grafton and vicinity, and on the northern extension of Halifax's underclass district around City Street. The visits made by Morton and Grierson, about which we have the most information, confirm many of the unsavoury features of these streets. Prominent among the temporary and permanent residents they encountered were sailors, prostitutes, servants, liquor sellers and soldiers' wives. They included a high proportion of blacks. The residents generally lived in crowded and filthy conditions. Respectable families, some of which the missionaries acknowledged to be pious, were not completely lacking in these streets. In October 1863 Morton reported that the dozen Protestant households which he visited in one street included eight passable families. But they lived cheek by jowl with three households comprised of drunks and four of prostitutes.[7]

120

In another neighbourhood he visited, possibly City Street, he noted with careful regard for religion, race and gender that six adjacent households included a notorious brothel kept by a Catholic, a tenement owned by a black Methodist woman and occupied also by two young Anglican women of "doubtful reputation" and two ex-prostitute Catholics who used their flat as a house of assignation for the convenience of lustful men and their "victims." The third dwelling was occupied by a poor, black, Baptist family and the fourth was a brothel kept by a black Methodist woman whose half-dozen girls were both black and white. The last two houses he described were four-room cottages in which each of the eight rooms was occupied by a prostitute, six black and one white Baptist and one white Anglican.[8]

Morton's reports threw light on what he considered to be the deplorable involvement of women in the liquor trade both as purveyors and consumers. One of the former was the wife of a servant in a respectable family who opened a liquor shop and allowed dancing through which her children were introduced to sailors and prostitutes and seduced away to brothels and her husband became a "perfect sot" by which he met an early death. Another was the wife of a good but drunken artisan in City Street who decided to sell liquor in her small shop on the premise that if her husband must drink, she "may as well get the profit as any one else." Among the drinkers, Morton described the "wretchedness of a drunken mother of four" who was the wife of "an industrious mechanic" and the death of an old hag whose drinking habit had produced a spontaneous combustion. The woman's "mouth had the appearance as if a flame had issued from it; destroying the lower half of the nose, and burning the upper lip to a cinder. The tongue was also so much burned that the half of it fell out while the body was being washed." She too was a mother, having produced a drunken son who was so intoxicated at her funeral that he could not walk.[9]

Grierson also resorted to lurid details in his description of the drinking habits of the residents of the upper streets. He found prostitution and alcohol abuse to be inextricably connected. On Barrack Street prostitutes lived in thirty public houses and on Albemarle Street he reckoned there must be two or three times as many prostitutes as on Barrack Street, most of whom lived in the little shops which sold liquor either legally or illicitly. As we have seen, he strongly suspected the connivance of Albemarle Street parents in their daughters' harlotry. The family context of drunkenness, which he described, implicated fathers, mothers and children. The male heads of some twenty families he encountered in the upper streets violently abused their wives and children when they were drunk.

Mothers sacrificed their children's food in order to satisfy their craving for rum. It was not at all uncommon to find parents selling their furniture in order to pay for liquor. The unfortunate example was not lost on the children: Grierson often had to expel teenage boys from his evening and Sunday schools because they turned up drunk. However bad Halifax was supposed to be in this regard, one newspaper claimed that Grierson's account "so far exceeds anything we anticipated as to fill our minds with mingled deep regret and astonishment" and went on to quote from his 1866 report:

> One evening I found a mother lying in a dangerous state from kicks and blows given her by a drunken son—seven of whom were in the room, five confirmed drunkards, and four of them then drunk—the two youngest, 12 and 14 years, have both been the worse of liquor several times. In another house I saw a young man lying drunk on the floor of his mother's room, having procured the rum by stealing and selling his mother's bible—he had not been sober for ten weeks. I heard a man the other day calmly and deliberately reply, when he was told that drink would ruin both soul and body, "I will have a glass of gin if I go to hell in five minutes." I was visiting at a house where a hand-axe, which a drunken husband had thrown at a drunken wife, was still sticking in the wall; the man had been drunk for six weeks. In the same street, I know a father and mother who are drunk almost every day, and whose chief, if not only, support is obtained from their daughter's prostitution, which must be often carried on under their own eyes, as they all occupy the same room. [10]

Even if these reports were largely cautionary tales, they did nothing to enhance the reputation of the upper streets in the minds of respectable Haligonians.

The public reports of the missionaries prepared the authorities for the lobbying by the city's leading evangelical clergymen and other mission society members against a number of intractable evils they perceived to be associated with the culture of the upper streets. Three of the problems which the mission society drew to the particular attention of the city and provincial governments in the 1860s were prostitution, the liquor trade and infanticide. The public response to each culminated in 1875 with the opening of the Women's Home for prostitutes, the Grove for inebriates, and the Infants' Home for unwanted babies. Unfortunately we know very little about the nature of the mission's campaigns. The one related to prostitution was conducted in 1860 when the committee decided that a perceived increase in immorality required an investigation of the extent of "the social evil." For this, the secretary prepared a table of statistics which was transmitted to the aldermen of the various wards of the city through the good services of the mayor. In anticipation of the results, a subcommittee was established "for the purpose of making such arrangements, suggesting such plans, and calling the attention of the public authorities to some regulations that may be advantageous to this class of unfortunate and the community generally." The outcome of this initiative is unknown but mission supporters were always in the forefront of the efforts to launch and sustain refuges for prostitutes and encourage police raids on the most visible brothels.[11]

The liquor question was one which obviously exercised the attention of the members every time court proceedings indicated the inadequacy of the liquor laws and the missionary's reports revealed yet again the problems associated with virtually unregulated access to liquor. Whereas Isaac Sallis and his fellow NCOs despised Sergeant Elliott for informing on upper-street liquor sellers in 1856, the evangelical press applauded the sergeant's motives as pure and honourable when he exposed "the unlicensed pest-houses in which his comrades are being poisoned." The Reverend P.G. MacGregor, chairing the annual meeting of the mission in 1857, spoke of the "terrible effects" of the licensing system and in 1861 the mission committee presented a memorial to the mayor and council calling for more stringent measures for the granting of licences. Although the mission was only one of the parties interested in tightening up the liquor laws, it could claim to speak for a broad spectrum of Protestant, middle-class opinion in Halifax.[12] Under such continuing temperance influence, Rockhead drunkards such as Julia Kelly and Patrick Cody were occasionally discharged on condition that they took the pledge.[13] Temperance pressure in the early 1860s led to more satisfactory legislation in 1864 but legislation and practice remained far enough apart to sustain a running critique of existing regulations.

The missionaries and medical members of the Halifax City Mission urged the temperance organizations to press the legislature for the establishment of an inebriate asylum. While nothing immediately came of this initiative, the issue was subsequently taken up by the temperance leaders who petitioned the House of Assembly in 1868 and received an encouraging response. The temperance press also agitated for an asylum on the ground that "four-fifths of the pauperism and crime existing in our midst owes its origins to drunkenness." Even the prohibition fanatics recognized that only rehabilitation could help existing drunkards to kick the habit.[14] The institution was finally opened in 1875 after the government had passed legislation for the guardianship and treatment of habitual drunkards, a measure which more or less forced it to provide curative facilities for alcoholics, at least on an experimental basis. Modelled on the Appleton home in Boston, the "Grove," located like the lunatic asylum on

123

the Dartmouth side of the harbour, provided a "family" environment for up to twenty patients. Offering wholesome food, recreation, work and worship, the institution was based on the assumption that drunkenness knew no class. Soon after its opening the first drunkard was sent there from the Halifax police court. The institution, apparently for men only, did not outlive the 1870s.[15] Interest in the treatment of habitual drunkards revived only in the 1890s when the gold cure became the fashionable treatment.[16]

The third campaign centred on the concern over infanticide. Closely associated with a culture which encouraged prostitution and short-term military marriages, infanticide served in the nineteenth century as a form of birth control when abortions failed and as the last desperate resort of seduced servant girls who would lose both their jobs and their characters through the discovery of illegitimate births. It seems likely that the soldier-town/sailortown areas of Halifax were the source of most of the circumstances which gave rise to infanticide. According to a recent study, most of the babies' corpses were found in the area between the Citadel and the waterfront.[17] The *Presbyterian Witness* claimed that twenty-three cases of infanticide had occurred in the city in 1864 and there were at least fifteen cases of concealed newborn deaths in 1866. In 1867 the mission committee sent a delegation to the mayor to express concern over this continuing problem. Perhaps what troubled the mission organizers most was the fact that a foundling home had been opened in 1865 specifically to provide an alternative to infanticide for desperate women. In less than half a year it had rescued twelve "cast-away children" from destruction and seemed to be a successful addition to the city's benevolent institutions. But by 1867 it no longer appeared to be working.[18]

City mission interest in this problem helped to keep the need for effective measures before the public but it was not until 1875 that the Protestants opened the Infants' Home and 1886 that the Sisters of Charity opened the Home of the Guardian Angel. These homes, catering also to unwed mothers and their infants, reflected a shift in attitudes away from abhorrence of mothers as murderers to concern for the circumstances in which workingwomen, often single, had to provide care for their infants. If the foundling hospital of 1865 was directed against infanticide, the infants' homes of the last quarter of the century were established to eliminate baby-farming. According to one contemporary assessment, the clients of baby-farmers in Halifax were domestic servants, who paid child-minders no more than fifty cents a week out of their scanty $4-$6 monthly wages to 'care' for their illegitimate offspring, and unofficial soldiers' wives, who had to go out to work in order to support themselves and children in the absence of a husband's income.[19]

The mission's interests therefore were wide-ranging. Despite the primary aim to save souls, the efforts of the supporters, when it came to expansion and diversification, went not into the building of a mission house for religious services, but into the promotion of a number of institutions designed for various victims of the city's social ills. Several of these were aimed at the poorer members of the working class. In 1856 the mission addressed the plight of transient workers: railway labourers in the Halifax area and merchant seamen ashore. Out of these concerns grew a short-lived sailors' home in 1862 and continued agitation for attention to the spiritual welfare of sailors.[20] The other initiative that was designed to benefit the working class was the establishment of a penny savings bank in 1863. The press reported on its opening that a large number of people were availing themselves of the opportunity to deposit their spare coppers. Located on Albemarle Street and operated by a voluntary board of directors, the aim was "to encourage habits of frugality and economy, particularly among the poor."[21]

The rest of the mission's energies were directed towards the underclass. As an agency for spiritual salvation through knowledge of the bible, one of the first problems which the mission workers addressed was illiteracy and, given the little likelihood they entertained of success among adults, these efforts were directed specifically at children. The first missionary established a ragged school for slum children in 1852 after he found, during his first six months, 100 school-aged children who had never been to school. This mission day school, taught by a woman, expanded to include a class for blacks in 1856, as the middle class gradually drove a wedge between the integrated racial elements of the underclass. By 1857 about half of the ragged school children were Catholic, as compared to 40 per cent of the city's population. A ragged Sunday school followed in 1858 and an attempt to extend schooling to children who worked all day led eventually to the establishment of mission evening schools in 1866. The Sunday schools and evening schools drew on the voluntary services of twenty-two teachers. In the years before the introduction of free schools in the mid 1860s, the number of charitable places in the existing semi-public schools was limited and mission schools therefore performed an important educational function.[22]

With an emphasis on the spiritual and moral improvement of the children, the mission was also concerned about the prevention of delinquency. Under Archibald Morton, the mission was in the forefront in calling for the establishment of a juvenile reformatory but was unable to get this project off the ground until 1863 when the Halifax Industrial School was opened. While the mission did not actually establish the reformatory, the first in the city outside of Rockhead, it was certainly one of its stepparents. Under the guidance of Isabella Binney Cogswell, who was also its generous patron, it originated as a combined ragged school and house of industry for both boys and girls, employed in making paper bags, learning the shoemaking trade and acting as errand boys and shoe-blacks. The organizers wanted a residential facility to isolate the children "from old and injurious associations and have time and opportunity for improvement in all that is calculated to make them useful members of society."[23] Accordingly, in 1864 the ragged school was separated from the new residential industrial school, the former being located in the old Inglis (African) school in Albemarle Street and the latter in Spring Garden Road until it moved to Quinpool Road in 1870. The Industrial School was confined to boys, many of whom were 'street arabs' who, when returned to the streets during the work hours as shoe-blacks and errand boys, resorted to their customary misbehaviour, forcing the managers to discontinue these particular lines of work. Mission supporters and moral reformers soon began to agitate for the recognition of the Industrial School as an official reformatory, to which juvenile offenders might be sentenced instead of to Rockhead where the reformatory wing was considered to be "the merest sham."[24]

The connection between the Industrial School and the City Mission and a concomitant strengthening of the Protestant ambience of the school was reinforced in 1866 when city missionary John Grierson was appointed to superintend the Industrial School on a part-time basis. In 1867 he took on the job full-time though his voluntary services in the south mission area continued during most of his superintendency and resulted eventually in his return to city mission work in 1876 and his appointment as seamen's missionary in 1881. Under Grierson and his wife as unpaid matron, the industrial pursuits followed in the school expanded to include cabinet-making (Grierson was a carpenter), tailoring and, for the younger boys, carpet cleaning and production of kindling wood for the city's domestic consumption. The boys worked eight or nine hours a day after which they were obliged to attend evening school for an hour or more. No wonder they sometimes ran away. Grierson realized that it was during the early period of confinement that the boys found the restraint and discipline "most irksome." If they persisted for a year, he felt they would adjust satisfactorily to the rhythm of work and the ethic of industry. The desired results were achieved when industrial school graduates entered the city's workforce at wages of $8 or $9 a week.[25]

In the late 1860s the school supporters campaigned successfully for it to become, for Protestant boys, an alternative to the Rockhead reformatory. In 1870 they secured federal legislation and civic funding for this purpose. The sectarian nature of the school, known after 1865 as the Protestant Industrial School, was based on the presumed opposition of the Catholic Church to Catholic boys being sent there and on the arrogant Protestant assumption that the city prison, inhabited very largely by Catholics, was probably good enough for them in any case.[26] As a result a parallel institution for Catholic boys, the St. Patrick's Industrial School, was established by that church with similar funding in 1885.

The industrial schools catered to delinquent boys, to boys whose behaviour marked them out as future delinquents, to vagrants and destitutes and, after 1888, to truants. Boys sent from the police court received much longer terms in the schools than they were accustomed to spending in Rockhead. Recognized delinquents were not separated from the street children in the Protestant Industrial School because it was thought "quite accidental that only some of them had been convicted in Police Court." Those boys who were deemed the worst cases did not escape incarceration at Rockhead. George Meagher, for example, went to the Protestant home at the age of twelve in 1885. When he ran away for the fourth time in 1889, the magistrate sentenced him to serve out the remaining three years of his term in city prison where the failure to continue a juvenile department meant he would have to lodge and work with the adult prisoners. The institutions also took neglected children from broken homes. When jailbird Thomas Norbury and his wife were convicted in 1888 of neglecting their children, their son was given the opportunity of going to the Protestant Industrial School which he readily embraced as a chance to learn a trade. To other boys the industrial schools provided a degree of comfort they had never known. Lundy Morine, son of an Italian scissors-grinder, might have felt lucky to be in the Catholic home in 1889 when his family's abode was described in the press as one of the most wretched hovels on Grafton Street.[27]

In the meantime the problem of female delinquency was addressed through the prostitute rescue efforts spearheaded by the Halifax City Mission. The mission was directly responsible for the establishment of the House of Refuge in 1854, the first such undertaking in the city. When missionary Gordon visited the upper streets in the summer of 1852, he identified about fifty brothels in which young women indicated that they wanted to repent but felt that their fall was permanent and irreversible. When several of them said that they would leave the red light district if they had a place to go, Gordon suggested that a house of refuge might rescue them from their "pitiable condition." The mission issued an appeal to the public the following spring for the establishment of "a House of Refuge for the Penitent, and of Safety for Those whose homeless Condition exposes them to the Danger of a Vicious Life." After the opening, the city missionary acted as chaplain. The story of that refuge is told in Chapter Six. Since it did not survive long, the missionary was soon urging that the work be taken up again. The resumption of the work briefly in 1863 was applauded by Morton; but by 1866 his successor Grierson once more lamented the lack of a refuge and, now that an industrial school for boys had been established, called also for a similar institution for girls.[28]

The only home for girls that materialized before the 1890s was a denominational effort unrelated to the City Mission but informed by the same spirit that produced the Protestant Industrial School. This was the St. Paul's Alms House of Industry for Girls, established by the Anglicans on Tower Road in 1867, which in more recent times was known as Collins House. It was conceived entirely as a preventive institution "for the support and training of destitute young girls,—girls who if left to grow up in their present poverty and disastrous surroundings would be a prey to vice, but who will by this home be trained for lives of usefulness and virtue." The first social worker attached to the home was the ubiquitous volunteer and patron Isabella Binney Cogswell to whom was "given the onerous duty of naming to the committee girls for admission and of affording information relative to their age, character and circumstances." Like most institutions concerned with the female sex at this period, a male committee handled the finances while a female committee attended to the internal management of the home. The regimen was the familiar one: work, instruction and worship. In keeping with prevailing attitudes, the girls were trained as domestic servants. Although it was considerably smaller and funded entirely from non-governmental sources, the St. Paul's Home was considered to be the female equivalent of the Protestant Industrial School and every bit as necessary. While it did not take children from the police court, it accepted the children of police court clients. When Thomas Norbury's son went to the Protestant Industrial School, his daughter Alice was admitted to the St. Paul's Home. Both institutions therefore emulated the City Mission in reaching directly into the lives of the city's underclass.[29]

By the time the Halifax City Mission was dissolved in 1868, mission work had become divided into two zones. Workers in the south mission field continued to evangelize the disreputable upper streets of Barrack, Albemarle and Grafton through separate denominational missions organized by Anglicans, Methodists and Presbyterians with the addition, during most of the 1870s, of an interdenominational mission on Barrack Street under the aegis of the YMCA until the mission's benefactor, Edward Jost, turned it into a Methodist mission by the terms of his will.[30] In contrast, the north mission field remained interdenominational in the spirit of the earlier Halifax City Mission. The missionary concentrated on the area north of Jacob and Cogswell Streets which included the rough neighbourhood of City Street and its environs as well as respectable working-class streets inhabited by both blacks and whites. The mission, known as the North End City Mission, was founded in 1868 largely through the initiative of Foster Almon, curate of St. George's Anglican Church. With predominantly Anglican funding, a diminutive frame mission hall was opened on the corner of Gerrish and City Streets in 1869.[31] The mission battled urban ills alone in the area with the wide-spread though somewhat parsimonious financial help of evangelical Protestants until an endowment came its way in Thomas Beamish Akins' will in 1891.

The North End City Mission, which survived for a century, was guided through its first two decades by its lay missionary, Adam Logan, a Presbyterian, and by female mission workers consisting of school teachers, bible women and patrons. While the mission gave high priority to the conventional mission practices—religious services two evenings a week; the missionary's visitations for spiritual and charitable purposes to the dwellings of the 300-400 poor families in his area; combatting the evils of drink through weekly temperance meetings—it was also devoted to saving the children of the north end. Under Logan it pursued two policies over and above the maintenance of the usual mission Sunday schools. First, within a year of the opening of the new mission hall, the City Street Mission day school was begun. Supported in the short term by a local female philanthropist, the day school, like the Halifax City Mission's ragged school which preceded it, was designed for the very poor who were not attending the public schools. Since schooling was not even partially compulsory until the late 1880s, Logan and his workers had to think of ways of enticing the children to the mission. Certainly they had to supply clothing, the lack of which was thought to be the major reason why destitute children did not go to the free public schools. In an appeal for contributions of clothing in 1870, Logan claimed that it was not unknown for children "to come to this school with bare feet when the ground was frozen." Once clothed, the children were disciplined to attend by a game of chance. "The attendance of the children," the *Morning Chronicle* reported approvingly, "is secured by the ingenious plan of giving them a nice tea once in a while, without letting them know on what evening it is to be, so that the children are unwilling to be absent a day for fear of losing a good tea."[32]

The progress of children at the mission school was put to the test in 1874 when the boys' and girls' classes were examined by the city school commissioners. Between seventy and eighty were put through their paces in reading, arithmetic, geography and grammar. When the prizes were distributed, they were awarded not only for scholastic and vocational achievement but for tidiness, regular attendance and good conduct, the kind of virtues the middle class wished to inculcate. By the late seventies the mission was leasing its building during weekdays to the city school board for use as racially segregated day schools. The missionary acted as an unofficial truant officer for the white school and followed his own segregationist policies by limiting one of the two Sunday schools to whites, further evidence that the 'respectable' were far more racist in Halifax than was the underclass.

The second method for catering to the needs of neglected children and providing the opportunity for learning so central to the evangelical programme was to isolate the children from their unsatisfactory parents. A policy evolved in the 1870s of removing children from their city homes and sending them for the rest of their childhood to foster homes in the country. By 1878 the missionary reported that he had rescued forty-two destitute children from evil influences. In 1882 alone he obtained the consent of parents to find homes for twelve children in the country, the object being "to rescue them from the evils of poverty and lives of future crime and place them where they may become useful and valuable members of the community."[33] The fact that Logan was able to persuade parents to give up their children suggests that he was a key figure in his community. He might of course have suggested to reluctant parents that this course was a better alternative than calling in the Society for the Prevention of Cruelty to investigate family problems. Logan was described in 1880 as a "Society for the Prevention of Cruelty to Women and Children" of his own, and applauded for his efforts at finding "safe and comfortable homes for scores of boys and girls that he has rescued from ill-treatment or destitution or both. That one man has done a world of good by sending these poor children from their dismal environments into the country."[34] Logan's concern for the welfare of the children within the territory of his mission meant that he was also on the look out for baby-farmers and prostitutes in whose care young children were thought to be at the greatest risk.[35]

The mission maintained close links with the Society for the Prevention of Cruelty. In 1886 John Naylor, the agent of the SPC, asked Logan to try to reform the behaviour of one of his mission women, resident in Maitland

Street, who was constantly getting drunk and neglecting her family. The woman was Margaret Pettigrew (née Ford), a sister of jailbirds Mary and Cornelius. Ford family influence was apparently more compelling than that of Logan's; Mrs. Pettigrew did not respond to the missionary's entreaties. She remained an SPC case for at least two more years as a result of the complaints of her labourer-husband. The kind of letter she received from the SPC in 1888 reveals the hardline approach which the secular interventionist society took when religious influences like those of Logan's failed:

> You have been reported to this society for being a habitual drunkard and neglecting your family. I have advised your husband to have you arrested and placed in prison but he does not wish to do that without giving you another chance. I therefore write this to caution you that if you do not mend your ways, I shall have you arrested and punished and your child placed in some institution. Your husband can then leave you to shift for yourself. I trust that your better self will see the dreadful course you are pursuing and that you will straighten yourself up and endeavour to do better.

Margaret Pettigrew might have been able to read this threatening letter but she could not write a response since she was, like so many of her class, only semi-literate.[36]

The close connection between the North End City Mission and the SPC was paralleled by its equally strong links with the Association for Improving the Condition of the Poor. As the mission had no welfare fund of its own and was always begging for cast-off clothing, Logan needed the help of the AICP. But the AICP also relied on him: as a visitor to slum dwellings he acted as an agent for the association whose relief was based on prior domiciliary investigation. Through the intervention of the missionary, the poor received evangelization along with AICP food and fuel.

For the people of the north end, the mission became a source of spiritual guidance, social activities, welfare assistance and literary and practical education. Devoted to his flock, the missionary and his workers undoubtedly functioned as the first social workers in the area, a work that was carried on with more variety and somewhat greater fanfare after 1893 by Logan's successor Major Theakston, a Methodist printer from England, who already had experience as a city missionary in the south mission field and as the port's missionary to seamen.

Several years earlier in 1885, city mission work, especially in the south mission field, received a great boost when the Salvation Army 'opened fire' in Halifax, using as the first makeshift barracks the former Black Dog tavern once operated by Isaac Sallis. For almost ten years the Salvationists

131

contented themselves with evangelical work before diversifying into social work. Jailbird Hannah Baker fell under their influence as did many other lower-class inhabitants. Not all of them found their attachment to the Army to be an unmitigated blessing. Jane Hisket of Upper Water Street, servant to a butcher's wife on Windsor Street, complained that she was dismissed without notice or wages because she had attended Salvationist meetings. One newspaper claimed that "some of the army recruits here are undoubtedly of our toughest citizens." Among the recruits were prostitutes and drunks who, with the moral support of their new found friends, informed on their erstwhile associates for breaking the law.[37]

The 1891 census indicates the type of people who responded to city mission work since the Salvation Army was accepted as a census category, a distinction not available to the adherents of the indigenous missions. Although the number of professed adherents to Salvationism in Halifax in 1891 was not large enough to be statistically significant, the appeal to the working class, to women and to young people is abundantly clear. Of the sixty with occupations, fourteen were female domestic servants and twelve of them were in the fifteen to twenty-five age group where exploitation and degradation so often stalked. Of the other twelve workingwomen and girls, eight were in the needle trades, another low-paid area of employment. As charwomen, washerwomen and nurses the remainder worked at very low-status jobs. Half of the thirty-four workingmen and boys were employed in unskilled jobs, mostly as labourers and teamsters. The others were semi-skilled or skilled workers or petty bourgeoisie.

Women were attracted to the Salvation Army across the whole age and marital spectrum but in greater numbers as women on their own than were men, evidence perhaps of a yearning for a degree of security and respect in a male-controlled urban environment. Apart from the high proportion of young domestic live-in servants, young people were drawn to the Salvation Army as a form of generational rebellion. They included the twenty-year-old eldest of six stepchildren of a Presbyterian carriage trimmer; the twenty-four-year-old daughter of a Methodist couple; a twenty-four-year-old blacksmith and his twenty-five-year-old sister, living with their widowed Church of England mother; the eighteen-year-old daughter of a Roman Catholic tinsmith whose other three daughters remained faithful to their parents' religion; a fifteen-year-old pantsmaker, the daughter of a Church of England widow with four other children, all Anglican.

Before the Salvation Army began its social work in Halifax in 1894, therefore, it had won the adherence of local residents whose working and living conditions were sufficiently precarious to define them as former or potential members of the underclass. The Army's Canadian commandant claimed in 1893 that it was the "Poor Man's Religion" in Halifax and that the Army had been "if anything, more successful in Halifax in getting hold of the poor than any other place I know of in the Dominion."[38] City missions were reaching both the rough and respectable poor. For the rough, however, the voluntary associations and the city missionaries began to devise more concrete measures than visits and prayers.

Protestant Industrial School. (Public Archives of Nova Scotia)

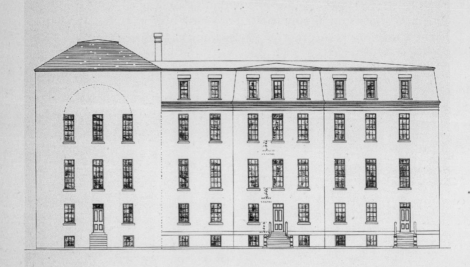

Architectural drawing of the Home of the Good Shepherd. (Public Archives of Nova Scotia).

# 6
# 'I HAVE NO REFUGE':
# HOMES FOR
# FEMALE OFFENDERS

When Mary Slattery went to jail in October 1868, one police court reporter opined:

> What a pity that something could not be done for this unfortunate class of females who occupy half the time of the Court. Released from prison in forty days, this Slattery girl will have to return again to her old course of life, the one she has led ever since she was in her teens.

In February 1869 she was back in court, asking if she might go to the house for 'fallen' women for a change instead of the city prison. The magistrate obliged by enquiring of the managers but they apparently declined the pleasure of Mary's company.[1] The evidence we have of contacts between prostitutes like Mary Slattery and the rescue homes is sketchy. In the public reports of these private facilities the identity of inmates was protected, ostensibly to enable them to re-enter society without the burden of what was seen as another handicap. The rescue efforts themselves were limited by lack of both collective and individual middle-class enthusiasm, particularly before the 1890s. If there were more R.H. Danas out in the streets trying to reclaim prostitutes, their work has gone largely unrecorded. A proprietress of a well-known boarding house reputedly engaged in prostitute rescue towards the end of the century but she was the exception. She is credited with having removed fallen women from brothels "amid curses and maledictions hurled at her head, but persevering through it all, and in many cases leading the girls to a better life by encouragement and getting places in families for them, where they were protected from the terrible temptations of city life."[2]

Historians have not been particularly interested in the rescue efforts of either individuals or houses of refuge, preferring instead to deal with the campaigns against prostitution itself or the double standard which perpetuated it. For our purposes, however, the rescue homes are worth studying because they attempted to recast along self-interested middle-class lines the lives of prostitutes and other women in trouble with the law.[3]

In Halifax the history of organized prostitute rescue and the related areas of alcoholic and ex-prisoner rehabilitation dates from 1853. Between 1854 and the end of the century at least nine homes for women threatened by the evils of the city were maintained for varying lengths of time to rescue or reform deviant women or prevent delinquency. Like most of the mid-century Protestant concern for the morals of Halifax, the first, the House of Refuge of 1854, grew out of the evangelical movement. An offshoot of city missionary Gordon's work and the creation of the city's evangelical clergymen, it was designed "to receive those only who seemed anxious to reform,—to enter on a new life,—and who, as a proof of their sincerity, were willing to be subject to strict rules, designed for their own improvement and the good order of the Institution."[4] The regimen included household chores, industrial work projects, primary education, and twice-daily religious instruction. One disadvantage of the home was its inability to attract "penitents": active recruiting on the upper streets does not seem to have been part of the scheme. Instead the management received applications for admission from women with a range of problems, from desertion or abuse by their husbands to physical disabilities. The male committee rejected a suggestion of the city missionary that preventive work in the form of a boarding house for country girls seeking employment might protect potential prostitutes "from the temptations and seductions of the designing."[5] Yet there was a clear and continuing need for a women's hostel for both single and married women. One of the women who applied to the House of Refuge in 1855, for example, was a soldier's wife "whose life was rendered wretched by the drunkenness, unfaithfulness and abuse of her husband." What she needed, but did not get, was a place to live until she could secure employment.[6]

The internal management of the home was "governed by love," according to the committee, and organized on the "family" model recommended by correspondents in similar institutions in Boston, Montreal, Philadelphia and Edinburgh. But it was clearly designed as a place of confinement; permission to go out was not granted except for special reasons at which time the inmate was accompanied by the matron. The women were kept at work; unwillingness to work meant expulsion. They did housework and covered palm leaf hats until 1856 when Isabella Binney Cogswell, who was a member of the ladies committee of the home, donated the money for the purchase of laundry equipment. The laundry soon became a standard part of women's reformatory work in the city, apparently on the assumption that active physical labour was more effective therapy than more sedentary pursuits. Cogswell's professed motive, however, was economic in nature. She hoped that a laundry would become the industrial enterprise to bring self-sufficiency to the home, an aim which made it "a sanctimonious sweatshop," like the Magdalene asylums of other cities.[7]

Within the very limited notion of prostitute rescue which the House of Refuge represented, the future options presented to the penitent women were marriage or domestic service. One woman from the House of Refuge, "respectably married" in April 1855, was back in the home by the following August after mistreatment by her new husband drove her to drink. Domestic service then became the alternative offered to her by the managers of the home.[8] They also provided inmates with a chance to return home—to the country, to the United States or to Britain. While this encouragement of emigration might resemble the banishment practised in police court, the initiatives came from the women themselves and the home paid the passages.

Given the experiences of Halifax's public prostitutes, it is hardly surprising that the home had to deal with a number of very hard characters. The committee considered the violence of one woman to warrant solitary confinement in the first instance with a threat to transfer her to police custody should isolation fail to subdue her. Indeed the occasional visit of a police constable was thought to be wise just to remind inmates that there was a thin line between benevolence and coercion.[9] The House of Refuge closed after three years when its building lease expired in 1857 and, in the absence of alternative premises, the inmates were removed to the poorhouse where some of the former ones had already been sent as feeble-minded.[10] A resident of Lockman Street, where the home was located, later claimed that "the disgraceful conduct of the inmates was the means of abandoning the Reformatory."[11]

Behavioural problems or rebellious resistance were even more obvious among the inmates of the second reformatory. This was the House of Mercy, established in 1862 by Thomas Connolly, Catholic archbishop of Halifax, in his summer home on the Northwest Arm. The archbishop's recruitment policy was entirely different to that pursued in the former Protestant institution. It was aimed specifically at jailbirds like Ann Mahoney and Henrietta McKegney, whom he encountered on his visit to Rockhead Prison in May 1862.[12] For what proved to be unrewarding rescue work, the archbishop chose the Sisters of Charity. Totally untrained in how to deal with delinquent women and isolated in the remote location of the archbishop's cottage, the nuns were unsuccessful in altering the behaviour of their charges. The first four inmates—three white and one black—made up for their lack of alcohol first with excessive unruliness and then by trying to run away. The number of inmates was never more than ten. "They were so discontented, idle and quarrelsome; they would dispute and come to blows for the merest trifle."[13] They were also unabashedly irreverant. Sister Mary Clare described a service given by a priest from St. Mary's parish during which one of the girls "barefoot, and without a dress," sat "on the top of the house, her bare legs dangling from the roof outside the Chapel window, shrieking while the Mass was going on below." The discipline of the Catholic Church was no match for the indiscipline of the residents and the Sisters of Charity gave up the venture after only one year.[14]

A second Protestant effort at prostitute rescue, encouraged by the rector of St. George's Church, Robert Fitzgerald Uniacke, was attempted in 1863, shortly after the Catholic House of Mercy failed. Considered to be a "resuscitation of the first house of refuge," it was a response to challenges thrown out occasionally by the Halifax City Mission and by such sensationalists of the Victorian press as a writer for the *Halifax Morning Sun* in 1862:

> Walk through our streets at nightfall, and glance at the numerous haggard wrecks of what was once the master-piece of God! Mark the hollow laughter in which there is no gladness;—note the factitious smile in which sparkles no gleam of joy. The outcast may flaunt in finery or shiver in rags; but in the vast majority of cases one may read the same secret written on her countenance, whether she be robed in satins and laces or huddled up in rags. The same tale is told. There is no happiness in those faces, and the words *I have no refuge* may be plainly read upon the blanched forehead.[15]

The home, modelled on the unsuccessful Connolly approach, soon foundered. This time it was middle-class female prison visitors who identified among the prisoners at Rockhead several adolescent women who would have little choice but to return to their former haunts once they were released from prison.[16] The central location of the house on Lockman Street might have been as much responsible for its failure as was the character of its inmates, who included such incorrigibles as Henrietta McKegney and Ellen Shefrow. Press coverage of the home's short existence indicates that people living in the vicinity felt threatened by the proximity of the home and worried about its effect on the sensibilities of their wives, daughters and sons. William Cunard, a prominent merchant, who donated the premises for the refuge to the ladies committee, acidly suggested that those same wives, daughters and sons were likely to learn more from the police court proceedings luridly detailed in the newspapers than "from walking past this establishment."[17]

The women's thwarted efforts were supplanted in 1867 when Uniacke's curate, Foster Almon, raised enough charitable funds to rent a house for rescue purposes at a short distance from the city and engage a married couple to manage the home. He established a ladies' committee to oversee the venture and a financial committee to support it.[18] Not to be confused with the concurrent home for servants known as the Temporary Home for Young Women Seeking Employment as Domestic Servants, Almon's refuge for fallen women, like its predecessor of the mid 1850s, was supported by a cross-section of Protestant churches as an essential part of city mission work. Indeed the wife of the North End City missionary was the matron. As the Church of England bishop of Nova Scotia remarked in 1869, it was no use for missionaries to talk to fallen women if there was no house ready to receive them.[19]

The refuge was another house of industry based, as the ideal, on a twelve-month stay followed by pre-arranged employment in the country. The problems of running a home were very much the same as in the 1850s; it was difficult to get 'fallen' women to resort to the refuge. Repeat offender Mary Clifford was an inmate but she ran away, taking clothes belonging to the home, and was shortly afterwards jailed for lewdness with a black man.[20] By 1869 the managers admitted that "the great majority had run away and returned to their old courses of iniquity" and that the remote location was a mistake. William Cunard again came to the rescue, offering the temporary use of a dilapidated house in Brunswick Street. With a sorry record in 1870 of an empty house which had a 50 per cent failure rate over the previous three years, some of the supporters suggested that the house should be discontinued and prostitute rescue work centralized in Saint John where a more successful effort existed. This suggestion was rejected in favour of the more explicit involvement of middle-class women in the day-to-day management of the home in the belief that "the refinement, tact and gentleness of Christian ladies was necessary."[21] But the ladies in question failed to save the home.

The lack of success through the first four institutional attempts at prostitute rescue may have been instrumental in finally promoting preventive work in the form of the servant girls' home of 1869. The aims of the Temporary Home for Young Women Seeking Employment as Domestic Servants were twofold: one was to promote a lodging house for country girls who came to the city looking for jobs in domestic service, the major form of employment for women in the nineteenth-century city. Without a safe lodging place, local observers knew what might happen to unsuspecting country girls. "Not long since," the *Halifax Daily Reporter* editorialized in a promotional article, "two girls from the country, ignorant of city ways and wiles were taken to a den of infamy and left there, to the great injury of their characters. One of them, we believe, felt so keenly her degradation that she refused to go home, preferring to sink into the abyss of ruin into which she had been treacherously cast."[22] The second aim was to provide a shelter for local servant girls between jobs.

The coexistence of the two refuges, the one for the innocent, the other for the fallen, underscores the dual concept of women's nature in the Victorian period: pure and polluted; angel and whore. Each home was seen to meet a particular need, which was reflected in the admission procedures. The servant girls required a certificate of good character in order to become boarders in the Temporary Home; the fallen women were referred to their refuge by people like the city marshal, the stipendiary magistrate and the city missionaries.[23] Despite the keen degree of self-interest manifested by Halifax's activist women towards the servant's home, it did not survive beyond 1875 at which time the same group of women, organized as members of the new Women's Christian Assocation, headed initially by Isabella Binney Cogswell, threw their weight behind the establishment of a reformatory for jailbirds, inebriates, vagrants and prostitutes. It superseded the servants' home and replaced the 1867 refuge for fallen women which did not survive beyond the end of 1872.[24] The new reformatory, known variously by a long list of names and incorporated in 1879 as the Women's Home, preoccupied the attention of Protestant rescue workers in Halifax for almost twenty years except for the additional, short-lived Inebriate Home run by Martha Harrison.[25]

The Women's Home became a facility to which the magistrate sentenced willing delinquent women and a shelter for women on their release from jail.[26] For the middle-class women of Halifax, the Women's Home represented part of their temperance crusade: "Drink," according to their second report, "is the great evil."[27] As a result the new Halifax Women's Christian Temperance Union took considerable interest in the home arranging for women, whose failing was public drunkenness, to be sent to

140

the home instead of prison. The home also represented a lack of confidence on the part of the élite in the existing penal institutions, which, as we have seen, had become a part of the underclass culture of survival. As the chair of the WCA reported in 1880: "prison is but a sad school of morals, and a term in prison is simply a term in vice."[28] Yet the stipendiary magistrate believed that in the hierarchy of punishments, the home would be preferred by offenders to the prison and his sentencing sometimes reflected this approach. In June 1878, a drunk and profane woman was "let off" in police court to go to the Women's Home. In September 1879 a woman, who was charged in police court for being drunk and incapable of taking care of herself, was sent to the Women's Home for six months on the understanding that she would get twelve months in Rockhead if she left that institution. Before long, parents of wayward girls turned to the Women's Home as a solution to their inadequate or unsuccessful parenting. In April 1881, a girl was given in charge by her mother for absenting herself from home without permission and sent to the Women's Home. Desperate women also began to sentence themselves to the home in much the same way as they had formerly done to the city prison.[29]

Given its disciplinary nature, it is not surprising that some Halifax street women resisted the regimen of the home. Women like Mary Ford Prendergast soon ran away in disgust.[30] The stipendiary magistrate magnanimously "allowed" escaped inmates to return to the Women's Home. When an escapee was given the choice of the home instead of prison, she sometimes preferred the former as its promoters hoped. But all too often young girls, either on initial sentencing or after escape, opted for the prison.[31] In 1883, when Minnie Porter was arraigned in police court for escaping from the home, she chose a thirty-day prison term over six months in the home. While the difference in the length of the sentences might have provided sufficient justification for her choice, Minnie claimed that her aversion to the home was based on the work she had to do as an inmate, a charge which produced an accusation of laziness from the Women's Home committee.[32] As Minnie Porter's complaint—justified or not—demonstrates, the normal length of stay for women considered to be delinquent was six months. Other women who applied for admission or returned to the home for shelter stayed anywhere from six weeks to six months.[33]

The home itself encountered considerable financial problems, its committee members blaming its precarious existence on the apathy and, in some cases, downright public hostility to the work. As we have seen, being "their 'Sisters' keepers" appealed to very few women in Halifax.[34] For the arrant women the routine in the small home, located first on Creighton

Street, then on Lockman and finally on Brunswick near North Street railway station, was depressingly institutional.

> The inmates rise at 6:30 and before commencing the duties of the day assemble for morning prayer, after which the work on hand is proceeded with. It may be washing, knitting, quilting, hooking mats or reseating cane chairs. Whatever work any of the women excel in she is given to do. At the close of the day they are again called together for evening worship, and all lights are put out at 9:30 p.m. Religious services are held every Thursday evening and Sabbath afternoon and on Sabbath as many as can, go out to church in the morning with the matron. [35]

Committee members sometimes spent two evenings a week at the home teaching the women how to read and write which might have been appreciated. The reports also refer to the provision of amusements of various kinds as well as books and papers. By 1888 the house was also equipped with an organ for musical entertainments and a sewing machine to encourage the women to make their own clothes.[36]

Yet the discipline of the home reveals that benevolent women of the 1880s found it no easier to deal with street women than had their predecessors. The rules, as the home managers themselves confessed, were quite strict, too strict according to some of the city's social workers. The inmates could not go out unchaperoned after it was discovered that allowing them walks or church visits on their own made them "more difficult to manage."[37] Sometimes the pacification methods did not work. In 1884, for example, the matron had to turn one young woman over to the police "for conducting herself in a disorderly manner."[38]

The Women's Home followed the example of similar institutions by basing its 'house of industry' on the incorporation of a laundry. From the beginning the home took in family washing to occupy the daytime hours of the inmates and to help support the establishment.[39] Even such menial work presented a challenge to rough women. The WCA reported that "in almost every case those who come in have to be taught *how* to work" in order to prepare them "to earn a respectable living."[40] The living was of course domestic service in country homes far away from the temptations of the city where the women were sent as soon as they were deemed to be proficient at housework and reliable in character.[41]

In order to reconcile themselves to the home's discipline and to ease the transition from rough to respectable, the women searched for connections with their previous lives. While the sources do not allow us to say anything very conclusive about this cultural adjustment, some of the women found that music helped. They were encouraged to sing; members of the local branch of the King's Daughters visited the home and led them in their singing. Their fondness for music meant that they sang anything and everything and the WCA members thought "wonderful the facility with which they commit to memory both words and tunes." What they were learning were not of course the racy ballads of soldiertown, but the rousing hymns of the mid-nineteenth-century revivalist movement. One inmate, who ran away and returned after spending a few days with her old cronies, told the matron that her friends had turned her out for singing the hymns she had learned in the home. For those who were able to reconcile themselves to the discipline of the home, the security it provided made them reluctant to leave. Like the jail, it provided a refuge against the dangers and uncertainties of underclass life. 'L.I.,' was still living in the home in 1888, eight years after she had been first admitted. She refused the other options held out to her and preferred to earn her living as a laundress in the home.[42]

Who were the women who lived in the home? We know that Mary Ford Prendergast was there for a spell and that many minor offenders of a later period also lived there. The women represented a broad range of ages. In 1879 thirty women between the ages of fourteen and sixty entered the home, in 1886 twenty-four women between the ages of eighteen and forty-five. Very young girls were sent on, if possible, to the St. Paul's Alms House of Industry for Girls. Women with young children needing shelter were sent to the poorhouse or to the Halifax Infants' Home or Home of the Guardian Angel.[43]

Women were referred to the Women's Home by a number of agencies and individuals besides the police court. In 1879 the inmates came from the prison, the police station, the Saint John WCTU, at a time when Saint John was between refuges, and others "applied for admission either to reform or for shelter." The Halifax WCTU continued to send homeless and inebriate women to the home. In 1890 a dozen women were admitted under WCTU auspices as a result of the visits to "the haunts and habitations of our fallen sisters" of the organization's superintendent of police work who was the wife of the sailors' home manager James Potter. In 1884 an incorrigible drunkard frequently before the court, described as an "Old Cumberland county Irish woman" was given a final chance of reform by being sent to the home. Mabel Peters, a young Scottish immigrant, who soon accumulated a jail record as a result of her "love for strong drink," was also sent to the home. Annie Malcolm promised to go to the home in 1889 after she had been forgiven in court by the woman she had assaulted.[44] The magistrate sent thirteen women to the Women's Home between 1889 and 1893, ten of them between seventeen and twenty-four years of age and three in their thirties. Prostitution, or suspicion of prostitution, and drunkenness accounted for eleven of the offences. The other two women were found guilty of larceny.

The city missionaries were active in rounding up recruits for the home and so was John Naylor, the busy secretary-agent of the Society for the Prevention of Cruelty. We find him advising relatives to have troublesome women arrested and sent to the home. He followed up on the advice of a nurse at the Victoria General Hospital that two country girls, one from Lockeport and the other from Prince Edward Island, wished to be taken out of the brothel known as the 'Stone Jug,' and sent to the home. In 1886, one of the police sergeants told Naylor about Matilda McMillan, a girl under eighteen years of age from Musquodoboit who was in a house in Maitland Street where she was likely to "be put to prostitution." Naylor went to the disreputable house in question and took the girl away to the Women's Home. In 1888 he was summoned by Garret Cotter, the city marshal, to take charge of Jane Hilchey, a sixteen-year-old who had been arrested for stealing and was known to be "going with soldiers." Naylor sent her to the Women's Home pending arrangements to send her back to Cape Breton. In another case, this time of a confirmed prostitute, Naylor referred Georgina Mason to the home after she left her place in service in Windsor and returned to town where she had lapsed into her old ways before applying to him to find her a job and remove her once more from temptation.[45]

Many of the women, then, were from out of town. In 1888 several were reported to be from rural areas of the province as well as from Newfoundland, Prince Edward Island and England.[46] Their rural backgrounds sometimes included sexual exploitation. There was the case of the fifteen-year-old Windsor girl who stole money from her mother in order to get away from home where her stepfather had raped her several times. For her the city and its refuges offered an escape from a dangerous and depraved home life.[47] Other childhood problems permanently scarred the character of inmates. "One, left without mother or father when a few months old, fell into the hands of people whose treatment of her was such that at the age of 7 she ran away, since which time she had been without a place she could call a home." The deprivation of her youth caused severe behavioural problems: "When she came to us," the matron reported, "her temper was so ungovernable, we felt that nothing could be done with her, and she was discharged for insubordination, but returned to us, begging to be tried again."[48]

The Women's Home prided itself on being equally welcoming to Catholics and Protestants, claiming that it interfered "with no one's peculiar Christian belief." During the first ten years when some 200 women were admitted, many repeatedly, the majority were nominally Catholic. But the Protestant management was seen to be an obstacle. The mayor referred in 1886 to the number of women prisoners who simply refused to go to the home "on account of the religious influences." SPC secretary-agent Naylor also regretted the aversion of young women to the policies of the Women's Home.[49]

By 1890 competition for the Catholic women came in the form of a Catholic monastery, the Home of the Good Shepherd. That, added to the rumour that the Salvation Army was going to open a rescue home and despair over the hopelessness of 'repeat' inmates of the Mary Ford ilk, resulted in a revision of the Women's Home policy in 1892, effective February 1893:

> We have decided to take a class of younger girls, and to make this successful we are compelled to exclude the older and more hardened ones, who for many years have come in during the winter months, only to avail themselves of home comforts and prepare for an early flitting in the spring. [50]

With few successes among the hardened members of the underclass, who had become in effect semi-permanent residents, the WCA gave up the rescue and rehabilitation work and concentrated on prevention and juvenile reformation. The organizers themselves put a positive gloss on the change:

> We gave up our work among the older and more abandoned ones, not because of its many discouragements, but because of the greater number of younger and more impressionable girls who were beginning the downward course with so many beckoning hands outstretched, but none to impede their fatal descent. [51]

The motives of the WCA members in favouring this change were not totally disinterested. During the three-year stay which they planned to impose on the new class of young inmate, the girls were to be trained in the arts of household service so that they might "meet the great want of the day, and our homes be again supplied with capable and conscientious servants," a priority confirmed by the initiation of a registry of servants in 1887. In fact few juvenile delinquents were sent from the police court to the home after the change in policy, despite considerable talk in the city in 1891 about the need for a Protestant reformatory for girls.[52] Its function as a reformatory remained entirely voluntary. From 1894 to 1898 it was known as the Home for Friendless Women (or sometimes Girls) and thereafter as the Girls' or Young Girls' Home, which was located after

1902 on College Street. In 1898, the WCA, recently reconstituted as the YWCA, also opened a boarding house for working girls on Hollis Street.[53]

In the meantime the Home of the Good Shepherd, armed with federal legislation in 1891 making it Nova Scotia's Catholic equivalent to Ontario's Mercer Reformatory, rapidly took in hand the problem of fallen women and delinquent girls. The Sisters of the Good Shepherd had turned their attention to Halifax as early as 1878 when their Ottawa home opened its doors to ex-prisoners collected from the east. The permanent settlement in Halifax in 1890 of members of the order was encouraged by a number of factors, one of which was the interest of Catholic middle-class women, like their Protestant counterparts, in securing a reliable supply of servants. In 1887 they had petitioned the archbishop in favour of the establishment of a servants' home "with a laundry attached and perhaps other remunerative accessories under the management of some religious order." They advocated the inclusion of a crèche both to allow needy mothers to go out as day workers and to provide child care experience for the trainee servants in the home.[54]

The Sisters of the Good Shepherd, who were trained especially for rescue work, ran a very closely controlled operation, consisting of an industrial refuge for wayward girls and a reformatory for convicted girls and women, which was out of sight of the middle-class citizenry in two respects. It was located on a large, austere estate devoted to Catholic institutions on Quinpool Road and the internal management of the home was not open to the scrutiny of the public in the same way as non-denominational and Protestant institutions were. Despite its aura of secrecy, the home was highly recommended by some Protestant social activists of the city. The Reverend Foster Almon, "eulogized the work of the monastery of the Good Shepherd" at the annual meeting of the Society for the Prevention of Cruelty in 1892 "and stated that since it had been at work the number of cases of vagrant girls had decreased and the work of the SPC had been lessened." John Naylor suggested that the reformatory branch of the home had "taken care of many girls who were giving us continual trouble. The institution was much wanted."[55] Unlike the Women's Home, whose managers agonized over the need to concentrate on particular problems rather than the whole range of outcast women's needs, the Sisters of the Good Shepherd clearly recognized three categories of women whom their institution might help.

1. Those who enter voluntarily (generally spoken of as "penitents"), the only condition being their desire to forsake the paths of shame—to get out of the way of temptation, and to lead new lives.

2. Young girls and children exposed and in danger, sent by parents, guardians or authorities, for stated periods. These are received on the principle that prevention is better than the cure.

3. A reformatory for women and girls sentenced by the courts under the Dominion statute. This class of girls may be received from any municipality in the province, contributing to their maintenance.

The penitents and prisoners had a chance on the expiration of their terms of confinement to become "magdalenes," that is, permanent residents of the religious community.

The nuns were much better able to cope with different categories of inmates than the Women's Home had been. For one thing, the staff of the monastery was a large one. In 1894 with fifty inmates at any one time, their needs, instruction and discipline were attended to by twenty-two nuns; in 1902, ninety-seven women were cared for by thirty-four nuns. Second, with a large staff and an ample facility, the nuns were able to keep the three categories of women and girls completely separate from one another and thereby avoid the bad influences which the hardened specimens were supposed to exert on the recently fallen in such places as the city prison and the pre-1893 Women's Home. This separation extended to the dormitories, bathrooms, dining rooms, classrooms, infirmaries and workplaces. In time-honoured rescue-home fashion, industry was centred on a laundry. Given the size of the institution, a viable laundry might have seemed possible but here again the women had to be disciplined to work and even a very experienced inmate was not permitted to earn more than her keep. Yet the scale of the operation was large enough to arouse the resentment of the commercial laundries towards a competing industrial establishment that did not have to pay taxes.[56]

According to a report in May 1894, the stipendiary magistrate had so far sentenced women sixty-six times to the reformatory branch of the home. Sixty-five of the sentences can be identified in the court registers. They were meted out to women who ranged in age from thirteen to sixty-five, with 20 per cent under sixteen and 50 per cent between the ages of seventeen and thirty. The charges ranged from drunkenness, through vagrancy and leading an idle life, to stealing, with various explicit prostitution charges in between. The sentences were much longer than terms in the city prison for the same offences, one and two years being quite usual. With one exception the women were Roman Catholic, and of the thirty-seven times an occupation was claimed, only one was not in domestic service.[57]

The Society for the Prevention of Cruelty was frequently involved in securing admission of wayward girls to the home. In most cases the

147

parents, who applied to the society to secure the incarceration of their daughters, dwelt in the rough neighbourhoods where children were exposed to the dangers of bad company and disreputable houses. Isabella Curley, living on the corner of Prince and Albemarle, reported that her fifteen-year-old daughter was incorrigible; Mary Ethel Brown of Grafton Street was worried about her twenty-three-year-old daughter "who is simple and unable to take care of herself and she is afraid that she will get into mischief." Charlotte Oakley, also of Grafton Street, wanted to get her fourteen-year-old daughter into a home because she stayed out all night, frequenting either the dance halls on her own street or the dives on Upper Water Street.[58] Fathers too applied to SPC agent John Naylor for help. In 1894, for example, two seamen of the SS *Halifax*, James Black and James Barry, each reported a young daughter who had "gone astray" or had "been staying out at night and generally disobedient." As a single parent, frequently at sea, Black was unable to give his daughter the supervision she required.[59] Young girls gone astray represented one type of admission to the monastery; another was that of alcoholic women or older, more hardened types. In 1897 Fanny Hollaran, a resident of Upper Water Street, reported that "her mother is a habitual drunkard and is acting disgracefully" and applied to have her admitted.[60]

The Home of the Good Shepherd became such a successful institution that it aroused the hostility of Protestant extremists and the anxiety of the underclass. The former opposed a civic grant to the home and tried to mask their religious prejudices by insisting that comparable Protestant institutions should not receive government funding either and that the city should on no account get into the female reformatory business.[61] In 1895 the *Presbyterian Witness*, the leading evangelical voice in the city, revealed the basic anti-Catholic bias of the opposition with its allegations about the "dark cells and solitary confinement" inflicted on disobedient girls. Such punishments were proof of the "danger in any sort of co-partnership between the civil authorities and any sect in carrying out the penal laws of the country," an argument aimed exclusively at female reformatories since both institutions for boys had received annual grants for years. In order to broaden support for their opposition to the proposed grant, the Protestants diplomatically dropped their objection to the idea of a state reformatory for women, interpreting it as the lesser of the two evils. A secular women's prison did not however materialize and the Home of the Good Shepherd finally received a civic grant in 1896 in recognition of the fact that it was the only institution in Halifax, other than the much criticized city prison, which was willing to do the job of the state.[62] As for underclass sentiments, Martha Kellum and Mary Crowe represented the

148

more hostile reaction when they entered the institution in 1897 with the intention of taking "charge of the place," an unsuccessful and sharply punished initiative.[63]

As if the Catholics were not enough, the militant Protestant fringe in the form of the Salvation Army and the Anglicans' Church Army started rescue work in the streets in the 1880s. The Salvation Army captured Hannah Baker, if only briefly. In 1894 the Salvationists took over a share of the institutional women's work in harmony with the Sisters of the Good Shepherd, because they made "it a rule not to keep Catholic girls unless specially requested to do so by that church."[64] Female army officers, like the nuns at the monastery, devoted themselves to rescue work in their capacities as full-time matrons, spiritual advisers and nurses. They also acted as jailers, despite the voluntary nature of the home. If women wanted to remain, they had to put up with considerable limits on their independence. Their money was confiscated on entering and their mail was censored. They helped to support themselves through the usual kind of menial labour promoted in these institutions. They were treated to large doses of salvation rhetoric and maudlin pronouncements on their experience of birth and death. From the beginning the home functioned also as an infants' nursery which soon became a maternity home for unwed mothers, the forerunner of the Grace Maternity Hospital.[65] With a high infant mortality rate typical of the period, the ceremony of death was used to good effect:

> ...the shadow of death that gathered on the tiny face of one of our Home babies not long ago seemed but to foretell the glorious dawning of immortal life, and as we knelt with sobbing mother besides the lifeless form of her darling, in the early dawn, and prayed for her salvation, we could but thank the tender Shepherd that another little lamb was safe in the fold—saved from ever being stained and marred by sin.
> At the funeral service four of the girls came out, and kneeling beside the little coffin, where the little body lay with pink blossoms resting against the icy face, they sought forgiveness for sin, purity for pollution. Since then the death angel has stolen into our Home with noiseless tread and borne away some of the other little ones. We believe in some cases their deaths have been a spiritual blessing to the poor mothers. [66]

The voluntary inmates of the Salvation Army home were for the most part prostitutes and friendless pregnant women. The home moved to three different buildings during its first few years and struggled for over a decade to secure adequate financial aid, experiencing much of the apathy which had earlier plagued the indigenous Protestant homes. Not till 1909 did the home become the Protestant counterpart to the Home of the Good Shep-

149

herd, with government support for its function as a reformatory for female prisoners.[67]

********

The supporters of the Salvation Army Rescue Home blamed the extent of prostitution in Halifax on its function as "a garrison town and a naval station."[68] It seems likely that Halifax's dependent military orientation also produced the relative silence on the wider issues raised by prostitute rescue. Very little evidence exists to suggest a critique of male sexual mores such as those found in campaigns in some cities under the impetus of moral reform and maternal feminism. What there was is widely scattered. We find the *Presbyterian Witness* suggesting in 1867 that major responsibility for jailbird Eliza Munroe's wretched life and early death must rest with "the men who directly or indirectly countenanced the 'social evil.' " Since Munroe's death related to her connection with a soldier, the undesirable influence of the military was another cause for concern.

> Think of "Eliza Munroe" brought up perhaps far away from the city —induced to come here for the purpose of making a livelihood— led into evil courses and ending in starvation! Her story is that of too many a girl who might be living happily in a virtuous home. Poor parents in the country cannot be too cautious in reference to their daughters when sent here to service. They are apt to take up with "soldier-beaux"—and then rapidly sink into a grave of infamy....[69]

Twenty years later the *Morning Herald* referred to the hypocrisy of a society that would reclaim with open arms its male prostitutes, by which it meant clients, while "trampling under foot the female" and in 1889, Bishop Courtney of the Church of England, called for the publication of the names of men who rented their properties for immoral purposes.[70]

It was not until the 1890s, however, that enough female activists became involved in the social problems of the city as missionaries, nuns, police matrons, doctors and members of the WCTU and WCA to produce a more critical approach to prostitution. Behind the scenes, the mother superior of the Monastery of the Good Shepherd urged action against commercial seduction. In 1892, for example, she claimed that the Crouch establishment on Albemarle Street was the cause of great harm by enticing young girls and "should be broken up."[71] Three years later Dr. Annie Hamilton, the first female medical graduate of Dalhousie, proclaimed on a public platform that she could name the perpetrators of the white slave trade in the city and condemned a society in which women, who were    "more sinned against than sinning," suffered "the awful consequences of their evil deeds while men escape scot free."[72] But such consciousness-raising came too late to make any difference to the lives of the mid-Victorian prostitutes. Their experience of the various short-lived refuges in Halifax in the second half of the nineteenth century suggests that they wanted to be able to come and go, using the homes as shelters in much the same way as they had tried to use the jail. The viewpoint of the managers and supporters of the rescue homes was quite different. They were not interested in refuges where women could drop in to escape winter hardship, get sisterly advice, talk over their troubles, explore alternative strategies for survival. They wanted to turn the female denizens of outcast Halifax into 'respectable' women who would take their rightful places as domestic servants in 'respectable' homes. The emphasis in these female houses of industry was on achieving self-sufficiency for the institution rather than on promoting the development of the potential of the individual women. Public response to the homes in such a conservative community was highly negative. They were thought to pollute the atmosphere and disturb orderly neighbourhoods. The greater acceptance of the Catholic and Salvation Army institutions was determined by the new public confidence in 'professional' rescue workers. The nuns and Sally Anns may also have exerted a more positive influence on some of the 'fallen.' One observer referred to the role-models which the Sisters of the Good Shepherd provided for their "children":

> The examples of piety and industry which are constantly given the inmates by their superiors, the atmosphere of cleanliness and order in which they live as well as the active interest taken in their individual welfare have a wonderful influence for good, which makes them anxious to regain the self-esteem they have lost. [73]

Although the homes, with their long sentences, undoubtedly helped to reduce the number of women coming before the police court and receiving committals to prison, they did not by any means replace the women's wing at Rockhead. Girls under sixteen were no longer sent there after 1892 but it remained the prison for outcast women, particularly black women, who were isolated from the mainstream of reform by an increasingly racist society.

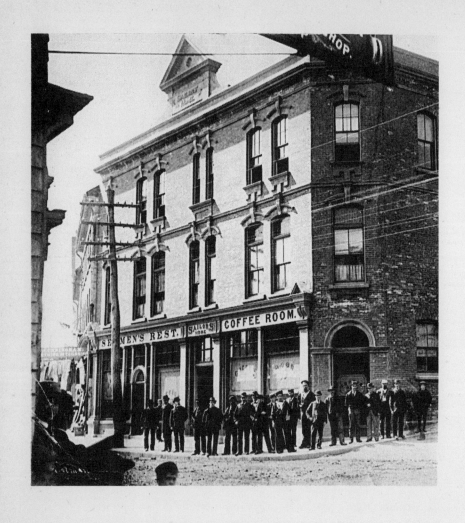

The Sailors' Home in which the Night Refuge was located. (Public Archives of Nova Scotia)

# 7
# 'HOW THE OTHER HALF LIVES': RELIEVING THE POOR AND SHELTERING THE HOMELESS

As we have seen the decades of the fifties and sixties were marked by considerable associational activities among the members of Halifax's élite as they banded together to attend to the morals, religious needs and material wants of the poor and outcast. These efforts included two poor relief agencies which, like the city missions, incorporated social investigation or 'friendly visiting' as part of their procedures. One was the St. Vincent de Paul Society, established in 1853, a Catholic, male, parish-level organization which was aided by women through their societies of the Children of Mary, begun in 1854.[1] The other was the Association for Improving the Condition of the Poor, a Protestant-run male organization of 1866. It too received some help from the city's womenfolk in providing employment for the poorer sisters and in visiting, especially late in the century when the WCTU became an active partner.[2] The two lay organizations, Catholic and Protestant, complemented each other. The St. Vincent de Paul Society expressed its appreciation of the work of the younger organization which "labored zealously in the same field as our own, and to whose zeal, impartiality, and freedom from sectarian prejudices" the members bore unanimous testimony.[3] They co-operated, characteristically, to differentiate between the "worthy and unworthy poor."[4]

For our purposes the AICP is the more relevant of the two because it directed its attention to a wider range of social problems and did not confine its material assistance to people of any particular religious persuasion. In 1871, for example, the society relieved Catholics as often as it did Anglicans but not to the same extent that it helped black Baptists in Africville. At the same time a large number of recipients were not churchgoers. One member claimed in 1889 that three-quarters of the people the AICP served were "nothingarians."[5] Only AICP

### AICP Relief, February 1871

|  | District 1 (Wards 1 & 2) | District 2 (Wards 3 & 4) | District 3 (Ward 5) | District 4 (Ward 6 & suburbs) |
|---|---|---|---|---|
| Families | 46 | 88 | 96 | 123 |
| Individuals | 150 | 294 | 364 | 474 |
| Catholics | 37 | 45 | 33 | 58 |
| Anglicans | 34 | 35 | 54 | 61 |
| Presbyterians | 3 | 24 | 42 | 10 |
| Baptists | 1 | 27 | 48 | 190 |
| Methodists | 5 | 20 | 13 | 27 |
| Religion unknown | 70 | 143 | 174 | 128 |

Source: AICP, 5th Report, 1871.

adherence to Protestant meeting rituals precluded the official partici-pation of Catholics, whose St. Vincent de Paul conferences concen-trated their support on respectable Catholic widows and abandoned wives and their familes. This preoccupation with the relief of female-headed families disturbed Archbishop O'Brien who suggested in 1888 that: "Because a being in the shape and form of a man was in the family was no reason why aid should not be granted."[6] In fact some women with problem husbands, like drunkards, were regularly relieved.[7] But both societies took a dim view of poverty thought to be caused by intemperance and equated it with being undeserving. The AICP also expected the recipients of its relief to discipline their children by sending them to school or into trades or service. Yet the nature of its procedures never excluded the 'undeserving' from its books. The need for references from supplicants was often mooted in order to discourage beggars and imposters but the requirement was never endorsed. The Poor Association therefore came into contact frequently with the underclass.[8]

A study of outdoor relief under the aegis of the AICP in Victorian Halifax is especially important given the failure of the civic authorities to provide non-institutional aid through the commissioners of the poor. The total reliance on indoor relief by the state made Halifax unusual in Canada where such equivalents to its poors' asylum as the almshouse in Saint John and the house of industry in Toronto accepted the responsibility for occasional poverty and did not insist on the disruption of families and incarceration of individuals as a prerequisite for relief. Regular visitors to the poorhouse from among our recidivist population, to say nothing of the 'respectable' poor, might have preferred to receive succour in their own abodes, however cramped or squalid: they had no choice before the formation of the voluntary agencies.

Modelled on its New York counterpart of twenty-four years earlier, the Halifax AICP was the first city-wide and long-lasting organization for the outdoor relief of the unemployed poor since the Halifax Poor Man's Friend Society of four decades earlier.[9] According to Smith-Rosenberg, the New York AICP grew directly out of city mission work and marked the "transition from evangelical piety to secular moralism." Its principles were "detection, discrimination, visitation." The same emphases apply to the Halifax society.[10] Until 1879 the AICP operated mainly through a system of volunteer visitors, supervised by four district committees, who systematically combed the streets of the city looking for those who were both needy and 'deserving.' The appointment of a paid inspector in 1879 and 1880 was followed in 1883 by the permanent employment of both a clerk and a visitor to man an office and investigate and relieve cases of application and referral from such organizations as the Visiting Dispensary, the SPC and the WCTU.[11] That administrative change was not without criticism. In January 1883 Mrs. Jane Haley died as a result of starvation in her room in West Street, near Maynard. A letter to the press claimed that the death would not have happened had the association appointed its usual cadre of visitors. How, asked "Humanity," was it possible for two persons paid by the AICP to do the work formerly performed by as many as eighty citizens?[12] The question vastly overestimated the enthusiasm of middle-class Haligonians for volunteer service as visitors to the slums.

The AICP was both a relief society and a referral service. If a problem emerged which should be handled by another agency, the association gladly made the appropriate arrangements. This applied in particular to the old, insane and infirm who were usually sent to the commissioners of the poor as likely candidates for admission to the poorhouse. Such human wreckage would only divert the Poor Association from its primary intention to elevate "the morals and physical condition of the poor." In other words, the AICP was interested primarily in the 'curable' poor whom it provided with supplies of food and fuel. In 1880 the association's benevolence amounted to some 5,829 loaves of bread and 5,876 bushels of coal. The old principle of 'less eligibility' still governed outdoor relief policies. In the case of provisions this meant that only the coarsest sort of food was provided; supposedly of worse quality than the wages of labour would be able to buy. Yet the poor could make quite a little feast out of the bread, cornmeal, oatmeal, molasses, tea, beef, sugar, flour, rice and potatoes supplied by the AICP.[13]

Like its forerunners earlier in the century the Poor Association was primarily a winter relief agency which its managers sometimes hotly denied.[14] The seasonality of poverty was a fact of life in Halifax since the onset of winter always affected employment levels and left labourers with little or no work during that time of year when prices were highest and living conditions most grim. In its second year, therefore, the Poor Association opened the customary stone-shed ostensibly to supply employment for unemployed men but also to provide a means of sorting out the deserving from the undeserving by making relief contingent on the willingness to work. Stone-breaking schemes had been a part of emergency winter relief since early in the century.[15] Payment to men willing to submit to the work-test was provided in cash at the rate of three cents per bushel of broken stone. Since the work relief scheme also reduced the need for relief in kind, which the association found increasingly difficult to provide, it became the cornerstone of AICP policy. In 1873 the stone-shed provided employment to fifty men at approximately forty cents a day during the winter months and the following year men were able to earn wages of $3 a week. The employment relief was restricted by 1875 to no more than two men from any one family but the rate had risen to three and a half cents a bushel. By 1876 when three-quarters of the stone-breakers were described as married men, the association imposed a maximum on possible earnings of fifty cents a day and tried to encourage the regular stone-breakers to make way for newcomers.[16]

In the late 1870s the employment scheme was placed in jeopardy, and thereafter experienced periodic cancellations, when the city reneged on its guarantee to purchase the broken stone for road-making, the stone produced by the 'undeserving' poor at the prison and by the habitual paupers at the poorhouse being cheaper.[17] When the stone-shed was restored in 1879, the city's niggardliness caused a drop in the wage-rate from three cents to two and a half cents a bushel. The AICP wage bill amounted to over $2100 in 1881 and when the city fell into arrears with its payments the association financed its operations with bank loans. The next year regular employment levels were high enough to cause the management to suspend the operation, a temporary interruption.[18]

Determined to render the association independent of the city council, the board searched for other customers including the new dry dock company and the Royal Engineer department of the British army. This initiative notwithstanding, the Poor Association continued to be dependent on the capricious city council which consistently failed to keep up its payment for the stone or failed to use up the stone it had contracted for, resulting in a surplus of unused stone the following year.[19] Despite the low and uncertain wages, the demand for the work steadily increased, with 80-100 men employed in 1891. The *Morning Herald* claimed that a man could earn between $5 and $7 a week, an amount that would feed his family though it was only 60 to 80 per cent of his normal earnings.[20] When the stone-shed failed yet again in 1894, the Poor Association began to function as a winter labour exchange putting prospective employers in touch with men needing work. In 1895 the employment register included the names of men looking for work as labourers, blacksmiths, machinists, grooms, teamsters, porters and nightwatchmen. The employment office coexisted with the stone-shed in the mid 1890s when large numbers of men were given some work for short periods in the winter, as many as 136 in 1893 and 150 in 1895.[21] The society's claim, that it did not aim at the abolition of poverty but rather at checking its increase, was reflected in the experience of Mr. Hartland of Maynard Street who made $3 a week during the six weeks he worked at the shed in 1896 but whose family was just as destitute in April as it had been at the beginning of the winter.[22]

The stone-shed, managed for many years by W.H. Neal, a dry goods merchant who was also the volunteer secretary, remained a feature of the Poor Association's approach to poverty for the rest of the century. Its importance depended on the general level of employment which prevailed at any one time. For example, unemployment peaked sharply during the depression in the mid 1870s and demand increased. In 1885 members found men who had left their jobs to help quell the Northwest Rebellion still out of work and requiring assistance. Unemployment rose again in the late 1890s, so much so that in 1897, when the society proclaimed its intention of closing the shed in early March after the city's order for broken stone had been filled, the stone-shed workers personally waited on the mayor and asked for a further order of stone which would give them another month's work. Unlike their counterparts in Liverpool, England, who in the spring of 1893 refused the wood-chopping work of the Central Relief Society on the ground that the pay was niggardly and the tools inadequate, Halifax men demonstrated for, not against, relief work. Continued demand for relief in 1898 led to married men being restricted to three days' work a week and single men to two. In 1900, however, existing employment opportunities, created by Boer War shipping, meant that only half the usual number of men were employed with sledge hammer and shovel.[23]

Members of the underclass were among those who looked to the AICP stone-shed as a way of coping with the winter season. On a pay day in January 1889 the three Kellum brothers and their relative George Deminas were reported to be "steadily at work" and making "a good average." They had come to accept AICP employment as part of their regular cycle of poverty and imprisonment. It had begun for them some years earlier. George Deminas, ensconced in his usual winter quarters at Rockhead, had been abruptly discharged in 1880 to enable him to take employment at the AICP stone-shed.[24] It was suggested in 1885 that winter "lodgers" at Rockhead might prefer the AICP stone-shed because they could as free men "make a comfortable living with no more labor than they are required to perform at Rockhead" under the rigorous management of Governor Murray. AICP members were convinced, perhaps with some justification, that the stone-shed kept men out of prison and the poorhouse.[25]

The persistent characteristics of poverty in the nineteenth century are nowhere better illustrated than in the Poor Association's approach to work for women. As early as 1869 the new association recognized the need for supplying women with employment. In response, a committee of ladies provided sewing for poor women in the winter of 1870. As long as Isabella Binney Cogswell was alive the work for women was continued despite a financial loss. Four years after her death, the association decided that it was time to provide work for women on the same work-test principle as applied to men in the stone-shed. A room was rented in Martha Harrison's private home for inebriates where poor women were employed for at least one season at mat-hooking. An employment register for women was opened in 1884 to try to put women looking for work by the day "at washing, scrubbing or cleaning" in touch with people needing such domestic help. Apparently this approach to domestic service on the part of the AICP was not successful because workplaces like offices and private homes already had their regular charwomen.[26] In 1885 and again in 1891 someone came up with the bright, but by then unoriginal, idea that a laundry should be opened to provide work for women. Of particular concern were "widows with families; grown girls; and wives and daughters whose husbands and fathers are unable from illness or other causes to work at the shed." It was thought that such women had no more work than one or two days' employment a week as part-time cleaners. This project too was dropped because of the reluctance of the AICP to make the initial outlay in machinery that was necessary to establish a viable operation capable of competing with the laundries located in the women's reformatories, to say nothing of the commercial ones.[27]

The AICP also recognized that the level of wages was a serious problem for women in Halifax. The exploitation of women in the needle trades attracted the association's particular attention in 1889, an interesting focus given the prominence of dry goods merchants in the AICP. In an appeal for subscriptions that year the executive indicated that:

> There are scores, hundreds, of women in this city whose only means of subsistence is by their needle. They are paid starvation wages, viz, 6 cents each for making shirts, 17 cents for making and pressing pants, 75 cents for coat and vest, etc. In the words of a skeleton living on Maitland St with a sick girl: "I have to work with my needle until midnight to earn the money to buy bread for tomorrow. And this is my hard experience everyday of the week, and every week of the year." [28]

By the end of the century the society found that it was becoming increasingly a relief agency for poor women as its Catholic counterpart, the St. Vincent de Paul Society, had always been. One-third of the AICP relief recipients were women, usually widowed with families, who had become, because of the regularity with which they applied, "pensioners, depending on the association to tide them over the winter when employment of any kind is hard to obtain." With one of its stated aims the increase of opportunities for employment and one of the realities of its operations the existence of a core group of women and men dependent on its relief year after year, the AICP was in reality an ersatz employer supported, at least in part, by those very businessmen and their wives who paid their workers inadequate wages.[29]

159

In the absence of AICP relief registers, we have to rely on other sources of information for identifying examples of people who received relief. The preferred objects for relief were families whose breadwinners were temporarily unable to provide the necessities of life. The Poor Association's own comments on its stone-shed suggest that the pressure for unemployment relief was greatest when opportunities for labour in the shipping industry were low. We can probably conclude therefore that the majority of the seasonally unemployed who looked to the AICP for help were casual port workers. Employment relief at the stone-shed and occasional supplies from the association's stockpile were not mutually exclusive forms of relief. When Mr. Hartland received his six weeks' employment in the stone-shed in 1896, his family also received material aid from the society in the form of four loaves of bread, four tickets for soup from the AICP soup kitchen and a pair of pants for their little boy. Despite the fact that the AICP claimed that this family was being cared for on a regular basis by the St. Vincent de Paul Society, Mrs. Hartland complained that they had no fire in their lodgings and that her children had to stay home from school in the absence of enough to eat. The insufficient level of occasional relief sent the destitute Hartlands looking for supplementary aid from the AICP. The family apparently needed more help than the St. Vincent de Paul Society was granting; yet they were not supposed to obtain aid at the same time from the Poor Association, other than what was available to Mr. Hartland in the stone-shed. Despite the professed policy, the AICP visitor was sympathetic enough to overlook such cases of the duplication of relief.[30]

The association's reliance on the stone-shed automatically excluded several important categories of the destitute from employment. First there were the men who could not perform physical labour of this variety. Matthew Walker, who relocated with his family in Halifax in 1885 after working in Amherst as a compositor, applied to John Naylor of the SPC for work. When Naylor sent him to the AICP, Walker was offered winter stone-breaking which he claimed to be unable to do. Another man who could not break stones was John Hays, a stevedore, living in Albemarle Street. He applied for relief in the winter of 1888, not because he could not get port work but because he was sick, as was also his wife. Another breadwinner too sick to work was Oscar Schroeter, a German immigrant, who had been ill with cancer for four years by the time his wife applied for aid for the five Schroeters.[31]

The other families excluded from stone-shed labour and dependent on relief were those headed by poor women. In 1884 Mrs. Power, a wi-

160

dow with three children living on Albemarle Street, needed a stove. The AICP could not supply one, sub-zero temperatures notwithstanding. Luckily for her, John Doull, a leading dry goods merchant, president of the Bank of Nova Scotia, and president of the association from 1870 to 1899, was in the habit of personally supplementing the AICP's aid. He fixed her up with a stove "to warm the shivering little ones."[32] In 1897 Mrs. Thomas Murphy's problem was her failure to receive regular remittances from her husband who was working in Kings County. Neighbours reported the destitution of the young woman and her infant son after she attempted several times to poison herself.[33]

A very large number of cases referred to the Poor Association related to the so-called 'undeserving.' Mrs. Jeannie Pringle, who lived in a tenement at the back of 37 Maynard Street, was refused aid in 1889 despite the fact that she was out of work and trying to support an eighteen-month-old child. She was apparently a soldiers' prostitute, a status which rendered her ineligible for relief. The Byrne family, immigrants from Newfoundland, were cut off by the association because of their bad character. The children were described as street beggars and jailbirds. The Coolens were also known as "dissolute people and confirmed beggars" but received coal and food from the AICP because one of the daughters had a sick baby whose welfare was of more concern to the society than the family's transgressions.[34]

The society's confrontations with the ravages of alcohol were frequent. The young McCann sisters of Grafton Street went out to beg to support their consumptive mother because their father was "a drunken worthless scamp." The drunkenness of William Miles, an ex-policeman living on Albemarle Street, resulted in his hospitalization in 1882 after he fell asleep in the street and suffered frost-bite. His wife and five children came to the AICP's attention because they were left without fire, food or clothing. When John Naylor referred a boy named McDermot to the AICP in 1886, he felt it was his duty to report that the father was a "drunken, worthless character."[35]

The association was also called upon to assist those people whom the vigour of the law had rendered helpless. In 1889, for example, Mrs. James Haley, her newborn infant and four other children were thought to be fit objects for relief after her husband was sent to Rockhead for illegally selling liquor. When the neglect experienced by long-suffering families of drunken men brought them into court to prosecute, it was sometimes discovered that the poor relief societies had been propping up the unsuccessful marriages. John Duffield was sent to jail for six months for wilfully neglecting his family which, in addition to receiving help from the St. Vincent de Paul Society for a number of years, had received from the AICP in 1883, 1884, 1886, 1887 and 1889 sundry supplies including 250 bushels of coal and fifty-two gallons of molasses.[36]

The most unfortunate members of the underclass also came within the purview of the AICP. In 1888 one of the Kellum tribe, Mary (Mrs. William Maxwell), was thought to be too degraded an object to receive assistance from the association. She lived with two male relatives and a white woman in a room in Albemarle Street. For this foul smelling accommodation, with holes in the ceiling and walls and almost no furniture, she paid $1.25 a week. But she and her associates were considered to be undeserving of relief because they drank and made no attempt to keep their room clean.[37]

Such experiences meant that by the 1880s the Poor Association began to toy with the idea of adopting policies other than ladling out soup, maintaining a stone-shed and dispensing small quantities of foodstuffs and fuel.[38] It turned to the conditions prevailing in underclass Halifax which contributed to the social problems associated with poverty. One issue was the effect of destitution and depravity on children. As a result of the concern for "young beggar waifs," the AICP formed a committee to agitate for the establishment of a general reformatory for children.[39]

The first suggestion that came out of this new interest on the part of the AICP was that it should contribute to the maintenance of delinquents in the Protestant Industrial School to keep them out of the prison and the poorhouse. The second suggestion related to begging. The association wanted to enforce the city ordinance against it, which the mayor proclaimed to be unenforceable, and to educate the public against "indiscriminate almsgiving." Ultimately the only concrete result was the maintenance of a boy named Lasher, whose mother was a drug addict, in the Protestant Industrial School for several years. But the association did remain concerned about promoting the welfare of children. In the 1890s, after the implementation of compulsory school legislation, it threw is weight behind making sure that children did attend regularly. It worked hand in hand with the truant officer and the school board to see that all children who needed clothing and footwear in order to go to school received them and that all children, so clothed, went to school. For the AICP, education became the preferred method for improving the condition of the poor in the twentieth century.[40]

Another major interest of the society was in promoting temperance and publicizing the evils of alcohol. Initially the AICP took a dim view of relieving any individual who appeared to be besotted by drink. Its by-laws required that each beneficiary abstain from intoxicating liquors. Yet the association's conclusion that drink was the foundation of poverty produced a less severe attitude when the families of drunks and alcoholics applied for relief. Concern over this matter led to such suggestions as removing drunken individuals from their families and placing them where drink was unobtainable and regulating the sale of liquor so that known tipplers would, like minors and Indians, be prohibited from obtaining it. With deserving and undeserving people coexisting within the same family unit, however, the association eventually decided to relieve the families of the undeserving because it was preferable to err on the side of mercy than to let the innocent suffer, a sentiment reflected by Archbishop O'Brien's advice to the St. Vincent de Paul Society that it was "better to be imposed on ten times than to refuse one deserving case."[41]

The most progressive causes which the Poor Association adopted, like its New York counterpart before it, emerged in the late 1880s and 1890s and related to the cost of commodities and the condition of housing. Poverty was considerably compounded and the gap between the rich and poor further widened by the inequitably high prices the poor were forced to pay for food, fuel and rent. Why, AICP members asked in the 1890s, were rentals higher for the poor than for the rich? Why were coal-hawkers allowed to sell coal to the well-to-do at $5 a chaldron but to the poor at $7.50?[42] These were questions that admitted of no easy solution but socially conscious members argued that the poor must be enabled to take advantage of the better prices. They advocated instruction in household economy as a means of alerting the poor to the discrimination of the marketplace.

An intense interest in housing conditions arose in 1887 when it came as something of a revelation to AICP members that the residences of the upper streets—notorious South Brunswick, Albemarle and Grafton—had no sanitation. As the Anglican bishop claimed at an AICP meeting in 1889: "if he had to live as he saw that a large number of people of this city had to live, it would be hell upon earth to him."[43] Feeling certain that such conditions must violate city ordinances, the AICP appointed a committee to investigate some of the tenements with the intention of reporting the deficiencies to the city council.[44] The three-man tour of inspection in January 1888, which included president John Doull and the AICP's paid visitor, fully revealed not only the lack of sanitary facilities but also the uninhabitable condition of the dwelling places of the poor, deserving and undeserving alike. In one boarded-up house, which the caretaker proclaimed to be unoccupied, the visitors found a family of five squatters crouched round a small fire.

> The room was absolutely devoid of furniture. In the corner of the rear room was a bundle of filthy rags. Underneath was the writhing form of a woman. The plaster was torn down and the biting cold rushed in through the cracks in the walls. Upstairs the windows were out; and through these and the holes in the roof, the snow, rain and ice had free course. On the floors were heaps of snow and ice, which sent waves of freezing air down on the helpless people.[45]

Since the inspectors were businessmen not given to excessive sentimentalism, there is no reason to doubt the sorry picture that emerged from their tour of the tenements.

For a month following the AICP tour of inspection, additional revelations of squalid housing and suggestions for reforms filled the press. The articles reveal not only the existence of many habitations unfit for pig sties, dog kennels or cattle stalls but also a cultural chasm of unbridgeable proportions between would-be reformers and the hovel-dwellers. Former mayor J.C. Mackintosh identified the most disgraceful housing to be "in the very heart of our city in the blocks bounded east by Argyle, west by Brunswick, north by Jacob and south by Blowers." A second tour of inspection in February 1888 by Doull, the AICP visitor, mayor, city medical officer, health inspector and reporters invaded Grafton, South Brunswick, Albemarle and Maynard Streets—the heartland of the underclass—and discovered the names of tenement owners, the rentals paid for the rookeries or "What dey calls rooms," as one black tenant in South Brunswick Street cryptically put it, and the abysmal state of the accommodations: "windows being an alternation of old hats, dirty rags and patched glass," yards always "horribly filthy" and everywhere a stench "disgusting and awful." Yet in these habitations the "wilfully poor" refused to give up their children to the industrial schools, refused to go to the poorhouse and refused to conform to health regulations by ceasing to prepare food to sell to their neighbours.[46]

With the realization that slum-dwellers were not willing to countenance such interference, the AICP concentrated on agitation for improvements in sanitation which helped to secure the city council decision of 1889 to provide drains for the upper streets. Continued pressure led to a legislative grant the following year to finance a sewage system after a series of AICP committees made further visits to the slums to investigate housing and sanitation.[47] The question of what to do about the tenements which were clearly unfit for human habitation

164

was the most controversial issue. The 1888 investigations led to suggestions that what was needed in Halifax was a Peabody to build model tenements; or a building society dedicated to replacing derelict housing; or a programme for building small houses in the suburbs at affordable prices combined with a system of rapid transport to the city's centre; or effective legislation to force owners to provide decent housing for their tenants.[48] These suggestions related specifically to the respectable poor. The rougher elements, the habitual slum-dwellers, would, according to J.C. Mackintosh, remain the rightful objects for the charity of the AICP, St. Vincent de Paul and individual church societies. According to the secretary-agent of the SPC, the disrespectable poor were in any case unfit for model tenements; the poorhouse and city prison were the appropriate abodes for undeserving paupers whose children alone were worth taking the trouble of trying to protect and reform in the city's institutions for child rescue.[49] Housing, even for the 'respectable,' remained a question for debate not for action; no public or charitable housing projects materialized in Halifax before the First World War. By the mid 1890s, when a tenement closing programme was in full swing, the Poor Association displayed a fundamental misunderstanding of the consequences by failing to stress the need to provide alternative housing for those left homeless by the clean-up of the upper streets. In 1897 no charitable agency came to the rescue of the members of the Kellum-Maxwell family when their shanty on Maynard Street was literally torn down around them after they had failed to take advantage of their one day's notice from the owner to vacate the premises.[50]

Despite investigations and suggestions, neither the AICP nor the St. Vincent de Paul Society directly undertook any housing of the poor. Nor did they sponsor any short-term shelters. Yet the need for refuges for the homeless was constantly felt in Halifax. The homelessness of men on their own or of families in transit or in trouble, who were destitute but not overtly criminal, resulted in the establishment of several refuges in the last quarter of the nineteenth century. To judge from the continued discussion of the need for a general refuge, the first effort begun in 1876, could not have been perceived by the public to be very successful or comprehensive. Small-scale and austere in its approach, it was the idea and for many years the responsibility of city missionary James Potter. Potter, an ex-soldier and reformed drunkard, began his work by selling cheap food to the poor in an establishment known as Potter's Workingmen's Refreshment Rooms on the Dartmouth Ferry Wharf, in which location he managed the AICP's second soup kitchen in 1876. Known as the Night Refuge for the Homeless, his new venture on Lower Water Street initially provided beds for twelve and cheap meals for both men and women. The SPC was known to take stray children to Potter for temporary care. Families too were sometimes lodged there. But by 1880 the Night Refuge had become to all intents and purposes a doss-house for men. Because many of the men were strangers and a goodly proportion of these were unemployed sailors, Potter's interest rapidly turned towards establishing a sailors' home, which opened in 1879. Nevertheless, the adjacent night refuge remained a charitable institution of the city into the 1890s. Its supporters looked on it as a way of preventing the sort of destitution and misbehaviour which would inevitably lead to the prison or poorhouse. The Night Refuge was not, however, well supported by the public which left the way open for the Salvation Army.[51]

By the early nineties the Salvation Army had become interested in replicating in Halifax its Toronto Lifeboat and Montreal Lighthouse or 'Joe Beef's Converted,' both shelters for homeless men and men on the tramp. As a result, the Salvation Harbour—the fifty-fourth Salvationist food and shelter depot worldwide—was opened in Hollis Street in 1894, providing inexpensive accommodation and food for the "hard-up, dead broke class" of men who had "formerly slept on the wharves or on the common."[52] Like the Night Refuge before it, the Salvation Army institution worked closely with the AICP and other relief agencies. Anxious to run a self-supporting home and to ensure that food and sleeping quarters were not "abused and made an excuse for laziness," the Salvation Army insisted that meals must be paid for and work performed by those who could not pay the ten or fifteen cents a night for a bath, clothes wash or fumigation and bunk bed with sheets and pillow. Chopping wood was the initial work-test but the Salvationists had to resort to a variety of additional employments and employment referrals until, some years later, they opened in Halifax, as elsewhere in the Salvation empire, a collection service for paper, junk and household materials. This gave haulage and repair work to the boarders and provided cheap, second-hand items for sale or distribution to the poor.[53] The approach met the approval of the charitable Protestant public. Foster Almon, the Anglican social activist, congratulated the Army on its determination "to solve the problem how to help the poor by enabling them to help themselves."[54]

Much larger than the Night Refuge department of the Sailors' Home and the St. Paul's Mission Shelter for poor men opened by the Anglicans on Albemarle Street in 1897, the Harbour could accommodate between fifty and seventy men and did a brisk business in economically depressed seasons like the winter of 1897 when it supplied 2880 beds and 4200 meals.[55] By then, the popularity of its restaurant with workingmen, who could obtain a three-course meal for about fifteen cents, and the pursuit of a strict style of management meant that the Harbour was indeed basically self-supporting.

While turn-of-the-century propaganda might give the impression that most of the clients of the shelter were drunks, Salvation Army "hoboes" came from a variety of conditions. It was reported that only "sometimes men come very much the worse for liquor...but if they show no disposition to become obnoxious, we take them in, and give them a special place apart from the rest." Lodgers sometimes proved to be untrustworthy. Patrick McDonough, an eighteen-year-old, stayed in the shelter for one night in June 1894 during which he helped himself to the pocket money of the officer in charge while everyone else was asleep.[56] We can imagine that Andrew Doyle or James Prendergast would have done the same.

********

The more notorious and pitiful members of the underclass lived in the wretched housing uncovered by AICP investigators and contributed to the need for public housing schemes and short-term refuges. For incorrigibles, like our mid-Victorian jailbirds, piecemeal public concern made no difference. Ex-soldier and ex-tavernkeeper Thomas Norbury is a case in point. Employed by the city for some years after the end of his 'criminal' career as a scavenger of dead animals, he was discovered by the police in January 1891 in a dying condition in "a hovel on Albemarle Street" which he called home. It contained: "Not a piece of furniture in the miserable room unbroken, the bed covered with a broken straw mattress looking as though with the slightest turn of its occupant it would collapse and smother him." Norbury himself, a longtime alcoholic, was "literally covered with vermin and presented a revolting spectacle."[57] In the annals of late Victorian Halifax Norbury's story was not unique especially among the old and sick.[58] He died of starvation and exposure in the kind of housing condemned by the AICP, an agency which did nothing to provide alternatives, and in a state of bodily filth deplored by the refuge keepers, whose concern with the here and now precluded their leadership in more far-sighted ventures.

167

Off-duty soldiers at their favourite pastime. (Public Archives of Nova Scotia)

Scene of domestic violence on Albemarle Street. (Public Archives of Nova Scotia)

# 8
# 'HALIFAX BELONGS TO GOD AND JOHN NAYLOR': THE SOCIETY FOR THE PREVENTION OF CRUELTY

The most active interventionist society in late nineteenth-century Halifax was the Nova Scotia Society for the Prevention of Cruelty. Established originally in 1876 as a humane society concerned with animals and more secular in its orientation than other voluntary organizations, it had moved by 1880 into the human sphere as instances of child and wife neglect and abuse came to light. The anti-cruelty movement, of which it was a part, has been virtually ignored by Canadian historians.[1] To the extent that there has been any analysis of this movement at all, attention has been focused on Toronto and the impression has been given that J.J. Kelso was the pioneer in the anti-cruelty and child saving movements.[2] This questionable emphasis on the Toronto Humane and Children's Aid Societies has neglected to account for the failure of the Toronto organizations, unlike their counterparts in Montreal and Halifax, to include women within their mandates and has erroneously credited Ontario with the first children's protection statute in 1893. In fact the SPC in Halifax secured two laws as early as 1880 and 1882 to enable it to prosecute under existing legislation all offences relating to children and to remove children from parents who failed to meet the SPC's standards for guardians.

The Nova Scotia anti-cruelty reformers were well aware of the pioneer nature of their work. As the secretary-agent claimed in 1882, before the formation that year of the Montreal Society for the Protection of Women and Children (inspired by the SPC according to its sources) and five years before the establishment of the Toronto Humane Society, "we are the only society in Canada that protects children."[3] During the 1880s the Halifax society frequently corresponded with fledgling societies elsewhere—both branch societies in Nova Scotia and new societies in other provinces—to which the SPC offered guidance and advice. The SPC also tried to promote national standards for the protection of children. In 1881, Matthew Richey, the president of the Nova Scotian society, unsuccessfully attempted, in his capacity as a member of parliament, to encourage the federal government to pass legislation to protect children, based on American and English statutes.[4] His lack of success left the initiative to the provinces with the predictable result that Ontario has claimed all the credit.

Failure to acknowledge the role of the Nova Scotian initiative also reflects the healthier financial state of the Toronto movement in comparison with emergent social services in parts of the country sinking into economic decline as capital and people fled the Maritimes. Insufficient voluntary and governmental financial support meant that the Nova Scotia society was always in a precarious position, a weakness which culminated in the inability of the society even to pay the secretary-agent's modest salary and in his occasional assumption of the full costs of the society's operations. The same economic circumstances meant that the pioneer Nova Scotian society was unable to maintain the leadership in the anti-cruelty and child saving movements. By 1892 the SPC had to confine its investigations and prosecutions entirely to the Halifax urban area because of shortage of funds, whereas the wealthy Toronto society was able to proselytize on behalf of the Children's Aid Society not only throughout Ontario but western Canada as well. The outreach of the SPC, which was so essential to deal with many cases in a highly mobile society, was considerably curtailed and the ability to add new services in Halifax, such as a children's temporary shelter like the one opened in Toronto in 1892, was stymied. The lack of public support was also apparent at the state level when the Nova Scotia legislature, which first provided a grant to the society in 1880, capriciously refused to vote any financial aid on several occasions in the 1890s. The history of the SPC in Halifax also provides another

172

illustration of the failure of maternal feminists to rally to social causes. After rescuing the fledgling society from financial ruin in the early 1880s, the ladies' auxiliary, founded in 1879, had dissolved by 1883 and, when it was revived in 1889, its relations with the parent society were debilitatingly ambiguous. This was in sharp contrast to Toronto where women played an important continuing role, a fact which impressed Nova Scotia SPC president J.C. Mackintosh on his visit to Toronto in 1891 to take part in the formation of the Canadian Humane Society. "One thing that struck him here," he was reported to have said, "was the number of ladies; in his society the active members were young businessmen."[5]

Young businessman might have been more accurate. For, as Carroll Smith-Rosenberg has noted with respect to Robert M. Hartley's role in the New York AICP, the SPC in Halifax was "the lengthened shadow of one man."[6] John Naylor, the secretary-agent of the society was, from its inception in 1876 until his resignation in 1899, the driving force behind the SPC's campaign to prevent and punish cruelty. An assessment of Naylor's varied career and his SPC caseload provides relevant background for examining the effect of the anti-cruelty movement on the experiences of some of our repeat offenders as well as the gender, class and family issues involved in late Victorian interventionism.

Like other activist moral reformers of his day such as John Grierson, James Potter and Major Theakston, Naylor came from a relatively modest background and was a new Canadian. Born in Calcutta in 1847, the son of a soldier, Naylor immigrated to Halifax from Bradford, Yorkshire in 1875. His major livelihood was real estate. In his private business his placards were so widespread that one visitor remarked that Halifax, with its many churches, appeared to belong to God and John Naylor.[7] He pursued a number of other employments besides selling and leasing property. These included employment agent, contract carter (for watering and cleaning the streets and removing furniture), poultry farmer, census enumerator in 1881 and chief inspector for the district of Halifax under the federal liquor licence law (McCarthy Act) in the mid 1880s. He was also paid, at least nominally, as agent and secretary of the SPC.[8]

As a newcomer who had to establish his credentials, Naylor initially secured support for his anti-cruelty work from his religious and associational confrères.[9] He was an Anglican and chose to be a member of the bishop's chapel, St. Luke's which, as a non-evangelical church, helped to make him acceptable to Catholics. He belonged to both the Independent Order of Good Templars and the Sons of Temperance and was

173

active also in his ethnic society, the St. George's Society, as well as in the masonic order. His initiative in organizing the watering of the dusty streets in the late 1870s secured him the goodwill of Halifax's businessmen. He was disappointed in some of his ambitions such as his failure to win an aldermanic seat or to secure appointment as the liquor licence inspector under the Nova Scotia act of 1886, which replaced the unconstitutional McCarthy Act. He also applied unsuccessfully for the job of Halifax chief of police in 1893 on Garret Cotter's retirement, a singular disappointment for a man who had functioned for many years as a police officer with "a right to interfere in any cases relating to a child under 16 and in regard to women."[10] Perhaps he was too much of a meddler for the authorities in Halifax. Only his dogged persistence, unremitting campaigns against cruelty and solid virtues as a citizen enabled him to overcome the suspicion generated among the middle class by his frequent interventions in such a taboo area as family life. What lower-class Haligonians thought of their 'cruelty' man is far more difficult to unravel given the mixture of dependence and resentment which arose in specific cases. But some indication is provided by the fact that they sought him out for help as often, if not more often, than he pursued them. The contact between Naylor and such repeat offenders as we encountered in Part One of this study, began when the SPC was still concerned exclusively with animal cruelty.

As a SPCA during its first four years, the society devoted its efforts in particular to promoting the humane treatment of horses, which involved everything from the provision of drinking fountains to the destruction of old or injured beasts. Central to the campaign was the legal prosecution of humans for mistreating their animals. Naylor's interest must have been essentially that of an animal lover. His own work involved the ownership of horses and he was a charter member of the Nova Scotia Kennel Club. This was the period when Isaac Sallis came up against Naylor for wilfully maiming horses. Perhaps they were rival carting contractors; certainly the facts of the case, as we have seen, are unclear but we do know that Sallis was acquitted, an outcome which Naylor sourly attributed to the pro-Sallis composition of the jury.[11] The attack on Sallis' new found respectability, which the prolonged and costly case represented, did not mean that Sallis became a sworn enemy or an indifferent observer of the activities of the SPC or that Naylor held any personal grudges against Sallis. Four years later Naylor willingly turned over to the erstwhile animal abuser an orphan boy of thirteen to be cared for and raised as an apprentice. On another

occasion Sallis conscientiously reported a suspected case of child desertion and neglect to the society.[12]

Prosecuted by the society one day; assisting it in its work or seeking
its protection the next—this was a common response to the interventionist policies of the SPC. Plebian resort to the society was not primarily related to a shift from rough to respectable which the example of
Sallis' experiences might lead us to expect. After the expansion of the
SPC from an animal protection society to a human-oriented one, both
the most incorrigible and pitiful jailbirds can be found being prosecuted one day and seeking protection or advice the next. The society
insisted on confining its assistance to those people who were incapable
of taking measures to resolve their problems by themselves. This meant
that the work of protection was aimed largely at poor women and
children though categories of helpless men, such as visiting merchant
seamen, were also considered suitable objects for the society's attention.
With respect to cases which did not fall within the society's very flexible
mandate, Naylor was always willing to offer advice and suggest
appropriate sources of help. As we have seen in previous chapters he
was well connected with the missions, poor relief societies, charitable
homes and individual churches. He performed a great variety of functions: policeman, detective, para-legal worker, social worker, marriage
counsellor, ombud, employment agent, health inspector and surrogate
parent.

Confronted with a possible case of cruelty or neglect, which he
construed to come within the terms of reference of the SPC, Naylor was
careful first to investigate the veracity of the complaint and thereby
"guard against deception, petty spite by one neighbour to another,
&c&c."[13] If the information was well founded, the nature of the case
determined the next stage. It might be a warning, particularly to a
husband to stop mistreating his wife; it might consist of gratuitous
advice; it might end in prosecution. Since he was not himself a lawyer,
Naylor did not prosecute personally but he worked hard to ensure that
the society had the legal right to intervene. The provincial legislation
of the 1880s respecting children, which was expanded in the 1890s, was
largely his doing. Violence against wives, on the other hand, was
prosecuted under the inadequate federal Offences Against the Person
Act and the complaints were frequently withdrawn before they reached
the court by women worried about their husbands' revenge or the
interruption of their means of support. It was not until 1889 that
legislation was obtained to allow a third party to prosecute when the

175

wife hesitated. Legislation, then, was the means by which the interference in family life was achieved.

But not all the cases were those of cruelty, narrowly defined. The human cases which Naylor investigated in the course of a year were varied and complex, as we can see from the ninth annual report.

### SPC Cases, 1 March 1884 - 1 March 1885

*Children* (sometimes involving more than one child)

| | |
|---|---:|
| Sent out begging by worthless parents | 20 |
| Neglected by drunken father | 42 |
| Neglected by drunken mother | 6 |
| Neglected by baby-farmers (8), ill-treated by aunt (6); father(10); adoptive parents (5); strangers (6); stepmother (1); mother (3) | 39 |
| Abandoned by father (4); mother (3); mother & father (3) | 10 |
| Persons with vicious dogs that injured children | 3 |
| Excessive punishment by school teacher | 1 |
| Rescued from improper houses or company—girls under 16 | 5 |
| Clothes provided (7); food, etc., when sick (6) | 13 |
| Cautioned at request of parents 3 boys & 4 girls | 7 |
| Homeless—sent to homes or institutions | 14 |
| Reward to boy for rescuing drowning child | 1 |

*Women*

| | |
|---|---:|
| Neglected by drunken husbands | 28 |
| Ill-treated by husbands | 24 |
| Husbands eloped with women | 2 |
| Husbands improperly conducting themselves with wife's sister | 2 |
| Neglected by sons legally liable for their support | 3 |
| Absconding husbands traced & made to support | 4 |
| Assaults by various persons | 4 |
| Illegal distress of goods | 4 |
| Death supposed by violence at hands of husband | 2 |
| Assisted to get stove & other articles | 3 |
| Rescued from bad life | 2 |
| Insane, advised & assisted relatives | 3 |
| Temporary assistance until brought to notice of proper authorities—to families | 7 |
| Homeless—suitably provided for | 8 |

*Men*

| | |
|---|---:|
| Seamen ill-used by captains | 9 |
| Sick, homeless or oppressed | 5 |
| Destitute & in search of work | 7 |

Source: Nova Scotia SPC, *9th Annual Report*, 1885, p. 18

The case books indicate a considerable diversification during the next decade. In 1892, a typical year, we find women going to Naylor with complaints about their husbands which not only included abuse and neglect but also desertion, quarrels and drunkenness.[14] Wives also asked him to get their husbands out of jail in order to restore to the family the major means of their support. A few husbands also complained that their wives were drunken, had deserted or were bad mothers. The major change was the resort by wives to Naylor as a go-between to arrange with the police magistrate for separation and maintenance orders which had become as popular in Halifax as in Boston.[15] Cases relating directly to children included complaints against parents—a demand by a daughter that her father pay for her education; an objection by a son to his father taking half his wages—and complaints by third parties that underaged children were working in the cotton factory. A variety of cases related to tenant-landlord disputes, wage disputes, harassment, rape and incest. Many of the problems were not single ones. For example, women who were deserted were also usually destitute. We do not know how many of the actionable cases ended up in court but we do know that almost two-thirds of the cases were brought to Naylor's attention by the parties directly involved rather than being discovered by him or another third party. Moreover, anywhere from one-half to two-thirds of the society's cases related to the protection of children. Children's problems brought the SPC into contact with such incorrigibles as Andrew Doyle and Thomas Norbury, two of the infamous 92.

Andrew Doyle was prosecuted by the SPC in 1882 as a child molester.[16] He had by that time been before the courts on many occasions for twenty years and in jail repeatedly. His first term in jail was in July 1863 when he was committed for drunkenness and using abusive and threatening language towards his father, Matthew. Doyle's relationships with his father and other kinfolk provide the key to his delinquency because at least twelve of his first twenty-nine terms in city prison resulted from family violence in which Doyle was the aggressor and members of the family the complainants. After his father, he next turned to his brother, whose butcher stall windows he broke in 1864 at the cost of thirty days in jail. Over the next ten years or so he continued to assault or threaten his principal relations: not only his father and brother but also his mother, sister, sister-in-law and brother-in-law. Usually given in charge by his father and always convicted, Doyle was at first given short sentences and bound over to keep the peace. In 1867 the magistrate resorted to the catch-all sentence of vagrancy, which enabled the court to imprison him for twelve months. On this occasion Doyle proclaimed that he did not care if he got ten years, for which the magistrate cited him for contempt of court. Because of the prevailing remission practices, Doyle's first year for vagrancy was a five-month one and it did nothing to alter the pattern of his drunken violence. If he was not bashing the authority figure represented by his father, he was taking on the city policemen. Tired of trouncing his vulnerable female relations, he committed the above-mentioned criminal assault on a little school girl in 1882, on whose behalf John Naylor intervened. While this offence, prosecuted by the SPC, resulted in a trial in the supreme court, the sentence Doyle received of one year in the county jail was not particularly novel for him. But it was combined with a flogging: twenty lashes with a cat-o'-nine tails, thought to be only the second time in the new nation's judicial history that the lash had been used as part of a sentence on a civilian prisoner. Here, thought the chief justice, was surely a way of shaming a man for whom all other methods had failed.

Contemporaries might have wished that the lash had been applied to Doyle by his shoemaker-father twenty years earlier. Yet Andrew was legally an adult by the time he served his first sentence. It was too late for family punishment of a corporal nature. The resort of lower-class families to the courts was, as we have seen, an important feature of family discipline in the nineteenth century. The court co-operated with this family to seek a definitive solution. The way of resolving the problem was thought to be banishment. It was unsuccessful. In common with Cornelius Ford and James Prendergast, Doyle had some experience as a sailor which removed him from the city at least temporarily. In April 1870, for instance, we find him deserting from the SS *City of Halifax* and spending three days in the county jail until his vessel sailed. He does not appear in the records again until November which seems to suggest that he did indeed go to sea. In 1872, however, his family, harassed afresh, made a concerted attempt to evict him from the city. Released from jail in April, after having served only a few days of a ninety-day sentence for disorderly conduct, on condition of leaving the city, his father made arrangements for his departure and paid for his passage. On 1 May Doyle prevaricated. He expressed his opposition to the scheme by assaulting his sister-in-law and creating a disturbance in his father's house. Doyle told the magistrate that "he refused to go because the papers had reported that he was being transported, and he would not go under such circumstances, and, moreover, that he was not as bad as the papers represented him to be." Unimpressed, the magistrate sentenced him to a year's imprisonment as a vagrant to which Doyle, ever mindful of his dignity, responded: "All right, I'll serve the year out, and then I can walk the streets as free and independent as you can."[17]

Since it is unlikely that his family was conspiring against Doyle—certainly he never charged any of them with assaulting him—we are probably dealing with a seriously flawed personality, further aggravated by alcoholism. But what a personality: Irish blarney, loquacious charm, deviousness and arrogance—all these traits emerge from the record. He commanded enough respect from Halifax street people for them to rescue him from the police in 1869 after he assaulted his brother. In November 1870 he ingratiated himself with Major Kidd, a former US army officer, who considered him such "a jolly good fellow" that he invited him to Brown's Restaurant in Hollis Street and, in the course of the meal, Doyle repaid his hospitality by allegedly picking $60 from the major's pocket. A reporter from the *Acadian Recorder*, who knew his record well, showed no sympathy for Doyle after his lashing in the county jail execution yard at the end of his year's imprisonment in October 1883:

> Doyle [he pronounced] is an arrant humbug. To hear him talk before the Police Court, one would think him to be not a fallen individual, but a fallen saint. He is most plausible with his vows of reformation, and has great power of bathos and glibness....He was probably only imposturing yesterday when affecting to be suffering from the blows—in fact is reported to have said so; and the whipping has resulted in nothing practical.[18]

In the meantime by the mid-seventies, Doyle's health had begun to deteriorate under the ravages of his dissolute life. In 1876 he was treated in hospital for primary syphilis. In 1879 and 1880 his alcoholism took him to the medical ward of the hospital. By 1881 his *delirium tremens* had reached a critical stage: he could not eat or sleep, he suffered violent pains in his head and had well marked tremors. His medical history described him as "a worthless idle fellow. And though of good family and apparently well educated," in a state of intoxication all the time. His normal condition over the previous fifteen years was summed up in one word: "tight." The week he spent in hospital in October 1881 gives us some idea of his psychosis. Admitted on 25 October, he was described as a "bummer" whose DT's were so bad that he was locked up. Shortly after he used his eloquence on the surgeon who obligingly freed him. Once liberated he escaped from hospital through a kitchen window, attired only in his shirt and drawers. The next morning he was returned to the hospital, still in shirt and drawers, but now complete with beaver hat. On 31 October he again talked his way out of confinement into a hospital ward where he proceeded to wheedle enough brandy from a fellow patient to get drunk and turbulent. Locked up again, he kept up a horrible row all that night and in the morning expressed his displeasure by relieving himself all over the floor. The casebook concludes: "He seems to be more a subject for Mount Hope than for this institution."[19]

But to the Mount Hope Insane Asylum he appears not to have gone. After prison terms in 1883 and 1884 he spent time in the poorhouse. He presented "a horrible spectacle" in court in 1887, suffering from DTs, when he was arraigned for stealing a pig's head and a counterpane.[20] He narrowly avoided a supreme court trial for larceny by dying in the poorhouse in January 1889.

The nature of Doyle's pathological aggressiveness may have been exacerbated by physical problems. In 1875 a newspaper reported that while in city prison, he got hold of an axe and chopped off the four fingers of his right hand. While the report proved to be wrong, it did reveal that Doyle had lost all the fingers of his left hand in a saw-mill accident some years earlier. We must therefore allow that his physical disability may have adversely affected his quest for a livelihood as much as his drinking affected his mind and made him wish in 1875 "for a knife to cut his throat."[21] Thirteen years later, near the end of his life, when he pleaded guilty to the charge of being a common vagrant, he again indicated his wish to end his miserable existence.

Even a hopeless derelict like Doyle turned to the SPC for help despite his previous incarceration and whipping at Naylor's instigation. In the mid 1880s, not long after he had completed the sentence for criminal assault, he complained to John Naylor about the cruelty of William Murray, the governor of Rockhead Prison. Naylor's records do not reveal an investigation of this complaint, though he was certainly not averse to taking on Halifax's institutions. But Doyle did not forget his grievance. The year before he died, while awaiting arraignment in the supreme court on the larceny charge in the spring of 1888, he summoned Naylor to the county jail to discuss ways of proving that Governor Murray mistreated prisoners.[22] He saw the SPC, then, as a vehicle for justice, not just for himself, but for his fellow prisoners. The society had taken him to task; he now expected Naylor to give equal attention to prosecuting the oppressor of the criminal poor.

It is perhaps not surprising that Doyle lacked the credibility to encourage Naylor to pursue the matter. But the society showed no such hesitation to criticize the prison authorities in the case of a black boy, John Brown, whose treatment in prison was so inhumane that his feet froze. The information concerning this case came from the boy's grandfather, a resident of Africville. The society demanded an inquiry. As a result, hearings were held before the city prison committee. Governor Murray argued that the prison doctor had been summoned to tend to the boy's feet and also that the state of his wounds has been aggravated by his 'filthy' habits, a reference apparently to bed-wetting or more general incontinence. In the event the prison governor was absolved of any blame and Naylor was outraged by the result. This was only one of a number of SPC inquiries into conditions in public and private institutions. Others featured the Protestant Industrial School and the Home of the Good Shepherd, facilities on which the SPC normally depended for the care of victims of cruelty and neglect.[23]

But the vast majority of cases investigated by the SPC involved family problems and it was in this context that Thomas Norbury, who eventually ended his life as the verminous city scavenger, came to Naylor's attention. Norbury initially belonged to the rough and tumble, frequently illicit, world of the marginal tavernkeeper in disreputable Barrack Street.[24] Most of his fellow publicans, such as Isaac Sallis, avoided jail by paying their fines. Norbury was not always so lucky when he appeared before the court between 1868 and 1883. A British soldier, his army career as a sergeant ended when he met Mrs. Eliza Kane (Cain) with whom he set up house. She purchased his discharge from the army at a time when he was said to be "one of the best specimens of physical manhood in Halifax" and he obliged her by buying from Mr. Kane "all the right, title, and interest in the latter's wife for $6."[25] This informal variety of divorce may have been in conformity with popular practice but it did not in this instance produce marital bliss or prevent confrontation with the legal husband. In February 1868, Mr. Kane successfully charged Norbury with assault and keeping a disorderly house. Thereafter Norbury was frequently in court. In April 1868 Norbury and Eliza Kane were discharged after two separate charges of stealing customers' property in their tavern, a resort apparently for soldiers and gold prospectors. Then he was convicted of keeping a disorderly house and served fifteen days of his ninety-day sentence before Eliza Kane came to the rescue. He rewarded her in May by assaulting her but she decided to drop the prosecution and turned her attention instead to abusing Norbury's new girlfriend. Kane then hired her new boyfriend Hugh Griffiths as a bartender and body-guard to protect her against "her purchaser," much to Norbury's displeasure.

Norbury, with whom Eliza Kane lived in "adulterous intercourse," as she put it, threatened the new bartender who countered by taking him to court.[26] As a result both Norbury and Eliza Kane were fined $20, as much for their irregular relationship as for the assault on Griffiths. Norbury alone went to jail until Eliza Kane decided to pay his fine. A month later Norbury and a female servant were convicted of stealing five dollars from Benjamin Bailey during a Sunday morning drinking and card-playing session in the Norbury establishment. Norbury appears not to have gone to jail but the next charge against him, for selling liquor without a licence, which resulted in a fully-served jail term of twenty days, was on information given by the same Benjamin Bailey whom he had recently robbed.

Two of Norbury's court appearances in 1868 and 1869 centred on his own prosecution of men who had attempted or threatened to stab him. He was next convicted in February 1869 when he and Eliza Kane went to jail for larceny. He served his ninety-day sentence while she secured an early release on payment of the fine. When he returned to Rockhead in 1872 he did so as a vagrant. Following four terms in jail for assaults and selling liquor without a licence in 1873, he again joined forces with Eliza Kane in April 1874 to sell liquor illegally. Andrew Doyle, one of the witnesses in the case, claimed that he had obtained rum in Thomas' and Eliza's house on a Sunday. Norbury went to jail and Eliza Kane was discharged. Later that year, Norbury's deteriorating status was reflected in the first of several incarcerations for drunkenness and drinking-related offences.

By 1876 Norbury had parted from Eliza Kane and entered into a legal marriage which he soon proceeded to destroy by refusing to support his wife and babies. First in 1880 and again in 1883, after the family had been forced to return to the city from their refuge with Mrs. Norbury's mother in the country, Norbury refused to provide for them. Found destitute in the streets on the second occasion, the wife and children were rescued by the police and referred to John Naylor who intervened with Norbury on their behalf, but to no avail. Consequently, the SPC took Norbury to court for neglecting his family for which he received ninety days at hard labour. When a local commentator remarked that Norbury would enjoy "a warm bed, comfortable food, medical and religious attendance, easy work for the winter in Rockhead, while his family was left destitute," Naylor explained that the family had been admitted to the poorhouse. The proceeds of Norbury's stone-breaking labour in jail would pay for their support.[27] In the spring the family left the poorhouse just as ex-prisoner Norbury arrived there. Subsequently,

Norbury's continued over-indulgence in alcohol and his wife's resort to prostitution led to a complete breakdown of the marriage.

Where did Norbury turn for help? To none other than to John Naylor who had barely finished prosecuting him. Norbury wanted the SPC to assume responsibility for the care of his children but before that could be arranged, Mary Norbury spirited them away again to her mother's home at Porter's Lake in the country and Norbury, described by his brother-in-law as an able man of fifty, continued to refuse to pay anything towards their support. Mary Norbury returned to Halifax but lived separately from her husband. When her mother died late in 1887, Mary was released from a term in city prison to take care of the children on condition that she join her brother as a servant at the lake. Instead she brought the children to town, continued as a prostitute, and in the absence of any help from her husband, she now asked Naylor to get the children, aged eleven and nine, admitted to homes. He recorded in his journal: "This couple are a disreputable lot and it would be a blessing to get them [the children] homes away from them."[28] Although Naylor doubted that Norbury was capable of supporting the children because he was now crippled, Naylor none the less summoned him under the Act to Prevent and Punish Wrongs to Children and charged him, and, by implication, his wife, with abandoning William and Alice. The stipendiary magistrate gave the girl in charge of the SPC to be placed in the St. Paul's Alms House of Industry. "He asked the boy if he would like to go to the Industrial School who said yes with a delighted expression," according to the press reports.[29] It is hard to imagine a child looking forward to the prospect of five years in an institution but in this instance it provided security for a boy virtually abandoned by his father and neglected by his mother.

Although historians might view the institutionalization of children as punishing the victim, Naylor's object in taking the children away from their parents was "to save them," especially from the influence of their mother who continued to pursue her disreputable occupation and her 'criminal' career.[30] William Norbury's fate is unknown. In 1891 he was still a pupil at the Protestant Industrial School, learning the shoemaker's trade. But the records allow us to trace Alice Norbury's life for another five years. In 1888 Naylor described her condescendingly as "a nice little creature and not at all vicious—having been for the past six years in the country with its grandmother where it was well looked after." To the secretary-treasurer of the home he wrote: "I think you will like the looks of the child as it is not at all illmannered."[31] Alice stayed in St. Paul's Alms House of Industry for nearly three and a half years. During that time her father, the city's drunken scavenger, died and her mother repeatedly applied for permission to see her. The ladies who managed the home decided that it was in the child's best interests to refuse her mother's requests. Their concern to protect Alice from her mother "and the influence of all other of her former companions and surroundings" and to protect the younger children in the home from Alice, now somewhat older than the average St. Paul's girl, encouraged them to find her a home in the country. She was sent to New Glasgow.[32] A year later her foster mother died and she was handed over to another matron of the same town where she remained until 1896. In the meantime in 1894, her mother, remarried and living on Albemarle Street, applied to Naylor to intercede on her behalf with the managers of the home for the purpose of restoring her daughter to her. It seems likely that Naylor, wary of prostitute-mothers, refused and when Alice Norbury finally returned to Halifax in 1896, it was to live not with her mother, who might have since died, but with her aunt in Albemarle Street. Naylor's last known involvement with the Norbury family centred on seventeen-year-old Alice. She followed her parents' habit of seeking him out with her troubles when she reported later that same year that she was pregnant by James Johnstone, a travelling sewing machine agent. Naylor, used to this problem, issued a bastardy warrant against Johnston who gave bonds and cleared out.[33]

********

Naylor dealt with such a variety of problems encountered by the poor, helpless and derelict that he probably had little time to reflect on the causes of all the misery he encountered. But his known attitudes reflect the moral, cultural and environmental explanations suggested by recent studies of violence and the anti-cruelty movement.[34] We do not have to look far for his critical assessments of underclass moral values. Naylor automatically condemned prostitutes like Mary Norbury as neglectful mothers. It was inconceivable to him that a woman who sold her body for a living could possibly be a good parent. Not surprisingly, the most common cultural reason he suggested for cruelty and neglect was excessive drinking. Naylor claimed that 80 per cent of the people he had to caution or prosecute were addicted to drink.[35] As an active temperance advocate and sometime federal liquor licence inspector he believed that "whatever tends to make the people more temperate makes them also more humane."[36] Feminist historians have

184

suggested that it was easier for social agencies to blame persistent problems of anti-social behaviour on patterns of drinking than to criticize patriarchy directly.[37] Indeed, violent men themselves often blamed their overindulgence for their attacks on the weak, as if their own responsibility for their behaviour stopped at the cork of the bottle. But when an abused wife denied that her husband was drunk at the time of the assault, she implicitly confirmed that male aggression, pure and simple, like that of James Prendergast towards his wife Mary Ford, was an equally important cultural explanation for cruelty. Neglect and violence were also caused by the pressure imposed on the poor and outcast by the environment in which they lived: crowded housing, frequent bouts of unemployment, large families, persistent illnesses, all contributed to an explosive atmosphere in which frustration, exhaustion and anxiety produced quarrels, fights and unpremeditated violence. No one knew about the terrible housing conditions better than Naylor both in his capacity as the SPC's official visitor and in his role as a real estate agent. In 1880 when the society officially launched into human cruelty cases, Naylor wrote about widespread unemployment and poor wages.[38] The SPC was not however a radical social organization and it did not explicitly make connections between hardship and cruelty, between the lack of economic opportunity and the neglect of children.

In the last quarter of the nineteenth century, the interventionism of the SPC was characterized by a mixture of social amelioration, social control and lower-class opportunism. Endangered females were rescued from violent males, starving children from parents unable to cope or past the point of caring, young people from exploitative employers, old people from unfeeling children. Such interventions necessarily involved control of the offending party in order to protect helpless people. In other cases, however, helpless people encountered the moral disapproval of the society. The SPC denied some members of the underclass access to its services. Naylor stated quite categorically in 1888 that he considered incorrigible drunks and beggers unworthy of assistance outside the poorhouse and the prison.[39] And yet his pronouncements were one thing; his actions another. The names of even the most notorious characters in the city could be found in his casebooks as clients. As the examples of our jailbirds indicate, he might well be prosecuting them one day and defending them the next.

Yet the society's willingness to go after employers, landlords and even the city's penal institutions on behalf of its clients indicates that the social control it tried to exercise was as horizontal as it was vertical.

In cases where it appeared to shun the responsibility to investigate inhumane treatment in the higher classes of society, the explanation was one of cost, not policy. Like its counterparts elsewhere, the SPC believed that cruelty and all forms of inhumane treatment could be found at every level of society. But normally victims of means could resort to the courts directly to solve their own problems; the corollary unfortunately was that defendants of means could use their resources to involve the SPC in lawsuits it simply could not afford.[40]

Although the bulk of SPC cases occurred within the working-class and the underclass, the majority of the investigations carried out by Naylor were initiated by the victimized clients themselves. This was not unique to Halifax. Linda Gordon found that 60 per cent of the complaints of known origin addressed to the turn-of-the-century Massachusetts Society for the Prevention of Cruelty to Children came from family members, the great majority women and children.[41] As was the case with the prison and the poorhouse, the lower classes did not allow themselves to be manipulated by the anti-cruelty societies. They took advantage of those institutions at least in so far as their circumscribed conditions permitted. The SPC functioned then, at least in part, as a vehicle of lower-class opportunism. Most of the secretary's work was initiated and defined by the self-expressed needs of the clients. Mothers asked him to caution their wayward children, wives looked to him to warn their abusive husbands, single mothers brought their many problems to him. In small children's cases, for obvious reasons, an intermediary was usually involved, typically a neighbour. Gradually the anti-cruelty society became an integral part of lower-class life and an oft-used and trusted resource. Unlike the missions, refuges, homes and poor relief agencies, the SPC proposed a range of practical solutions for individual supplicants and this accorded them a degree of dignity and choice consistent with a sense of control over their own lives.

Architectural drawing of the chateau-like poorhouse of 1869. (Public Archives of Nova Scotia)

# CONCLUSION

We reconstruct the lives of others at our peril. One major pitfall is that the experiences of the Victorian underclass are reflected through the biased prism of middle-class sources. In addition, human nature and the social relations of the past are so enormously complex that they defy sweeping generalizations and academic theories. Yet it is important to try to understand the course of deviant life-cycles, family conflict, cross-class contacts and the evolution of social policy historically because many of the same problems persist in our advanced capitalist society. We still have people who are delinquent before they reach maturity, people who drink and drug themselves to ruin and death, men who beat their wives or rape the girl next door, parents who batter their infants, adolescents who risk disease and violence to prostitute themselves in order to secure an adequate living or assert their independence, desperate people whose fate is prison, mental illness or suicide. Not all of them are poor, disadvantaged and dependent of course; nor were they in the nineteenth century. And that is why class-based explanations do not provide all the answers.

This study has been specifically concerned with the biography of Haligonians who became well known in the city because of their frequent encounters with the criminal law. Some repeat offenders, like our 92 mid-Victorians, went to jail and other institutions on a regular basis because they were unable to overcome problems caused by their gender, colour, family relationships, individual personalities or acquired habits. Others, including their kinfolk, neighbours and underworld employers, avoided Rockhead as a result of material advantages,

189

better luck, more self-discipline, greater natural or learned intelligence or access to caring relatives or friends. Altogether, as a result of shared experiences and shared space, the jailbirds and their associates formed a loose connection of underclass people. In varying degrees they were subject to economic, cultural and familial pressures.

The underclass included the very poor who were driven to petty crime by destitution. Women were especially vulnerable but so too were blacks of both sexes and casual labourers of the two races represented in the upper streets. Crime as a strategy for survival had a long tradition among marginalized people in pre-industrial society and as long as the poor stole from each other or from transients, they were treated by the authorities more as a nuisance than a threat, an attitude confirmed by their short jail sentences. The containment of crime within the rough neighbourhoods suggests a low level of class consciousness on the part of the poor as well as a hand-to-mouth approach to survival typical of people generally lacking experience in capital accumulation. As we have seen, petty capitalist success by erstwhile members of the underclass depended both on externally determined status like military honours and on astute use of strong-arm tactics and underworld influence. The Isaac Sallises of the upper streets climbed to worldly comfort on the backs of their less fortunate friends and relatives. But they started at the same point, a fact graphically illustrated by the divergent careers of Sergeants Sallis and Norbury in civilian life.

Because Halifax retained much of its pre-industrial character through its industrial revolution, the seasonality of winter continued to contribute substantially to the definition of poverty and the hardship of people on the margin of a subsistence livelihood. Seasonal unemployment swelled the ranks of the residents of the prison and the poorhouse, particularly those of the men. Women were affected more by stages in their life-cycles than by the change of seasons. Young women who had to make or wanted to make their own way in life turned to prostitution as employment in a city devoid of other adequate ways to make a living; the pool of marriage partners included a high proportion of unreliable providers with military and seafaring jobs; the chances of poverty-stricken widowhood or separation were high in a city with such a mobile male workforce.

The frequent preference by the repeat offenders for the 'comforts' of the public institutions tells us much about the typical quality of underclass home life. If they preferred the rats of Rockhead to the hovels of the upper streets, we can appreciate how bleak their housing normally was. Indeed specific descriptions of the conditions endured

190

by the Kellum family as they were hounded from one upper-street shanty to another and by Thomas Norbury in old age provide evidence of the comparative advantages of the jail cell.

A second common feature which upper-street residents shared was a way of life which constituted a distinct subculture. It was a loud, boisterous, hard-drinking culture that spilled out of the taverns and dance halls into the streets. The innumerable times that the repeat offenders were transported drunk to the lock-up indicate the opportunities for over-indulgence the licensed and illicit rum shops offered to a resident and transient population still largely untouched by the temperance movement. Few of the 'crimes' committed by the 92 were unconnected with drunkenness. Liquor flowed in hundreds of upper- and lower-street locations; whatever money the weaker members of the underclass were able to earn through their labour was invested in refreshment of the liquid variety. They were victims of the drink culture which turned them into hoboes, hooligans and very sick alcoholics.

And yet, for all the problems which overindulgence caused the frequenters of the taverns, those semi-public places were central to the recreation, leisure and sociability of lower-class life. People outside the immediate circle of down-and-out, skid-row types depended on the grog shops for fellowship, food, accommodation, news, entertainment, relaxation, warmth and variety in their otherwise humdrum existence. Some well-run houses there must have been; yet both orderly and disorderly houses were threatened by the tightening of the liquor laws.

Before the legal abolition of the tavern in the 1880s, the culture which flourished in the houses of the upper streets was centred not only on drink and sex, but also on music which played an important role in the lives of the lower classes. We know very little about the nature of the music because it was often proscribed and rarely documented. Much of it was designed for dancing, was performed on the fiddle or piano and included rousing singing. Some of the music of the underclass was also derived from their religious experiences. The Kellums were inveterate gospel singers and probably learned some of their hymns through participation in the black Baptist and Methodist churches. Perhaps it was music which encouraged some residents of the rough neighbourhoods to respond to the mission of the Salvation Army, with its loud, brass band.

This subculture was particularly offensive to the middle class in its street manifestations. From the 1860s on, increasing numbers of social reformers had occasion to frequent the unfamiliar streets of soldiertown and sailortown on their various missions. Their moral standards together with the establishment of respectable institutions in these alien spaces meant that, by the 1880s, the upper streets represented a contested terrain. The middle class clamped down on the vulgarity of the residents. Since a considerable proportion of the greatly increased police court business in the 1890s was accounted for by prosecutions for profane, obscene and blasphemous language, genteel standards of propriety had apparently been adopted also by the residents of the upper streets themselves, especially by wives bent on correcting their husbands' rough behaviour.[1]

A third feature of the biography of repeat offenders is the importance of the family as both a positive and a negative influence. Threatened from the outside, the family could draw together and provide the kind of solidarity which the experiences of the Kellums demonstrate. But, more often, we find conflict to be the central feature of family relations. Lower-class residents of Halifax used the law enforcement agencies and the prison to discipline their problem children. Delinquents and misfits were born not only to people at the bottom of the socio-economic scale, needless to say. But parents with the financial means could pay to have their abnormal and subnormal children locked away. This avenue was not available to the poor, whether respectable working class or disrespectable underclass. The conflict between children and parents admits of no easy explanations. But clearly sometimes the parents were overbearing, unduly demanding or, in the case of fathers, sexually abusive or tyrannically patriarchal. This is not to say that children were always in the right, but they were accorded little of the benefit of the doubt or acknowledgment of maladjustment common a century later. Problem or oppressed children suffered untold miseries from the concepts of childhood which guided the attitudes of their elders. Imagine the trauma involved in rejection by one's family and prosecution by one's closest kin. Examples of the constant conflict in the relationships of children and parents which lay behind the court appearances are legion. That being the case, it is hardly surprising to find also conjugal and other forms of family disagreement and violence in the annals of the underclass.

Yet parental and marital failure are insufficient to explain the behaviour of some of the hard cases included in the 92. Every society has its share of black sheep. They often ran away to sea or joined the army or, in the case of women, escaped from the family home to live wild, sexually promiscuous lives in company with other refugees from the accepted social norms. Halifax naturally attracted its share of such rebels. They brought a great deal of misery to those close to them and ultimately to themselves. Every society also has its share of disabled people. In the nineteenth century they were considered a burden by both their families and the state and frequently treated like deviants.

When the 92 repeat offenders featured in this study first embarked upon their unfortuante careers, very few facilities existed outside the family and the penal and poor law systems to cope with their problems. Nor were their transgressions monitored by any community group other than their immediate neighbours. During the remaining years of the century, however, circumstances changed. A range of new voluntary associations and institutions intervened in underclass life. They provided alternatives to prison and different approaches to the seemingly uncontrollable excesses of outcast society. None of this cross-class interventionism was unique to Halifax, but the timing, methods and personnel all had distinctive local features including military exigencies, racial discrimination and Protestant-Catholic rivalry.

The stream of friendly and not-so-friendly visitors that invaded the upper streets during the last quarter of the nineteenth century expanded from the policemen and city missionaries of the mid-century to include the truant officer, agents of the poor relief and anti-cruelty societies, the liquor licence inspector, health officers, middle-class ladies preaching temperance and more aggressive agents of the almighty like the Salvationists. They shared a number of assumptions whether their efforts were neighbourhood or city-wide, Catholic or Protestant, state-subsidized or privately supported.

The first assumption was that the members of the underclass could be rescued from their folly, but only if they were reached before they had sunk too far. The *Halifax Herald* speculated in 1892 that: "There are men and women in Halifax today, who have spent from one-third to half of their lifetime in prison, or the poorhouse, who might have been good citizens had an effort been made to save them when they started on their careers of crime."[2] Timing therefore was crucial and the prominence assigned to child rescue reflected this concern.

The second assumption shared by the critics of the subculture was that the customs of the underclass—begging, taverngoing, serial monogamy and other flexible sexual relationships and juvenile precosity—were unacceptable and must be eradicated. When the public campaigns of the social activists were combined with the intervention of the state, new legislation was enacted or existing legislation more effectively enforced to prohibit people from pursuing their living in the streets; to outlaw the social gatherings centred on the bar-room; to destroy irregular marital and guardianship arrangements, especially those with an inter-racial dimension; to protect children from exploitation by adults of their own class; and to ensure that all children were imprisoned in the schoolroom for a large part of their time. Contemporaries believed that universal reforms, like compulsory schooling, would diminish the need for institutions aimed at the underclass such as the industrial schools.[3]

The third assumption was that the existing traditional institutions of social control—the poorhouse and the prison— did more harm than good in reshaping the morals and attitudes of the underclass. The poorhouse, for example, was thought to be "worse for children than the streets."[4] Much late nineteenth-century effort was therefore devoted to providing alternatives to the poorhouse and the prison and to helping people in the police station as they teetered on the brink of a jail career. At the other end of the spectrum, a start was made at addressing the problems of prisoners on their release from jail. Prison-gate work was in particular promoted by women's organizations and the managers of the women's homes "to save the wrecks which the manhood of the city has cast out."[5]

The fourth assumption was that the best way to rehabilitate delinquents was to get them away from the evil influences of the city—be it their parents, their neighbourhood, their exploiters or their employment—and introduce them instead to life in rural Nova Scotia. Not all the child apprentices and adoptees in the country were British home children; many of them were Halifax's own underclass youth, whose removal from the city had been arranged by the city missionaries, the Catholic religious, the SPC or the industrial schools. The preferred location for servant trainees from the women's homes was also the country. In their concern for the rural reformatory, reformers were admitting that the excesses of the city were beyond their control.

The regimentation of life and deprivation of traditional cultural forms involved in social reform, inspired initially by "religious ardour" and then by "domestic ideology," presented a new challenge to the underclass.[6] Their response was a traditional one. They adapted to the new circumstances. What Michael Katz has said about the poor in American cities also applies to the disadvantaged, delinquent and dependent people represented in this study. They "found ways to exploit the interstices of the system and to manipulate institutions to their own purposes."[7] Their proprietorial attitude to the poorhouse and the jail was expanded to include the private and semi-public institutions opened for children, women and men. They often asked to have their children admitted to the reformatories and refuges; women sought out the rescue homes and some even wanted to remain there; men participated in the work schemes and patronized the hostels. Another major interventionist organization that they tried to turn to their advantage was the Society for the Prevention of Cruelty. Specifically designed for the protection of the weak, helpless women used it against their abusers and harassers. When a downtrodden wife punished or humiliated her violent husband, she attacked traditional male authority within the family. For her, cross-class intervention in the family was preferable to continued male tyranny. As Linda Gordon has suggested: "If we reject the social premises of liberalism (and marxism), that gender and the sexual division of labour are natural, then we can hardly maintain the premise that familial forms of social control are inherently benign and public forms malignant."[8]

In the final analysis, social reformers still had a long way to go to understand underclass Halifax and convince its members that they understood and cared about the social, familial, gender and racial problems faced by people on the margin. They had closed the barrooms and thereby attacked the subculture of the upper streets but they had abandoned alcoholic rehabilitation as a strategy for helping the victims of drink. They had broached the sanctity of the family to expose neglect and abuse; yet the call for a permanent shelter for endangered women and their children had gone unanswered. They had backed the eradication of slum conditions but done nothing about the crying need for cheap and decent housing in the upper streets. They made life increasingly difficult for prostitutes and searched diligently for white-slavers but they raised only tentative opposition to the double standard of sexual morality. They did not question a legal system which imprisoned people because they could not pay their fines. The segregation of the city's black population was reinforced rather than undermined by middle-class interventionism. These were some of the legacies bequeathed to the twentieth century by the dark side of life in Victorian Halifax.

---

# NOTES

---

## NOTES TO PREFACE

1. *Evening Express*, 6 June 1862.
2. Paul Craven, 'Law and Ideology: The Toronto Police Court 1850-80,' in David H. Flaherty (ed.), *Essays in the History of Canadian Law*, II (Toronto, 1983), p. 249.
3. *Morning Chronicle*, 21 Sept. 1865, 19 Feb. 1884; *Acadian Recorder*, 25 June 1874, 24 Oct. 1889; M.M. Mathews (ed.), *A Dictionary of Americanisms on Historical Principles* (Chicago, 1951), vol. 1, pp. 846-7.
4. See Ken Auletta, *The Underclass* (New York, 1982); William Julius Wilson, 'Cycles of Deprivation and the Underclass Debate,' *Social Service Review*, vol. 59 (Dec. 1985), 541-59 and *The Truly Disadvantaged: The Inner City, the Underclass, and Public Policy* (Chicago, 1987).
5. A term used by Linda Gordon, among others: 'Child Abuse, Gender, and the Myth of Family Independence: A Historical Critique,' *Child Welfare*, vol. 64, No. 3 (1985), 216.
6. Gareth Stedman Jones, *Outcast London: A Study in the Relationship between Classes in Victorian Society* (London, 1971); Gertrude Himmelfarb, *The Idea of Poverty: England in the Early Industrial Age* (London, 1984).
7. K.S. Inglis, *Churches and the Working Classes in Victorian England* (London, 1963), p. 328; Gilbert A. Stelter and Alan F.J. Artibise (eds.), *Power and Place: Canadian Urban Development in the North American Context* (Vancouver, 1986), p. 10.
8. Greg Marquis, ' "A Machine of Oppression Under the Guise of the Law": The Saint John Police Establishment,' *Acadiensis*, vol. XVI, No. 1 (Autumn 1986), 58-77; E.H. Monkkonen, *Police in Urban America, 1860-1920* (Cambridge, 1981); Nicholas Rogers, 'Serving Toronto the Good: The Development of the City Police Force 1834-1880,' in V.L. Russell (ed.), *Forging a Consensus: Historical Essays on Toronto* (Toronto, 1984), pp. 116-40; Craven, 'Law and Ideology: The Toronto Police Court, 1850-80,' in Flaherty (ed.), *Essays in the History of Canadian Law*, II, pp. 248-307; Brian Harrison, *Drink and the Victorians: the Temperance Question in England 1815-1872* (London, 1971); Elizabeth Pleck, *Domestic Tyranny: The Making of American Social Policy against Family Violence from Colonial Times to the Present* (New York, 1987); Linda Gordon, *Heroes of Their Own Lives: The Politics and History of Family Violence, Boston 1880-1960* (New York, 1988); George K. Behlmer, *Child Abuse and Moral Reform in England, 1870-1908* (Stanford, 1982); Susan E. Houston, 'The "Waifs and Strays" of a Late

Victorian City: Juvenile Delinquents in Toronto,' in Joy Parr (ed.), *Childhood and the Family in Canadian History* (Toronto, 1982), pp. 129-42; Margaret May, 'Innocence and Experience: The Evolution of the Concept of Juvenile Delinquency in the Mid-Nineteenth Century,' *Victorian Studies*, vol. XVII, No. 1 (Sept. 1973), 7-29; Anthony M. Platt, *The Child Savers: The Invention of Delinquency* (Chicago, 2nd ed. 1977).

9. *Acadian Recorder*, 29 Dec. 1897.

# NOTES TO INTRODUCTION

1. T.W. Acheson, 'The National Policy and the Industrialization of the Maritimes,' *Acadiensis*, vol. I, No.2 (Spring 1972), 3-28; James D. Frost, 'The "Nationalization" of the Bank of Nova Scotia, 1880-1910,' *Acadiensis*, vol. XII, No.1 (Autumn 1982), 3-38; L.D. McCann, 'Staples and the New Industrialism in the Growth of Post-Confederation Halifax,' *Acadiensis*, vol. VIII, No.2 (Spring 1979), 47-79; Eric Sager, 'Sources of Productivity Change in the Halifax Ocean Fleet, 1863-1900,' in D. Alexander and R. Ommer (eds.), *Volumes Not Values* (St. John's, 1979), pp. 91-116; Eric Sager, 'Labour Productivity in the Shipping Fleets of Halifax and Yarmouth, 1863-1900,' in R. Ommer and G. Panting (eds.), *Working Men Who Got Wet* (St. John's,1980), pp. 155-84; D.A. Sutherland, 'The Personnel and Politics of the Halifax Board of Trade, 1890-1914,' in L.R. Fischer and Eric Sager (eds.), *The Enterprising Canadians* (St. John's, 1979), pp. 203-29.

2. The published material on urban government relates to an earlier or later period. See J.M. Beck, *Joseph Howe*, vol. 1 (Kingston and Montreal, 1982); Henry Roper, 'The Halifax Board of Control: The Failure of Municipal Reform, 1906-1919,' *Acadiensis*, vol. XIV, No. 2 (Spring 1985), 46-65. For the period under discussion, see P.B. Waite, *The Man from Halifax: Sir John Thompson Prime Minister* (Toronto, 1985), part one.

3. The only scholarly approach to these questions has been the biographical one as exemplified in the *Dictionary of Canadian Biography* which is useful for all élites in Halifax.

4. Gwenyth Andrews, 'The Establishment of Institutional Care in Halifax in the Mid Nineteenth Century,' B.A. honours essay, Dalhousie University, 1974; Judith Fingard, *Jack in Port: Sailortowns of Eastern Canada* (Toronto, 1982); Ian McKay, 'The Working Class of Metropolitan Halifax, 1850-1889,' B.A. honours essay, Dalhousie University, 1975; Ian McKay, 'Capital and Labour in the Halifax Baking and Confectionary Industry,' *Labour/Le travailleur*, vol. 3 (1978), 63-108; Ian McKay, *The Craft Transformed: An Essay on the Carpenters of Halifax, 1885-1985* (Halifax, 1985), ch.1; Ian McKay, 'Class Struggle and Merchant Capital: Craftsmen and Labourers on the Halifax Waterfront, 1850-1902,' in Bryan D. Palmer (ed.), *The Character of Class Struggle: Essays in Canadian Working-Class History, 1850-1985* (Toronto, 1986), pp. 17-36; M.K. Morrison, 'The "Social Evil" in Halifax in the Late Nineteenth Century,' B.A. honours essay, Dalhousie University, 1979; Brenda Lee Potter, 'Poor Relief in Nova Scotia in the 1880s,' B.A. honours essay, Dalhousie University, 1978; Kenneth G. Pryke, 'Poor Relief and Health Care in Halifax, 1827-1849,' in Wendy Mitchinson and Janice Dickin McGinnis (eds.), *Essays in the History of Canadian Medicine* (Toronto, 1988), pp. 39-61.

5. Phyllis R. Blakeley, *Glimpses of Halifax 1867-1900* (Halifax, 1949).

6. *Morning Journal*, 15 June 1855.
7. Robert Everest, *A Journey through the United States and Part of Canada* (London, 1855), pp. 4-5.
8. Blakeley, *Glimpses of Halifax*, ch.2; Melody Himmelman, ' "For Whom the Bell Tolls": Marriage Patterns, Halifax, 1871-1881,' B.A. honours essay, Dalhousie University, 1979; McKay, 'The Working Class of Metropolitan Halifax, 1850-1889,' ch.5; D.A. Sutherland, '*Warden of the North* Revisited: A Re-examination of Thomas Raddall's Assessment of Nineteenth-Century Halifax,' *Transactions of the Royal Society of Canada*, Series IV, vol. XIX (1981), 89.
9. Sutherland, '*Warden of the North* Revisited: A Re-examination of Thomas Raddall's Assessment of Nineteenth-Century Halifax,' 89; Thomas H. Raddall, *Halifax, Warden of the North* (Toronto, 1948); Bruce Galloway, 'The Life of the British Soldier in Mid-Victorian Halifax,' B.A. honours essay, Dalhousie University, 1983.
10. *Presbyterian Witness*, 22 Feb. 1862; *Morning Herald*, 10 Dec. 1889; *Morning Chronicle*, 6 May 1882.
11. *Morning Herald*, 13 Oct. 1891; Blakeley, *Glimpses of Halifax, 1867-1900*, pp. 5-6.
12. Susan Buggey, 'Building Halifax 1841-1871,' *Acadiensis*, vol. X, No.1 (Autumn 1980), 90-112; A.J.B. Johnston, 'Popery and Progress: Anti-Catholicism in Mid-Nineteenth-Century Nova Scotia,' *Dalhousie Review*, vol. 64, No.1 (Spring 1984), 146-63; T.M. Punch, 'The Irish in Halifax, 1836-1871: A Study in Ethnic Assimilation,' M.A. thesis, Dalhousie University, 1975; B.E.S. Rudachyk, 'The Most Tyrannous of Masters: Fire in Halifax, Nova Scotia, 1830-1850,' M.A. thesis, Dalhousie University, 1984.
13. Alan A. Brookes, 'Out-Migration from the Maritime Provinces, 1860-1900: Some Preliminary Considerations,' *Acadiensis*, vol.V, No.2 (Spring 1976), 26-55; Patricia A. Thornton, 'The Problem of Out-Migration from Atlantic Canada, 1871-1921: A New Look,' *Acadiensis*, vol.XV, No.1 (Autumn 1985), 3-34.
14. Blakeley, *Glimpses of Halifax 1867-1900*, ch.2; Fingard, *Jack in Port: Sailortowns of Eastern Canada*, ch. 1.
15. *Morning Chronicle*, 9 Oct. 1883.
16. Charles Roger, *Glimpses of London and Atlantic Experiences* (Ottawa, 1873), pp. 11-12.
17. *Presbyterian Witness*, 20 Dec. 1856; *Hutchinson's Nova Scotia Directory* for 1864-5 and 1866-7.
18. *Presbyterian Witness*, 2 May 1863; A.J. Wright, 'The Halifax Riot of April, 1863,' *Nova Scotia Historical Quarterly*, vol.4 (1974), 299-309.
19. *Sun*, 6 Feb. 1885.
20. Halifax Visiting Dispensary Registers, Oct. 1866-Mar. 1868 and Sept. 1882-Dec. 1887, Dalhousie University Archives MS 2-240.
21. Punch, 'The Irish in Halifax, 1836-1871: A Study in Ethnic Assimilation,' ch.6. I am also drawing on the research of John Grenville and Linda Lever.
22. R. Barclay-Allardice, *Agricultural Tour in the United States and Upper Canada* (Edinburgh & London, 1842), p. 3.
23. Robert F. Lucid (ed.), *The Journal of Richard Henry Dana, Jr.*, vol. 1 (Cambridge, Mass., 1968), p. 79.
24. *Novascotian*, 29 Mar. 1847.
25. Halifax City Mission, *Report for 1866*.
26. *Morning Chronicle*, 20 Apr. 1866.
27. *Morning Chronicle*, 3 Aug. 1870.
28. *Morning Herald*, 23 July 1885.

29. *Novascotian*, 14 Nov. 1864.
30. *Journal of the House of Assembly*, 1838, App. No. 18, p. 71.
31. Halifax City Mission, *Report for 1862*.
32. Halifax Garrision Orders (also includes locations of unnamed houses), PANS, MG 12, HQ, No. 106-123, 125, 127, 129 (1860-1879); MG 12, Miscellaneous General (1879-1884).
33. *Morning Chronicle*, 4 Dec. 1871.
34. *Morning Herald*, 9 Nov. 1880.
35. Address to Grand Jury, 8 Oct. 1883, and Meeting of Grand Jury, 18 Oct. 1883, PANS, RG 34-312, Series P, vol. 24.
36. J.H. Grenville, 'The Halifax Police Department, 1864-1893: The Cotter Years,' unpublished research paper.
37. *Morning Chronicle*, 24 Dec. 1885.
38. *Presbyterian Witness*, 6 Sept. 1856.
39. *Presbyterian Witness*, 11 Jan. 1862.
40. *Halifax: "Its Sins and Sorrows"* (Halifax, 1862), pp. 13, 20.
41. *Halifax: "Its Sins and Sorrows"* p. 14; Halifax City Mission, *Report for 1863*.
42. Nova Scotia Statutes, 27 Vic, cap. 81; see Canada, *Sessional Papers*, 21 (1894), vol. XXVII, No. 12, Royal Commission on the Liquor Traffic—Minutes of Evidence, vol. 1 (Maritimes), 1893.
43. *Acadian Recorder*, 1 Feb. 1868.
44. *Morning Chronicle*, 16 June, 10 Nov. 1883.
45. *Presbyterian Witness*, 1 Jan. 1870.
46. *Presbyterian Witness*, 21 Jan. 1860, 6 Feb. 1864.
47. *Presbyterian Witness*, 31 July 1869.
48. *Acadian Recorder*, 16 Jan., 6, 13, 20, 27 Feb. 1869; *Presbyterian Witness*, 15 Apr. 1871.
49. *Acadian Recorder*, 1 Feb. 1868.
50. *Acadian Recorder*, 25 Jan. 1868.
51. *Acadian Recorder*, 6 June 1868.

# NOTES TO CHAPTER 1

1. *Morning Chronicle*, 22 Nov. 1869. A reference no doubt to "The Wickedest Man in New York" of 1868, see Paul Boyer, *Urban Masses and Moral Order in America, 1820-1920* (Cambridge, Mass., 1978), p. 127.
2. *Acadian Recorder*, 29 May 1869; *Morning Chronicle*, 29 May 1869.
3. *Acadian Recorder*, 28 Nov. 1868.
4. *Morning Chronicle*, 13 Apr. 1868.
5. *Morning Chronicle*, 9 Jan. 1872.
6. *Acadian Recorder*, 18 Apr. 1868. Howard's biography is compiled from the following sources: City Prison Records, Registry of Inmates, PANS, RG 35-102, Series 18B, vols. 2 and 3; Police Court Minutes, PANS, RG 42, Series D, vols. 19-23; Police Court Minutes, Halifax Police Museum; Poor House Records, PANS, RG 35-102, Series 33A, vol. 2; *Morning Chronicle*, 9 Dec. 1865, 9 Mar., 14 Apr., 29, 31 May, 27 June 1866; 13 Apr. 1868, 29 May, 1 Oct., 22 Nov. 1869, 9, 16 Jan., 7 Aug. 1872, 14 Apr. 1874, 9 May 1879; *Acadian Recorder*, 18 Apr., 28 Nov. 1868, 29 May, 28 July 1869.
7. Statistics compiled from City Prison Records, Registry of Inmates, PANS, RG 35-102, Series 18B, vols. 2 and 3.

8.  E.H. Monkkonen, *The Dangerous Class: Crime and Poverty in Columbus, Ohio, 1860-1885* (Cambridge, Mass., 1975); Michael B. Katz, Michael J. Doucet and Mark J. Stern, *The Social Organization of Early Industrial Capitalism* (Cambridge, Mass., 1982), ch. 6; John Weaver, 'Crime, Public Order, and Repression: The Gore District in Upheaval, 1832-1851,' *Ontario History*, vol. LXXVIII, No. 3 (Sept. 1986), 176-207.

9.  For institutional studies, see David Rothman, *The Discovery of the Asylum* (Boston, 1971); Michel Foucault, *Discipline and Punish* (New York, 1978); Michael Ignatieff, *A Just Measure of Pain* (New York, 1978). For statistical studies, see Monkkonen, *The Dangerous Class*; Katz, Doucet, and Stern, *The Social Organization of Early Industrial Capitalism*, ch. 6. For social crime see G. Rudé, 'Protest and Punishment in Nineteenth Century Britain,' *Albion*, vol. 5 (1973), 1-23. On the failure to provide criminal biographies for the 19th century see V.A.C. Gatrell, 'The Decline of Theft and Violence in Victorian and Edwardian England,' in V.A.C. Gatrell, B. Lenman and G. Parker (eds.), *Crime and the Law: The Social History of Crime in Western Europe since 1500* (London, 1980), p. 335; H.J. Graff, 'Crime and Punishment in the Nineteenth Century: A New Look at the Criminal,' *Journal of Interdisciplinary History*, vol. VII (1977), 477-91; Monkkonen, *The Dangerous Class*, p. 74; G. Rudé, *Criminal and Victim: Crime and Society in Early Nineteenth-Century England* (Oxford, 1985), p. 2. For a description of the lives of more serious criminals see Philip Priestly, *Victorian Prison Lives: English Prison Biography 1830-1914* (London, 1985).

10. According to the 1861 census, the native born (i.e. in the Atlantic region) constituted 74 per cent of the population, including of course young children unrepresented among the recidivists. *Censuses of Canada 1665-1871*, vol. IV, pp. 346-7.

11. For Doyle's biography, see Chapter 8.

12. Jones, *Outcast London*, pp. 77-78.

13. *Morning Chronicle*, 29 Nov. 1872; *Acadian Recorder*, 31 Jan. 1889.

14. *Morning Chronicle*, 7 Sept. 1868.

15. *Acadian Recorder*, 20 Jan., 28 Mar., 3 Oct. 1868.

16. Police Court Minutes, 10 Oct. 1863, PANS, RG 42, Series D, vol. 18; 9 Oct. 1865, *ibid.*, vol. 21; *Morning Chronicle*, 25, 27 June, 27 Oct. 1866; *Acadian Recorder*, 30 May 1868.

17. *Acadian Recorder*, 7 May 1875.

18. Police Court Minutes, 13 July 1865, PANS, RG 42, Series D, vol. 21; *Morning Chronicle*, 26 May, 26 June 1866; *Acadian Recorder*, 25 Jan., 15 May 1868.

19. *Morning Chronicle*, 15 Mar. 1865.

20. Police Court Minutes, 30 May 1864, PANS, RG 42, Series D, vol. 19; 10 Aug. 1865, *ibid.*, vol. 20; 6 Sept. 1867, *ibid.*, vol. 22; 26 Sept., 3 Oct. 1868, 2 Feb. 1869, *ibid.*, vol. 23; 17 Apr. 1874, *ibid.*, vol. 25; Entry for 12 Mar. 1869, City Prison Records, Registry of Inmates, PANS, RG 35-102, Series 18B, vol.2.

21. See Chapters 3, 4 and 8; also J. Fingard, 'Jailbirds in Mid-Victorian Halifax,' *Dalhousie Law Journal*, vol. 8, No. 3 (June 1984), 81-102, and *Jack in Port: Sailortowns of Eastern Canada*, pp.50-52.

22. Police Court Minutes, 8 July 1865, PANS, RG 42, Series D, vol. 20; 22 Aug. 1867, *ibid.*, vol. 22; Coroner's Inquest on Eliza Munroe, 1 Mar. 1867, PANS, RG 41, Series C, vol. 41; Medical Case Books, Victoria General Hospital Papers, PANS, RG 25, Series B, Section III, vol. 5, p. 281; *Morning Chronicle*, 24 Oct. 1868, 7 Jan. 1870, 11 Mar. 1872, 26 Apr. 1875, 4 Nov. 1882. The Elizabeth Johnston included in this analysis represents three different black women of the same name with overlapping jail records.

23. Police Court Minutes, 18 June 1864, PANS, RG 42, Series D, vol. 19; 10 May 1865, *ibid.*, vol. 20; 1 Nov. 1867, *ibid.*, vol. 22; Medical Case Books, Victoria General Hospital Papers, PANS, RG 25, Series B, Section III, vol. 4, p. 423; Surgical Case Book, *ibid.*, Section IX, vol. 1.

24. Medical Admissions Ledgers, Victoria General Hospital Papers, PANS, RG 25, Series B, Section II, vol. 45; Surgical Record Books, *ibid.*, Section IV, vol. 18.

25. Police Court Minutes, 3 Aug. 1868, PANS, RG 42, Series D, vol. 23; *Morning Chronicle*, 4 June 1869, 1 Oct. 1870, 3 Feb., 12 Nov. 1873, 30 June 1875.

26. Surgical Record Books, Victoria General Hospital Papers, PANS, RG 25, Series B, Section IV, vol. 18; *Morning Chronicle*, 11 Feb. 1874. Other recidivists treated for various forms of venereal disease included: Mary Barry, Hannah Baker, Mary Cahill, Andrew Doyle, Robert Hilton, James Hogan, Robert Hamilton, Charles McInnis. See Medical Admissions Ledgers, Victoria General Hospital Papers, PANS, RG 25, Series B, Section II, vol. 45; Surgical Record Books, *ibid.*, Section IV, vol. 18; Surgical Case Books, *ibid.*, Section IX, vol. 3.

27. Police Court Minutes, 14 June 1858, PANS, RG 42, Series D, vol. 9; 12 Aug. 1865, *ibid.*, vol. 21; 21 Oct. 1867, *ibid.*, vol. 22; 22 July 1871, *ibid.*, vol. 24; *Morning Chronicle*, 21 July 1869, 21 Dec. 1870, 13 Apr. 1871.

28. County Jail Registers, PANS, RG 34-312, Series J, vol. 12; *Morning Chronicle*, 24 May 1864, 15 Mar. 1866.

29. Police Court Minutes, 3 July, 9 Sept. 1865, PANS, RG 42, Series D, vol. 21; 28 July 1871, *ibid.*, vol. 24; Queen vs Elizabeth Johnston, Supreme Court Records, PANS, RG 39, Series C, Box 269; *Morning Chronicle*, 11 Sept. 1865, 16 Mar. 1866, 6 Aug. 1869, 8 May 1872; *Acadian Recorder*, 6 Dec. 1867, 6 June 1868, 11 Aug. 1869.

30. Police Court Minutes, 21 Oct. 1868, PANS, RG 42, Series D, vol. 23; *Morning Chronicle*, 22 Nov. 1876, 18 Oct. 1877, 1, 2 Mar. 1880, 2 Feb. 1885.

31. *Acadian Recorder*, 4 Apr. 1868.

32. *Acadian Recorder*, 2 May 1868.

33. Police Court Minutes, 4 Jan. to 23 May 1868, PANS, RG 42, Series D, vol. 22; 2 Apr. to 29 Dec. 1868, *ibid.*, vol. 23; *Acadian Recorder*, 2, 30 May, 19 Dec. 1868; *Morning Chronicle*, 6 Apr. 1881.

34. *Acadian Recorder*, 30 May, 6 June 1868.

35. *Morning Chronicle*, 16 Jan. 1865, 21 Nov. 1868; *Acadian Recorder*, 29 May 1868.

36. *Morning Chronicle*, 27 July 1865; Police Court Minutes, 2 Jan., 6 Feb. 1867, Halifax Police Museum; Poor House Records, PANS, RG 35-102, Series 33A, vols. 1a-18 (1860-1900).

37. Poor House Records, PANS, RG 35-102, Series 33 A, vol. 2; Entries for 19 Feb. 1866, 28 May 1868, City Prison Records, Registry of Inmates, PANS, RG 35-102, Series 18B, vol. 2.

38. *Morning Chronicle*, 20 Aug. 1868, 23 June 1869, 1 Mar. 1880, 30 Jan. 1882; *Acadian Recorder*, 7 Nov. 1868.

39. Entries for 4 Jan. and 4 Apr. 1873, City Prison Records, Registry of Inmates, PANS, RG 35-102, Series 18B, vol. 2; Entry for 28 Nov. 1879, *ibid.*, vol. 3; City Prison Committee Minutes, 15 May, 4 July 1872, City Prison Records, Minute Book, 1861-1872, Series 18A, vol. 1; *Morning Chronicle*, 19 July 1870, 24 and 25 July 1873, 17 May 1877, 30 Nov. 1878, 28 Nov. 1879, 21 Mar. 1881, 23 Jan. 1882.

40. Entries for 21 Mar. 1861, 2 Sept. 1872, 5 Mar. 1873, City Prison Records, Registry of Inmates, RG 35-102, Series 18B, vol. 2; City Prison Records, Prison Committee Minute Book, 1861-1872, PANS, RG 35-102, Series 18A, vol. 1; *Morning Chronicle*, 22 May 1866, 27 Apr. 1870, 29 Oct. 1879, 13 Aug. 1885, 13 Jan. 1886.

41. Graff, 'Crime and Punishment in the Nineteenth Century: A New Look at the

Criminal,' 483; Katz, Doucet, and Stern, *The Social Organization of Early Industrial Capitalism*, p. 237.

42. Police Court Minutes, 18 June 1859, PANS, RG 42, Series D, vol. 10; 20 Aug. 1864, *ibid,*. vol. 19; 22 Aug. 1867, *ibid.*, vol. 22; 12 July 1871, *ibid.*, vol. 24; 13 and 28 May, 1 June 1874, *ibid.*, vol. 25; *Morning Chronicle*, 18, 30 Jan., 30 May, 21 Sept. 1865, 26 Jan., 21, 23 Aug. 1866, 19 Jan. 1870, 16 May 1872, 18 Apr. 1876; *Acadian Recorder*, 4 Aug. 1866, 2 May 1868, 25 June 1874.

43. Police Court Minutes, 9 Dec. 1867, PANS, RG 42, Series D, vol. 22; *Morning Chronicle*, 9 Nov. 1866, 13 Jan. 1868, 30 July 1881, 18 Jan., 11 July 1868.

44. *Evening Express*, 6 June 1862; *Novascotian*, 5 Jan. 1863; *Morning Chronicle*, 26 Jan., 29 Oct., 18 Dec. 1864, 6 Jan. 1865, 21 Jan., 3 May, 4 Oct. 1866, 9 Jan., 1, 4 Feb. 1867, 22 Jan., 18 Dec. 1868, 6, 9 Feb., 3 Mar. 1869, 7 Mar., 4, 21, 30 Apr. 1872, 4 Jan. 1873; *Acadian Recorder*, 30 Jan. 1869.

45. City Prison Committee Minutes, 5 Feb., 2 Apr. 1863, 7 Jan., 2 Nov. 1864, 26 Sept. 1872, City Prison Records, PANS, RG 35-102, Series 18A, vol. 1; 16 Nov. 1864, Halifax Police Museum; Report of Special Committee Appointed to Inspect City Prison, 27 Aug. 1873, Halifax City *Annual Report*, 1872-73, pp. 93-95; *Morning Chronicle*, 29 Dec. 1866, 20 Mar. 1873, 2 May 1874, 12 Aug. 1879; *Acadian Recorder*, 18 July 1868, 12 Aug. 1897.

46. County Jail Registers, PANS, RG 34-312, Series J, vol. 12; Police Court Minutes, 29 Aug. 1857, Halifax Police Museum; 29 June 1858, PANS, RG 42, Series D, vol. 9; 4 July 1862, *ibid.*, vol. 16; 27 Sept. 1862, *ibid.*, vol. 17; 7 Sept. 1863, *ibid.*, vol. 18; 19 Oct., 25 Nov. 1867, *ibid.*, vol. 22; *Morning Chronicle*, 11 Nov. 1862, 23 Nov. 1869.

47. Police Court Minutes, 3 June 1864, PANS, RG 42, Series D, vol. 19; 13 Nov. 1866, Halifax Police Museum; *Acadian Recorder*, 2 May 1868; *Morning Chronicle*, 6 Sept. 1881.

48. Police Court Minutes, 29 Mar. 1856, PANS, RG 42, Series D, vol. 8; 18 June 1860, *ibid.*, vol. 12; 29 Apr. 1861, *ibid.*, vol. 14; 5 Oct. 1863, *ibid.*, vol. 18; 3 and 19 Aug. 1864, *ibid.*, vol. 19; 12 May, 19 June 1865, *ibid.*, vol. 20; 16 Sept., 20 Oct. 1865, *ibid.*, vol. 21; 21 Sept. 1867, *ibid.*, vol. 22; 7 Dec. 1866, Halifax Police Museum; Entry for 28 Aug. 1880, Stipendiary Magistrate Court Records, PANS, RG 42, Series D, vol. 28; *Morning Chronicle*, 7 Jan., 24 Sept., 11 Oct. 1864, 16 Apr., 27 June, 6 Aug., 12 Sept., 7 Nov. 1866, 9 Oct. 1869.

49. Police Court Minutes, 1 Apr. 1856, PANS, RG 42, Series D, vol. 8; Coroner's Inquest on William Henry Kehoe, PANS, RG 41, Series C, vol. 45; Coroner's Inquest on Ann Wilsonhome, *ibid.*, vol. 46; *Morning Chronicle*, 20 Aug. 1864, 25 May 1874, 27 Dec. 1875, 4 Sept. 1880; *Acadian Recorder*, 5 May 1874.

50. *Acadian Recorder*, 6 Oct. 1897.

51. *Acadian Recorder*, 2 June 1880, 2, 8 May 1889; Potter, 'Poor Relief in Nova Scotia in the 1880's,' B.A. honours essay, Dalhousie University, 1978, p. 35; Michael B. Katz, *Poverty and Policy in American History* (New York, 1983), ch. 2.

52. Poor House Records, PANS, RG 35-102, Series 33A, vols. 1a-18; *Morning Chronicle*, 1 Nov. 1877. John McDonald was sent to the insane asylum but the only reference is to John McDonnell, another recidivist (1866-72:13). This is a case where McDonald and McDonnell may be one and the same offender but they have been counted as two. Nova Scotia Hospital Papers, PANS, RG 25, Series A, No. 8. There is a mention of John Hamilton being sent to the asylum in *Morning Chronicle*, 6 Aug. 1866, and the public hospital authorities believed Andrew Doyle was certifiable.

53. Coroner's Inquest on Ann Wilsonhome, PANS, RG 41, Series C, vol. 46; *Morning Chronicle*, 6, 11 Nov. 1871.

54. *Morning Chronicle*, 24 June 1874.
55. Coroner's Inquest on Johanna Power, PANS, RG 41, Series C, vol. 54.
56. Coroner's Inquest on Alice Donnelly, PANS, RG 41, Series C, vol. 55; *Morning Chronicle*, 5, 6 Aug. 1880.
57. Coroner's Inquest on Patrick Cody, PANS, RG 41, Series C, vol. 57; *Morning Chronicle*, 12 Sept. 1882.
58. *Morning Chronicle*, 8 and 9 Nov. 1882.
59. Coroner's Inquest on Eliza Munroe, PANS, RG 41, Series C, vol. 41; *Morning Chronicle*, 4 Mar. 1867.
60. Coroner's Inquest on Mary Slattery, PANS, RG 41, Series C, vol. 50; Police Court Minutes, 16 and 17 Jan. 1865, Halifax Police Museum; *Morning Chronicle*, 2, 4, 30 Apr., 4, 19 May 1874.
61. Coroner's Inquest on Julia Martin, PANS, RG 41, Series C, vol. 56; *Morning Chronicle*, 12, 18, 19 Oct. 1881; *Acadian Recorder*, 19 Oct. 1881.

# NOTES TO CHAPTER 2

1. Police Court Minutes, 18 June 1859, PANS, RG 42, Series D, vol. 10; 14 and 27 July 1863, *ibid.*, vol. 18; 13 June 1857, Halifax Police Museum; City Prison Register, 1 Sept. 1857, PANS, RG 35-102, Series 18B, vol. 1.
2. *Evening Mail*, 20, 22 Aug. 1904; *Daily Echo*, 20, 22 Aug. 1904. Only the silver medal for distinguished conduct was an individual medal. The others were campaign medals won by the regiment. H.C. Wylly, *History of the Manchester Regiment (late the 63rd and 96th Foot)*, vol. 1 (London, 1923), p. 241.
3. *Evening Mail*, 29 Aug. 1904; *Daily Echo*, 29 Aug. 1904; Inventory and Appraisement in the Estate of Isaac Sallis, deceased, 11 Nov. 1904, Halifax Court of Probate, No. 5967. Jane Painter Sallis, the only child who survived, was born in Halifax on 23 Nov. 1866. PANS, Births, Halifax County, mfm reel 119, p. 89, No. 341.
4. Peter DeLottinville, 'Joe Beef of Montreal: Working Class Culture and the Tavern, 1869-1889,' *Labour/Le travailleur*, vol. 8/9 (Autumn/Spring 1981/82), 9-40.
5. Peter Bailey, ' "Will the Real Bill Banks Please Stand Up?" Towards a Role Analysis of Mid-Victorian Working-Class Respectability,' *Journal of Social History*, vol. 12, No. 3 (Spring 1979), 348.
6. General Order No. 1, 11 March 1857, Halifax Garrison Papers, PANS, MG 12, Series HQ, No. 50.
7. Police Court Minutes, 13 June and 21 Oct. 1857, Halifax Police Museum; Marriage Licence, 1 May 1857, PANS, RG Series M, Halifax County, 1857, No. 18.
8. Police Court Minutes, 13 June 1857, Halifax Police Museum; *Sun*, 15 June 1857; City Prison Register, 22 May 1858, PANS, RG 35-102, Series 18B, vol. 1; Police Court Minutes, 25 Sept. 1859, PANS, RG 42, Series D, vol. 11.
9. Police Court Minutes, 21 Oct. 1857, Halifax Police Museum.
10. *Unionist and Halifax Journal*, 11 Dec. 1865; *Morning Chronicle*, 16 May, 17 Nov. 1866, 16, 22 Apr. 1869.
11. Halifax City Assessment, 1862, PANS, RG 35, Series A, vol. 4.
12. Police Court Minutes, 5 July 1858, PANS, RG 42, Series D, vol. 9; 18 June 1859, *ibid.*, vol. 10; St. Paul's Church Records, Marriages, 2 May 1857, Register 7.
13. Besides the Sallises, there were four adults and three children. Soldier lodgers and their 'official' families should not but may sometimes be included in the count. It

is impossible to know about 'unofficial' wives and families. Census of 1861, Halifax Polling District No. 3, Abstract No. 16; Police Court Minutes, 5 Aug. 1863, PANS, RG 42, Series D, vol. 18.

14. Police Court Minutes, 17 Oct. 1857, Halifax Police Museum.
15. Police Court Minutes, 30 Apr. 1861, PANS, RG 42, Series D, vol. 14.
16. Police Court Minutes, 21 Jan. 1867, Halifax Police Museum; Coroner's Inquest on Jesse Heathfield, 4 Nov. 1867, PANS, RG 41, Series C, vol. 41, No. 22.
17. Police Court Minutes, 14 July 1863, PANS, RG 42, Series D, vol. 18; 6 June 1860, *ibid.*, vol. 12; 14 May 1862, *ibid.*, vol. 15; *Morning Chronicle*, 1 May 1888.
18. Police Court Minutes, 10 Oct. 1864, Halifax Police Museum; *Morning Chronicle*, 25 Nov. 1862, 5 Nov. 1867; *Sun*, 22 June 1859, 6 Nov. 1867.
19. Police Court Minutes, 30 Apr. 1861, PANS, RG 42, Series D, vol. 14; 17 June 1863, *ibid.*, vol. 18; 24 Aug. 1864, *ibid.*, vol. 19; 28 Oct. 1864, Halifax Police Museum; *Morning Chronicle*, 30 Dec. 1865, 31 July 1866.
20. Police Court Minutes, 17 Aug. 1862 and 3 Jan. 1863, PANS, RG 42, Series D, vol. 17; 17 June 1863, *ibid.*, vol. 18; *Morning Chronicle*, 28 Aug. 1862, 21, 27, 28 Feb., 10 Mar., and 16, 22, 24 May 1866; *Acadian Recorder*, 24 Feb. 1866.
21. *Morning Chronicle*, 3, 11, 21 Aug., 27, 31 Oct., 8, 10 Nov. 1866; *Sun*, 26 Oct. 1866.
22. Police Court Minutes, 6 June 1860, PANS, RG 42, Series D, vol. 12; 17 July and 26 Aug. 1863, *ibid.*, vol. 18; *Morning Chronicle*, 20 Oct. 1864.
23. Police Court Minutes, 31 Dec. 1860, PANS, RG 42, Series D, vol. 13; 4 July 1861, *ibid.*, vol. 14; 14 May 1862, *ibid.*, vol. 15; 20 Dec. 1864, Halifax Police Museum; Coroner's Inquest on Jesse Heathfield, 4 Nov. 1867, PANS, RG 41, Series C, vol. 41, No. 22; *Novascotian*, 7 Jan. 1861, 31 Aug. 1863; *Sun*, 9 Aug. 1865.
24. *Novascotian*, 25 Aug. 1856.
25. Police Court Minutes, 7 Jan. 1859, PANS, RG 42, Series D, vol. 9; *Morning Chronicle*, 21 Sept., 4, 27 Nov., 7 Dec. 1865; *Unionist and Halifax Journal*, 23 Oct. 1865; *Sun*, 8 Dec. 1865.
26. Police Court Minutes, 20 July 1868, PANS, RG 42, Series D, vol. 23; *Morning Chronicle*, 22 July 1868.
27. *Morning Chronicle*, 5 May, 29 Aug. 1870, 22 Apr. 1871. Sallis' peregrinations can be traced in the provincial and city directories: *Hutchinson's Business Directory* for 1863, *Hutchinson's Nova Scotia Directories* for 1864-5 and 1866-7, *McAlpine's Nova Scotia Directory* for 1868-9; *McAlpine's Halifax Directories* for 1869-70 to 1904-5.
28. 1871 Census, ward 3, division 2, p. 51, family 227.
29. *Acadian Recorder*, 15 May 1871.
30. *Morning Chronicle*, 14 Dec. 1871, 8 Nov. 1872, 8 Apr. 1873; *Acadian Recorder*, 8 Apr. 1873.
31. *Morning Chronicle*, 5 June 1874, 5 Sept. 1878, 12 Mar. 1885. For information on out-of-bounds streets and houses, 1860-1885, see Halifax Garrison Orders, PANS, MG 12, Series HQ, Nos. 106-112, 114-18, 120-3, 125, 127, 129, and MG 12, Series Miscellaneous General, vol. 8. Restrictions on naval sailors were separate and not necessarily the same.
32. *Morning Chronicle*, 6 Oct. 1875.
33. Deeds: Transaction 1009 (1869), Book 162, p. 567; Transaction 378 (1873), Book 186, p. 122; Transaction 375 (1876), Book 205, p. 88.
34. *Morning Chronicle*, 18 Aug. 1877.
35. Police Court Minutes, 20 Dec. 1864, Halifax Police Museum; *Morning Chronicle*, 25 Nov. 1862, 27 Oct., 2 Dec. 1876, 31 July 1878.
36. County Jail: Committals and Discharges, PANS, RG 34-312, Series J, vol. 18,

pp. 117-18, 121-2, 139-40; *Morning Chronicle,* 16, 21, 23, 25, 29 Oct., 5, 19 Nov. 1879; *Morning Herald,* 21 Oct. 1879; *New Times and Reporter,* 18 Nov. 1879.

37. *Morning Chronicle,* 5 and 20 Dec. 1879; *New Times and Reporter,* 29 Nov. 1879.
38. *Acadian Recorder,* 19 Dec. 1868, 5 April 1880; *Citizen,* 5 Apr. 1880.
39. *Morning Chronicle,* 31 Mar., 20, 21 Apr. 1880.
40. 1881 Census, Ward V, second section, subdivision 2, p. 62; 1891 Census, Ward Vi, p. 18, No. 81; *Acadian Recorder,* 5 Nov. 1897.
41. Deeds, PANS, RG 47, mfm reel 1022, vol. 253, 14 July 1885; *ibid.,* reel 1026, book 258, 30 June 1887; *ibid.,* reel 1037, vol. 272, 1889; County Jail: Committals and Discharges, PANS, RG 34-312, Series J, vol. 17, pp. 7-8, 185-6, 285-6; *Acadian Recorder,* 6 Sept. 1884; *Morning Herald,* 29 Mar., 3 June 1887, *Morning Chronicle,* 21 Feb. 1888; *Halifax Herald,* 9 Nov. 1894, 3 Sept. 1898.
42. *Morning Chronicle,* 20 Aug., 1, 3 Sept. 1884. Later society publications claim the veterans first organized in 1872.
43. *Morning Chronicle,* 2, 10 Sept. 1886; *Acadian Recorder,* 9 Sept. 1889.
44. *Evening Mail,* 5 June, 13 Sept. 1900.

# NOTES TO CHAPTER 3

1. The analysis of the Kellums includes at least two generations. The older one is composed of John, Charles, Henry, Martha and Mary and their kinsman George Deminas (whose blood relationship is unclear but who was one of several people with other surnames, including Fletcher, Pears and Maxwell, who constantly interacted with the Kellums). The younger generation includes Edward, George, and some children with the same names as the older generation. In some cases it is possible that the analysis confuses the generations. The institutional sources are the same as those used in Chapter 1.
2. The Ford/Prendergast deviancy is largely one-generational. The main characters are Cornelius and his sister Mary. Mary married James Prendergast, a comrade of Cornelius. The parents of both the Fords and Prendergast played significant supporting roles in this family drama. The institutional sources are the same as those used in Chapter 1.
3. Jerry White, *The Worst Street in North London: Campbell Bunk, Islington, between the Wars* (London, 1986), especially chs. 5-7. For a biographical account of turn-of-the-century lumpen home life, see Raphael Samuel (ed.), *East End Underworld: Chapters in the Life of Arthur Harding* (London, 1981).
4. *Morning Chronicle,* 31 July 1868.
5. For information on John Kellum see: City Prison Records, Registry of Inmates, PANS, RG 35-102, Series 18B, vols. 2 and 3, and Registry of Visitors, RG 35-102, Series 18H, vol. 1; County Jail Registers, PANS, RG 34-312, Series J, vols. 12 and 14; Police Court Minutes, PANS, RG 42, Series D, vols. 19-24; Stipendiary Court Records, PANS, RG 42, Series D, vols. 28-31; Poor House Records, PANS, RG 35-102, Series 33A, vols, 6 and 18; 1881 Census, Halifax, Ward I, Subdivision 2; *Morning Chronicle,* 28 June 1864, 10 Apr. 1865, 5 Oct. 1866, 3 July, 3 Aug. 1868, 6 Dec. 1869, 21 Dec. 1870, 20 March, 22 Apr., 18 June, 15 Oct. 1872, 7 Nov. 1874, 9 Aug., 21 Oct. 1875, 6 May, 31 Oct., 30 Nov. 1878, 19 Mar., 25 Aug. 1883, 22 July 1885; *Acadian Recorder,* 8 Apr. 1867; *Halifax Herald,* 29 Jan. 1895; *Evening Mail,* 7 Aug., 27 Nov. 1895, 21 Apr. 1903; *Evening Echo,* 26 May 1899.
6. *Acadian Recorder,* 8 Apr. 1867.
7. *Morning Chronicle,* 15 Oct. 1872.

8. *Halifax Herald*, 29 Jan. 1895; *Evening Mail*, 21 Apr. 1903.
9. *Morning Chronicle*, 29 May 1863.
10. *Morning Chronicle*, 31 Oct. and 30 Nov. 1878.
11. *Morning Chronicle*, 28 Nov. 1879.
12. *Morning Chronicle*, 23 Jan. 1882.
13. *Morning Chronicle*, 19 Mar. 1883.
14. *Acadian Recorder*, 21 and 29 July 1897.
15. *Morning Chronicle*, 6 May 1878.
16. *Morning Chronicle*, 25 Aug. 1883; *Acadian Recorder*, 14 Mar. 1889.
17. *Morning Herald*, 25 Nov. 1889.
18. *Morning Chronicle*, 16 Oct. 1878.
19. *Morning Chronicle*, 10 Nov. 1881.
20. *Morning Chronicle*, 15 Sept. 1885.
21. *Acadian Recorder*, 4 Aug. 1880; *Morning Chronicle*, 19 Feb. 1884.
22. *Morning Chronicle*, 27 Feb. 1883.
23. *Morning Chronicle*, 8 June 1883.
24. *Morning Chronicle*, 13 Aug. 1883.
25. Victoria General Hospital Papers, PANS, RG 25, Series B, IV.18.
26. For example, *Acadian Recorder*, 19 June 1880.
27. *Acadian Recorder*, 29 Jan. and 1 Aug. 1889.
28. *Halifax Herald*, 24 July 1895; *Acadian Recorder*, 3 July 1897; *Evening Mail*, 7 July 1897; Dorchester Penitentiary Convict Register, No. 1176, PANS, Misc. P. micro reel 3.
29. *Acadian Recorder*, 19 June 1880; *Evening Mail*, 9 Apr. 1904; Halifax County Marriages, vol. 71, f. 256, No. 506, PANS, RG 32, Series WB.
30. *Morning Chronicle*, 29 Mar. 1876.
31. *Evening Mail*, 27 Nov. 1895.
32. *Evening Mail*, 9 May 1895.
33. *Acadian Recorder*, 25 June 1874.
34. *Acadian Recorder*, 4 Aug. 1880.
35. *Morning Chronicle*, 16 June 1885.
36. *Halifax Herald*, 1 Sept. 1893.
37. *Acadian Recorder*, 6 Sept. 1884; *Morning Chronicle*, 6 Sept. 1884.
38. *Morning Chronicle*, 22 July 1885.
39. *Morning Chronicle*, 10 Sept. 1885, 9 Jan. 1886.
40. *Acadian Recorder*, 9 May and 25 Nov. 1889.
41. For information on Mary Ford Prendergast see: City Prison Records, Registry of Inmates, PANS, RG 35-102, Series 18B, vols. 2 and 3; County Jail Registers, PANS, RG 34-312, Series J, vol. 12; Police Court Minutes, PANS, RG 42, Series D, vols. 19-24; Stipendiary Court Records, PANS, RG 42, Series D, vol. 28; Poor House Records, PANS, RG 35-102, Series 33A, vol. 6; Victoria General Hospital Papers, PANS, RG 25, Series B, Section II, vol. 45, Section III, vol. 5, and Section IX, vol. 3; PANS Halifax Marriage Registers, 1872, p. 249, No. 606; 1881 Census, Halifax, Ward IV, Subdivision 1; SPC Daily Journal 1885, 31 Jan. 1885, PANS MG 20, vol. 516, No. 6; PANS, Holy Cross Cemetery Records; *Morning Chronicle*, 21 June, 28 July, 22 Oct., 24 Dec. 1864, 24 July 1865, 19 Jan. 1866, 4 Sept. 1868, 4 June 1869, 16 May, 28, 29 Aug. 1872, 7, 8 Aug. 1874, 9 Sept., 11 Dec. 1875, 29, 30 Nov. 1876, 7, 11 Dec. 1878, 29 Apr., 5 Aug. 1879, 6 Sept. 1881, 2 Feb. 1885. For proof of her illiteracy see Coroner's Inquests, PANS, RG 41, Series C, vol. 54 (Johanna Power).
42. See entry in the jail register for 5 Sept. 1861, PANS, RG 35-102, Series 18B, vol. 2.

43. *Morning Chronicle*, 24 July 1865.
44. *Morning Chronicle*, 4 June 1869.
45. *Morning Chronicle*, 16 May 1872.
46. *Morning Chronicle*, 28, 29 Aug. 1872.
47. *Morning Chronicle*, 9 Sept., 11 Dec. 1875.
48. *Morning Chronicle*, 6 Sept. 1881.
49. Surgical Case Book, Victoria General Hospital, PANS, RG 25, Series B, Section IX, vol. 3, p. 109; Medical Case Book, VGH, PANS, RG 25, Series B, Section III, vol. 5, p. 281.
50. *Acadian Recorder*, 6 Dec. 1867; *Morning Chronicle*, 24 Oct. 1876, 13 Aug. 1877.
51. Entry for 28 Aug. 1880, Stipendiary Court Records, PANS, RG 42, Series D, vol. 28; *Morning Herald*, 4 Sept. 1880; See Chapter 1.
52. *Morning Chronicle*, 19 June 1884.
53. *Morning Chronicle*, 5, 6 Mar. 1877.
54. *Morning Chronicle*, 28 July and 23 Sept. 1876, 27 July 1878.
55. Halifax County Marriages, vol. 66, f. 341, No. 356, PANS, RG 32, Series WB.
56. *Halifax Herald*, 4 May 1894.
57. *Morning Chronicle*, 5 Mar. 1877. Prendergast's career is detailed in *Jack in Port*, pp. 50-52.
58. *Morning Chronicle*, 1 Mar. 1880, 6 Sept. 1881.
59. *Morning Chronicle*, 11 Mar. and 1 July 1872, 8, 24 Apr. 1874, 17 July and 14 Sept. 1875.
60. *Morning Chronicle*, 28 Feb. 1880, 30 Jan. 1882.
61. *Morning Chronicle*, 28 Mar. 1885.
62. *Morning Chronicle*, 6 Sept. 1881.
63. For problems endemic to the black and Irish segments of nineteenth-century urban society in North America see Leonard P. Curry, *The Free Black in Urban America 1800-1850: The Shadow of the Dream* (Chicago, 1981) and Michael B. Katz, *The People of Hamilton, Canada West: Family and Class in a Mid-Nineteenth-Century City* (Cambridge, Mass., 1975).

# NOTES TO CHAPTER 4

1. Jean Lawrence L'Esperance, 'Woman's Mission to Woman: Explorations in the Operation of the Double Standard and Female Solidarity in Nineteenth-Century England,' *Histoire sociale/Social History*, vol. XII, No. 24 (November 1979), 316-38; Linda Gordon and Ellen DuBois, 'Seeking Ecstasy on the Battlefield: Danger and Pleasure in 19th Century Feminist Sexual Thought,' *Feminist Studies*, vol. 9, No. 1 (Spring 1983), 7-15; Judith R. Walkowitz, 'Male Vice and Female Virtues: Feminism and the Politics of Prostitution in Nineteenth-Century Britain,' in Ann Snitow, Christine Stansell, and Sharon Thompson (eds.), *Desire: The Politics of Sexuality* (London, 1984), pp. 43-61; Ronald Hyam, 'Empire and Sexual Opportunity,' *The Journal of Imperial and Commonwealth History*, vol. 14, No. 2 (Jan. 1986), 34-89.
2. Judith Walkowitz, *Prostitution and Victorian Society: Women, Class and the State* (Cambridge, 1980); Paula Petrik, 'Prostitution in Helena, Montana, 1865-1900,' *Montana: The Magazine of Western History*, vol. 31 (1981), 28-41; Luise White, 'Prostitutes, Reformers, and Historians,' *Criminal Justice History*, vol. 6 (1985), 201-27, and 'Domestic Labor in a Colonial City: Prostitution in Nairobi, 1900-1952,' in Jane Parpart and Sharon Stichter (eds.), *Patriarchy and Class:*

*African Women in the Household and Workplace* (Boulder, Colorado, 1988), pp. 139-60.

3. Jill Harsin, *Policing Prostitution in Nineteenth-Century Paris* (Princeton, 1985). In Canada legal historians have been active in this area. See Graham Parker, 'The Legal Regulation of Sexual Activity and the Protection of Females,' *Osgoode Hall Law Journal*, vol. 21 (1983), 187-244; Constance Backhouse, 'Nineteenth-Century Canadian Prostitution Law: Reflection of a Discriminatory Society,' *Histoire sociale/Social History*, vol. 17 (Nov. 1985), 387-423; J.P.S. McLaren, 'Chasing the Social Evil: Moral Fervour and the Evolution of Canada's Prostitution Laws, 1867-1917,' *Canadian Journal of Law and Society*, vol. 1 (1986), 125-65.

4. David J. Pivar, *Purity Crusade, Sexual Morality and Social Control, 1868-1900* (Westport, Conn., 1973); Barbara Berg, *The Remembered Gate, Origins of American Feminism, The Woman and the City, 1800-1860* (New York, 1978); Mark Thomas Connelly, *The Response to Prostitution in the Progressive Era* (Chapel Hill, 1980); Carroll Smith-Rosenberg, 'Beauty, the Beast, and the Militant Woman: A Case Study in Sex Roles and Social Stress in Jacksonian America,' *American Quarterly*, vol. 23 (1971), 562-84; Ruth Rosen, *The Lost Sisterhood: Prostitution in America, 1900-1918* (Baltimore, 1982).

5. *War Cry* (Toronto), 28 Apr. 1894.

6. *Morning Herald*, 13 Jan. 1885, 14 Oct. 1894; Melody Himmelman, ' "For Whom the Bell Tolls": Marriage Patterns, Halifax, 1871-1881,' B.A. honours essay, Dalhousie University, 1979.

7. Halifax City Mission, *Report for 1866*, p. 8.

8. *Ibid.*, p. 12; Walkowitz, *Prostitution and Victorian Society*, ch. 10. On casual prostitution among working-class women and girls in mid-nineteenth-century New York, see Christine Stansell, *City of Women: Sex and Class in New York, 1789-1860* (New York, 1986), pp. 176-92.

9. Myna Trustram, *Women of the Regiment: Marriage and the Victorian Army* (Cambridge, 1984), pp. 131, 134.

10. Police Court Minutes, 22 June 1854, PANS, RG 42, Series D, vol. 6.

11. *Halifax: "Its Sins and Sorrows"*, p. 24.

12. Halifax City Mission, *Report for 1866*, p. 8.

13. Police Court Minutes, 9 Sept. 1864, PANS, RG 42, Series D, vol. 19; *Morning Chronicle*, 13 Jan. 1863; Police Court Minutes, 20 Dec. 1864, Halifax Police Museum.

14. Police Court Minutes, 23 July 1862, PANS, RG 42, Series D, vol. 16; *Morning Chronicle*, 24 July, 19 Aug. 1862; *Acadian Recorder*, 3 July 1879.

15. *The Journal of Richard Henry Dana Jr.*, vol. 1, pp. 76-78, 82-83.

16. Halifax City Mission, *Report for 1866*, p. 6.

17. Police Court Minutes, 14 July 1864, PANS, RG 42, Series D, vol. 19.

18. Police Court Minutes, 17 Oct. 1857, Halifax Police Museum.

19. Halifax City Mission, *Report for 1866*, p. 6; *Morning Chronicle*, 15 Nov. 1862; Police Court Minutes, 11 July 1861, PANS, RG 42, Series D, vol. 14; 4 Aug. 1865, *ibid.*, vol. 21.

20. Police Court Minutes, 8 July 1859, PANS, RG 42, Series D, vol. 10; 10 May 1856, *ibid.*, vol. 8.

21. Police Court Minutes, 10 May 1856, PANS, RG 42, Series D, vol. 8.

22. For example, Police Court Minutes, 11 Apr. 1855, PANS, RG 42, Series D, vol. 7.

23. Police Court Minutes, 8 Mar. and 11 Apr. 1855, PANS, RG 42, Series D, vol. 7; 5 July and 9 Oct. 1858, *ibid.*, vol. 9.

24. Rosen, *The Lost Sisterhood: Prostitution in America, 1900-1918*, p. 33.

25. Police Court Minutes, 26 Feb. 1855, PANS, RG 42, Series D, vol. 7; *Acadian*

*Recorder*, 3 Mar. 1855; Police Court Minutes, 26 Apr. 1861, PANS, RG 42, Series D, vol. 14; 20 July 1864, *ibid.*, vol. 19.

26. See Chapter 1.
27. Police Court Minutes, 9 Sept. 1864, PANS, RG 42, Series D, vol. 19.
28. *Acadian Recorder*, 25 July 1866.
29. Linda Lever, 'The Black Community in Halifax, 1871-1881,' unpublished paper.
30. For example, Amelia Reynolds and Mary Ann Branden in 1855, Dinah Pickering and Susan Morgan in 1856, Ann Smithers in 1862, and Sophia Morris in 1866.
31. *Morning Chronicle*, 3 July 1865.
32. For information on Mahoney see: City Prison Records, Registry of Inmates, PANS, RG 35-102, Series 18B, vols. 2 and 3; Police Court Minutes, PANS, RG 42, Series D, vols. 14 to 25; County Jail Registers, PANS, RG 34-312, Series J, vol. 12; *Morning Chronicle*, 28 Nov. 1865, 8 Jan., 29 May, 2 June, 4 July, 3 Oct. 1866; 14 Aug. 1868, 18 May 1870, 4 Apr. 1874, 23 June 1875; *Acadian Recorder*, 11 July, 15 Aug. 1868.
33. *Acadian Recorder*, 3 Mar. 1855.
34. For information on Munroe, see: City Prison Records, Registry of Inmates, PANS, RG 35-102, Series 18B, vol. 2; Police Court Minutes, PANS, RG 42, Series D, vols. 10 to 21 and Halifax Police Museum; Poor House Records, PANS, RG 35-102, Series 33A, vols. 1a and 2; Coroner's Inquests, PANS, RG 41, Series C, vol. 41; *Morning Chronicle*, 3 Aug., 1, 30 Nov. 1865, 5, 16 June, 24 Sept., 22 Oct. 1866, 4 Mar. 1867; *Presbyterian Witness*, 9 Mar. 1867.
35. For example, Police Court Minutes, 8 July 1859, PANS, RG 42, Series D, vol. 10; *Morning Chronicle*, 8 Oct. 1866; Police Court Minutes, 9 Feb. 1869, PANS, RG 42, Series D, vol. 23; *Morning Chronicle*, 6 Sept. 1876.
36. *Morning Chronicle*, 23 Mar. 1867, 28 Nov. 1865; *Unionist and Halifax Journal*, 29 Nov. 1865; *Christian Messenger*, 29 Nov. 1865; *Morning Chronicle*, 22 Oct. 1866.
37. *Morning Chronicle*, 1, 3, 17 Aug. 1866; *Christian Messenger*, 22 Aug. 1866; *Morning Chronicle*, 5 Nov. 1866.
38. For example, Police Court Minutes, 17 Oct. 1863, PANS, RG 42, Series D, vol. 18; *Unionist and Halifax Journal* and *Morning Chronicle*, 12 Aug. 1867.
39. *British Colonist*, 3 Jan. 1856; *Acadian Recorder*, 3 Mar. 1855; Police Court Minutes, 10 May 1856, PANS, RG 42, Series D, vol. 8; 12 Feb. 1862, *ibid.*, vol. 15.
40. Police Court Minutes, 26 Feb. 1855, PANS, RG 42, Series D, vol. 6; 5 and 8 Mar. 1855, *ibid.*, vol. 7; 9 Oct. 1858 and 10 Jan. 1859, *ibid.*, vol. 9; 12 Feb. 1862, *ibid.*, vol. 15; *Morning Chronicle*, 5 Mar. 1866.
41. For example, *Acadian Recorder*, 10 Jan. 1868, *Morning Chronicle*, 26 Sept. 1872.
42. Police Court Minutes, 16 Dec. 1864, Halifax Police Museum; 21 June 1854, PANS, RG 42, Series D, vol. 6.
43. *Morning Chronicle*, 5 Nov. 1867, 7 Sept. 1868.
44. *Morning Chronicle*, 26 July 1862; *Acadian Recorder*, 5 July 1867, 15 Aug. 1868; Harsin, *Policing Prostitution in Nineteenth-Century Paris*, p. 232.
45. See Backhouse, 'Nineteenth-Century Canadian Prostitution Law,' 390-3.
46. Police Court Minutes, 10 Aug. 1857, Halifax Police Museum; Halifax Garrison Order, 6 Apr. 1874, PANS, MG 12, HQ, No. 121, p. 255.
47. *Acadian Recorder*, 20 June 1889.
48. *Acadian Recorder*, 14 Aug. 1897.
49. *The Journal of Richard Henry Dana Jr.*, vol. 1, p. 79.
50. *Halifax Herald*, 5 Nov. 1894.
51. Report of the Chief of Police, *Annual Report* of the City of Halifax, 1898-99, p. 70.

52. Police Court Minutes, 2 Jan. 1856; PANS, RG 42, Series D, vol. 8.
53. Police Court Minutes, 2 July 1859, PANS, RG 42, Series D, vol. 9.
54. For information on Julia Donovan see: Police Court Minutes, 9 June and 7 July 1865, PANS, RG 42, Series D, vol. 20; 17 July 1865, *ibid.*, vol. 21; *Unionist and Halifax Journal*, 22 Sept., 4, 16, 21, 23, 25 Oct., 6, 13 Nov., 11, 13 Dec. 1865, 7 Feb. 1866; *Morning Chronicle*, 7 Feb., 6 Oct. 1863, 10 June, 8, 18 July, 4, 7, 21 Sept., 4, 27 Nov., 7 Dec. 1865, 6 Feb. 1867.
55. *Acadian Recorder*, 28 Nov. 1868.
56. *Morning Chronicle*, 12 Aug. 1862.
57. *Morning Chronicle*, 26 July 1862.
58. Police Court Minutes, 16 Aug. 1860, PANS, RG 42, Series D, vol. 12.
59. Police Court Minutes, 4 June 1863, PANS, RG 42, Series D, vol. 18.
60. Police Court Minutes, 5 Aug. 1863, PANS, RG 42, Series D, vol. 18; 11 Nov. 1866 and 30 Jan. 1867, Halifax Police Museum.
61. Police Court Minutes, 28 Nov. 1862, PANS, RG 42, Series D, vol. 17; *Morning Chronicle*, 29 Nov. 1862.
62. Harsin, *Policing Prostitution in Nineteenth-Century Paris*, p. 229.

# NOTES TO CHAPTER 5

1. Most relevant to this study are Boyer, *Urban Masses and Moral Order in America, 1820-1920*; Inglis, *Churches and the Working Classes in Victorian England*; Jones, *Outcast London: A Study in the Relationship between Classes in Victorian Society*; Norris Magnuson, *Salvation in the Slums: Evangelical Social Work, 1865-1920* (Metuchen, N.J., 1977); F.K. Prochaska, *Women and Philanthrophy in Nineteenth-Century England* (Oxford, 1980); Carroll Smith-Rosenberg, *Religion and the Rise of the American City: The New York City Mission Movement, 1812-1870* (Ithaca, 1971); For the role of city missions in organizing the leisure activities of the poor, see H.E. Meller, *Leisure and the Changing City, 1870-1914* (London, 1976), chs. 6 and 7. For a catalogue of public and private charitable institutions in Toronto with some reference to evangelical influences, see Stephen A. Speisman, 'Munificent Parsons and Municipal Parsimony: Voluntary vs Public Poor Relief in Nineteenth Century Toronto,' *Ontario History*, vol. LXV, No. 1 (March 1973), 33-49. On the Salvation Army, see R.G. Moyles, *The Blood and Fire in Canada: A History of the Salvation Army in the Dominion 1882-1976* (Toronto, 1977).
2. Prochaska, *Women and Philanthropy in Nineteenth-Century England*, p. 189.
3. Smith-Rosenberg, *Religion and the Rise of the American City*, p. 272.
4. *Presbyterian Witness*, 16 June 1855, 11 Oct. 1856, 26 July 1861, 22 Feb. 1862, 21 Feb. 1863.
5. *Presbyterian Witness*, 11 Oct., 22 Nov. 1856, 26 Apr. 1862, 6 Feb. 1864, 2 Mar. 1867; *Halifax: "Its Sins and Sorrows"*, p. 23.
6. *Presbyterian Witness*, 6 Feb. 1864.
7. Halifax City Mission, *Report for 1863*.
8. Halifax City Mission, *Report for 1863*.
9. Halifax City Mission, *Report for 1862, Report for 1864*; *Halifax: "Its Sins and Sorrows"*, pp. 14-15.
10. Halifax City Mission, *Report for 1866*; *Novascotian*, 18 Mar. 1867.
11. Minutes, Halifax City Mission, 7 Nov., 5 and 21 Dec. 1860, PANS, MG 4, No. 42.
12. *Presbyterian Witness*, 6 Sept. 1856; Minutes, Halifax City Mission, 16 Dec. 1857,

3 July 1861, PANS, MG 4, No.42.

13. *Morning Chronicle*, 16 Jan. 1864; *Acadian Recorder*, 19 July 1889.

14. *Presbyterian Witness*, 21 Feb. 1863, 22, 29 Aug. 1868, 3 Apr. 1869.

15. *Morning Chronicle*, 30 Aug. 1875; *Journal of the House of Assembly*, 1875-9. Designed for men, alcoholic women were left to the care of the various homes for fallen women as well as to the poorhouse. *Morning Chronicle*, 16, 21 July, 16 Dec. 1875.

16. *Daily Echo*, 18 June 1895. On the gold cure see Cheryl Krasnick Warsh, 'Adventures in Maritime Quackery: The Leslie E. Keeley Gold Cure Institute of Fredericton, N.B.,' *Acadiensis*, vol. XVII, No.2 (Spring 1988), 109-30.

17. M.E. Wright, 'Unnatural Mothers: Infanticide in Halifax, 1870-1875,' *Nova Scotia Historical Review*, vol. VII, No.2 (1987), 13-29.

18. *Presbyterian Witness*, 7 Jan., 10 June 1865; *Morning Chronicle*, 18 Feb. 1865; Minutes, Halifax City Mission, 11 Mar. 1867, PANS, MG 4, No.42.

19. *Presbyterian Witness*, 9 Sept. 1891.

20. Minutes, Halifax City Mission, 8 Jan., 15 Aug. 1856, PANS, MG 4, No.42; Fingard, *Jack in Port: Sailortowns of Eastern Canada*, pp. 234-9.

21. Halifax City Mission, *Report for 1864*; *Christian Messenger*, 8 July 1863; *Presbyterian Witness*, 16 Jan. 1864.

22. Halifax City Mission, *Handbill*, PANS Ak B2 J13c; Minutes, Halifax City Mission, 8 Jan. 1856; 4 Feb. 1857; 6 Jan. 1858, PANS, MG 4, No.42; Halifax City Mission, *Report for 1866*.

23. *Presbyterian Witness*, 2 Apr. 1864; *First Annual Report of the Committee of the Halifax Industrial and Ragged Schools*, 1864.

24. *Presbyterian Witness*, 7 Jan., 13 Aug., 30 Sept. 1865; *Report of the Halifax Protestant Industrial School*, 1870. On other turn-of-the-century Canadian reformatories see Neil Sutherland, *Children in English-Canadian Society: Framing the Twentieth-Century Consensus* (Toronto, 1976), chs. 7 and 8; Paul W. Bennett, ' "Turning 'Bad Boys' into 'Good Citizens' ": The Reformatory Impulse of Toronto's Industrial Schools Movement, 1883-1920s,' *Ontario History*, vol. LXXVIII, No.3 (Sept. 1986), 209-27.

25. *Presbyterian Witness*, 20 July 1867, 1 Jan., 9 Apr. 1870.

26. *Presbyterian Witness*, 7 Dec. 1867, 27 Aug. 1870, 25 Feb. 1871; *Report of the Halifax Protestant Industrial School*, 1870.

27. *Report of the Halifax Protestant Industrial School*, 1865-66; on the Norburys see Chapter 8; *Acadian Recorder*, 24 June, 12 July 1889.

28. Halifax City Mission, Abstract of the Journal of the City Missionary for quarter ending 18 Aug. 1852, PANS Ak B2 H13c; An Appeal for a House of Refuge for those who are destitute of Reputable Homes, 5 May 1853, PANS Ak B2 H13c; Minutes, Halifax City Mission, 12 Nov. 1856, PANS, MG 4, No.42; Halifax City Mission, *Report for 1861*; *Report for 1864*, *Report for 1866*.

29. *Presbyterian Witness*, 16 Feb., 15 June 1867, 16 July 1870; *Unionist and Halifax Journal*, 27 May 1868; *Report of St. Paul's Alms House of Industry for Girls*, 1870, 1875, 1877; see Chapter 8.

30. For the Jost Mission in the twentieth century, see Christina Simmons, ' "Helping the Poorer Sisters": The Women of the Jost Mission, Halifax, 1905-1945,' *Acadiensis*, vol. XIV. No.1 (Autumn 1984), 3-27.

31. *Morning Chronicle*, 15 Oct. 1868, 30 Dec. 1869, 9 Dec. 1872; *Morning Herald*, 24 Jan. 1885.

32. *Morning Chronicle*, 2, 10 Dec. 1870; *Presbyterian Witness*, 2 Nov. 1884; North End City Mission, *Annual Report*, 1878, 1880, 1882.

33. North End City Mission, *Annual Report*, 1882.
34. *Evening Mail*, 28 Jan. 1880 from PANS, MG 20, vol. 519, pp. 49-50.
35. For example, SPC Daily Journal 1887, 2 and 23 Mar., 6 May 1887, PANS, MG 20, vol. 516, No. 7.
36. Naylor to Logan, 21 Aug. 1886, Naylor to Mrs. Pettigrew, 18 June 1888, PANS, MG 20, No.516, No. 3, pp. 120, 348; SPC Daily Journal 1885, 20 Oct. 1885, PANS, MG 20, vol. 516, No. 6; *Evening Mail*, 26 Nov. 1887, from PANS, MG 20, vol. 519, No. 1, p. 111; 1891 Census, Halifax, Ward 5g, p. 32, No. 170.
37. SPC Case Book, 1892-6, 2 Feb. 1893, PANS, MG 20, vol. 513, p. 113; *Morning Chronicle*, 2 Nov. 1885; *Halifax Herald*, 29 Oct. 1894; *War Cry*, 23 Jan. 1893.
38. *War Cry*, 25 Feb. 1893.

# NOTES TO CHAPTER 6

1. *Acadian Recorder*, 3 Oct. 1868, 27 Feb. 1869; City Prison Records, Registry of Inmates, 22 Feb. 1869, PANS, RG 35-102, Series 18B, vol. 2.
2. *Halifax Herald*, 26 Nov. 1897.
3. For rescue efforts and the maintenance of refuges see Edward J. Bristow, *Vice and Vigilence: Purity Movements in Britain since 1700* (Dublin, 1977), chs. 3 and 7; Magnuson, *Salvation in the Slums: Evangelical Social Work, 1865-1920*, ch. 6; Lori Rotenberg, 'The Wayward Worker: Toronto's Prostitute at the Turn of the Century,' in Janice Acton, Penny Goldsmith and Bonnie Shepard (eds.), *Women at Work: Ontario, 1850-1930* (Toronto, 1974), pp. 33-69; Prochaska, *Women and Philanthropy in Nineteenth-Century England*, ch. 6; Judith Godden, 'Sectarianism and Purity Within the Women's Sphere: Sydney Refuges during the Late Nineteenth Century,' *Journal of Religious History*, vol. 14, No. 3 (June 1987), 291-306.
4. *British Colonist*, 19 Aug. 1854; *Presbyterian Witness*, 23 Dec. 1854, 27 Jan. 1855.
5. Minutes of the Committee of the House of Refuge, 27 Mar. 1854, PANS, MG 20, No. 214/5.
6. Minutes of the Committee of the House of Refuge, 5 Nov. 1855, PANS, MG 20, No.214/5.
7. *Presbyterian Witness*, 3 Feb. 1855; Minutes of the Committee of the House of Refuge, 1 Apr. 1856, PANS, MG 20, No.214/5; *Morning Chronicle*, 8 Dec.1870; Bristow, *Vice and Vigilence: Purity Movements in Britain Since 1700*, p. 66.
8. Minutes of the Committee of the House of Refuge, Apr., 1 Aug. 1855, PANS, MG 20, No.214/5.
9. Minutes of the Committee of the House of Refuge, 18 Sept. 1855, PANS, MG 20, No.214/5.
10. *Presbyterian Witness*, 19 Jan. 1856, 20 July 1861; Minutes of the Committee of the House of Refuge, 25 Apr. 1857, PANS, MG 20, No.214/5.
11. *Evening Express*, 2 May 1864.
12. City Prison Records, Registry of Visitors, 2 May 1862, PANS, RG 35-102, Series 18H, vol. 1; *Morning Journal*, 5 May 1862.
13. *Hutchinson's Business Directory* for 1863; Journal of Sr. Mary Clare Connolly, 1849-1874, pp. 20-21, Archives of the Sisters of the Charity of Saint Vincent de Paul.
14. Journal of Sr. Mary Clare Connolly, 1849-1874, pp. 20-21.
15. *Sun*, 1 Oct. 1862; *Presbyterian Witness*, 16 Jan. 1864.
16. City of Halifax, *Annual Report*, 1862-3, p. 52.
17. *Evening Express*, 2, 4 May 1864.

18. *Presbyterian Witness*, 21 Dec. 1867; *Morning Chronicle*, 3 Jan. 1868.
19. *Morning Chronicle*, 16 Nov. 1869.
20. City Prison Records, Registry of Inmates, 5 Oct. 1867, PANS, RG 35-102, Series 18B, vol. 2; *Morning Chronicle*, 8 Dec. 1870.
21. *Presbyterian Witness*, 20 Nov. 1869; *Morning Chronicle*, 8 Dec. 1870.
22. *Halifax Daily Reporter*, 5 Jan. 1869.
23. *Morning Chronicle*, 25 Mar. 1869; *Presbyterian Witness*, 5 June 1869.
24. *Novascotian*, 22 Feb. 1869; *Presbyterian Witness*, 7 Dec. 1872.
25. *Morning Chronicle*, 13, 14 Feb. 1878; *McAlpine's Halifax Directory*, 1878-9, 1879-80. Harrison may have been the proprietress with the unusual interest in raiding brothels.
26. *Morning Chronicle*, 14, 18 Mar., 3 May 1876, 17 Jan., 11, 19 June, 13 Aug. 1878, 25 Apr., 2 Sept., 21 Nov. 1879, 2, 11, Apr., 13 Oct., 15 Nov. 1881, 6 June, 19 July, 11 Aug. 1883, 14 Jan., 19 Mar. 1884, 11, 22 May 1885.
27. *Presbyterian Witness*, 2 Dec. 1876.
28. *Presbyterian Witness*, 10 Apr. 1880.
29. *Morning Chronicle*, 1 June 1878; 2 Sept. 1879; 2, 11 Apr. 1881.
30. Stipendiary Magistrate Court Records, 24 Sept. 1880, PANS, RG 42, Series D, vol. 28; *Morning Chronicle*, 19 June 1878, 25 Apr., 21 Nov. 1879, 6 June, 19 July, 11 Aug. 1883, 11, 22 May 1885; *Acadian Recorder*, 24 Sept. 1883.
31. *Morning Chronicle*, 3 May 1876, 13 Oct. 1881; *Halifax Herald*, 11 Nov. 1892.
32. *Morning Chronicle*, 7, 17 June 1883.
33. Women's Christian Association (WCA), *11th Report*, 1885.
34. WCA, *14th Report*, 1888.
35. WCA, *5th Report*, 1879; *Morning Chronicle*, 8 Sept. 1886; *Acadian Recorder*, 12 Nov. 1889, from PANS, MG20, vol. 519, No. 1, p. 24.
36. WCA, *11th Report*, 1885.
37. WCA, *11th Report*, 1885, *12th Report*, 1886.
38. *Morning Chronicle*, 14 Jan. 1884.
39. WCA, *1st Report*, 1875; *Morning Chronicle*, 6 Aug. 1876.
40. WCA, *2nd Report*, 1876; *12th Report*, 1886.
41. *Morning Herald*, 26 Nov. 1890.
42. WCA, *2nd Report*, 1876, *14th Report*, 1888.
43. WCA, *2nd Report*, 1876, *5th Report*, 1879, *12th Report*, 1886.
44. WCA, *5th Report*, 1879; *Morning Chronicle*, 6 Apr. 1878, 19 Mar. 1884; *Morning Herald*, 3 Jan. 1887, 5 Feb. 1890; *Acadian Recorder*, 22 Feb. 1889.
45. *Acadian Recorder*, 12 Nov. 1889 from PANS, MG 20, vol. 519, No. 1, p. 240; SPC Daily Journal 1885, 21 July 1885, PANS, MG 20, vol. 516, No. 6; SPC Daily Journal 1887, 29 July 1887, PANS, MG 20, vol. 516, No. 7; SPC Daily Journal 1886, 8 Apr. 1885, PANS, MG 20, vol. 516, No. 6; SPC Daily Journal 1888, 8 Sept. 1888, PANS, MG 20, vol. 516, No. 8; Naylor to Miss Bentley, 1 Feb. 1890, PANS MG 20, vol. 516, No. 3.
46. WCA, *14th Report*, 1888.
47. Naylor to Mrs. Starr, 1 Dec. 1891, PANS, MG 20, vol. 516, No. 4, p. 135.
48. WCA, *2nd Report*, 1876.
49. *Acadian Recorder*, 12 Nov. 1889 from PANS, MG 20, vol. 519, No. 1, p. 24; WCA, *11th Report*, 1885, *12th Report*, 1886, *14th Report*, 1888; Naylor to Miss Campbell, 18 Feb. 1887, PANS, MG 20, vol. 516, No. 3, pp. 169-70.
50. *Halifax Herald*, 6 Dec. 1892. According to the 1891 census, the home's four inmates in April 1891 were all old enough to be incorrigibles at 33, 40, 46 and 64. Two were Catholic. See Ward 6b, p. 19, No. 108.

51. *Acadian Recorder*, 31 Oct. 1893.
52. *Morning Herald*, 12 Apr. 1887; 4, 9, Apr. 1891; Grand Jury Presentment, 1 Apr. 1891, PANS, RG 34-312, Series P, vol. 24.
53. *McAlpine's Halifax Directory*, 1894-5 to 1900-01; *Acadian Recorder*, 14 Dec. 1897; *Halifax Herald*, 30 May 1898, *Daily Echo*, 25 Feb. 1911. On the early work of the YWCA in Canada see Wendy Mitchinson, 'The YWCA and Reform in the Nineteenth Century,' *Histoire sociale/Social History*, vol. XII, No. 24 (Nov. 1979), 368-84; Diana Pedersen, ' "Keeping Our Good Girls Good": The YWCA and the "Girl Problem," 1870-1930,' *Canadian Woman Studies*, vol. 7, No. 4 (Winter 1986), 20-24.
54. *Morning Chronicle*, 3 Apr. 1878; *Morning Herald*, 16 Mar. 1887.
55. *Halifax Herald*, 9 Dec. 1892.
56. *Halifax Herald*, 16 May 1894, 10 Aug. 1895, Women's Extra, p. 6, 26 Nov. 1902; Backhouse, 'Nineteenth-Century Canadian Prostitution Law: Reflection of a Discriminatory Society,' *Histoire sociale/Social History*, vol. XVIII, No. 36 (Nov. 1985), 417.
57. 20 per cent were married or widowed. Magistrate Court Records, PANS, RG 42, Series D, vol. 31, 34.
58. SPC Case Book, 1892-6, 15 Feb. 1893, 15 Apr., 8 May 1895, PANS, MG 20, vol. 513, pp. 119, 244, 245.
59. SPC Case Book, 1892-6, 7 May 1894, PANS, MG 20, vol. 513, p. 188; Naylor to Mother Superior of the Good Shepherd, 5 Mar. 1894, PANS, MG 20, vol. 516, No. 4, p. 503.
60. SPC Case Book, 1896-8, 13 July 1897, PANS, MG 20, vol. 514, p. 90.
61. *Presbyterian Witness*, 9 Feb. 1895 from PANS, MG 20, vol. 519, No. 1, p. 54; *Halifax Herald*, 11, 28 Nov. 1892, 14 Mar. 1895.
62. *Presbyterian Witness*, 9 Feb. 1895; Canada, *Senate Debates*, 1891, pp. 194-200, 211-22; *House of Commons Debates*, vol. xxxii, 1891, pp. 3595-9; *Halifax Herald*, 29 Mar., 18 May 1895; City of Halifax, *Annual Report*, 1896-7.
63. *Acadian Recorder*, 9 Apr. 1897.
64. *Halifax Herald*, 15, 19 Feb., 13 June 1894; on the Church Army see *Acadian Recorder*, 24 May 1889.
65. *Halifax Herald*, 19 Sept. 1894; Ann R. Higginbotham, 'Respectable Sinners: Salvation Army Rescue Work with Unmarried Mothers, 1884-1914,' in Gail Malmgreen (ed.), *Religion in the Lives of English Women, 1760-1930* (London, 1986), pp.216-33.
66. *War Cry*, 22 June 1895.
67. *War Cry*, 28 Apr. 1894; *Evening Mail*, 4 Nov., 17 Dec. 1909; City of Halifax, *Annual Report*, 1910-11.
68. *Halifax Herald*, 19 Mar. 1894.
69. *Presbyterian Witness*, 9 Mar. 1867.
70. *Morning Herald*, 9 May 1887.
71. SPC Case Book, 1892-6, 19 May 1892, PANS, MG 20, vol. 513, p. 27.
72. *Halifax Herald*, 18 May, 6 Nov. 1895.
73. *Halifax Herald*, 10 Aug. 1895, Women's Extra, p. 6.

# NOTES TO CHAPTER 7

1. Potter, 'Poor Relief in Nova Scotia in the 1880s,' B.A. honours essay, Dalhousie University, 1978, ch. 2; *Morning Chronicle*, 24 June 1882.

2. AICP, *24th Report*, 1890, *25th Report*, 1891. Some of the reports are extant in pamphlet form, others appear only in the newspapers. *Morning Herald*, 10 Dec. 1889.

3. *Acadian Recorder*, 18 Jan. 1868.

4. *Morning Herald*, 10 Dec. 1889.

5. AICP, *5th Report*, 1871.

6. *Morning Herald*, 13 Feb. 1888; *Presbyterian Witness*, 3 Jan. 1891.

7. *Morning Herald*, 22 Feb. 1888.

8. AICP, *7th Report*, 1873, *18th Report*, 1884; *Morning Chronicle*, 29 Nov. 1884.

9. *Morning Chronicle*, 24 Sept. 1866, 22 Jan. 1867; G.E. Hart, 'The Halifax Poor Man's Friend Society, 1820-27, An Early Social Experiment,' *Canadian Historical Review*, vol. XXXIV (1953), 109-23.

10. Smith-Rosenberg, *Religion and the Rise of the American City: The New York City Mission Movement, 1812-1870*, pp. 253, 256 and ch. 9 generally. On other American AICPs, see Boyer, *Urban Masses and Moral Order in America, 1820-1920*, ch. 6. On an English equivalent, the Central Relief Society in Liverpool, see Margaret B. Simey, *Charitable Effort in Liverpool in the Nineteenth Century* (Liverpool, 1951), chs. 6-10.

11. AICP, *17th Report*, 1883.

12. *Morning Chronicle*, 9, 11, 12 Jan. 1883.

13. AICP, *1st Report*, 1867, *5th Report*, 1871, *14th Report*, 1880, *28th Report*, 1894.

14. AICP, *1st Report*, 1867, *2nd Report*, 1868, *3rd Report*, 1869, *5th Report*, 1871; *Morning Herald*, 28 Nov. 1891.

15. J. Fingard, 'The Relief of the Unemployed Poor in Saint John, Halifax, and St. John's, 1815-1860,' *Acadiensis*, vol. V, No. 1 (Autumn 1975), 44-45.

16. AICP, *2nd Report*, 1868; *3rd Report*, 1869, *7th Report*, 1873, *8th Report*, 1874, *9th Report*, 1875, *10th Report*, 1876, *25th Report*, 1891; *Morning Chronicle*, 28 Nov. 1891.

17. AICP, *11th Report*, 1877, *12th Report*, 1878; Minutes of AICP Annual Meeting, 30 Dec. 1878, PANS, MG 1, vol. 1, No. 285.

18. AICP, *13th Report*, 1879, *14th Report*, 1880, *15th Report*, 1881, *16th Report*, 1882, *23rd Report*, 1889, *26th Report*, 1892, *29th Report*, 1895.

19. AICP, *20th Report*, 1886, *21st Report*, 1887. The society claimed that the stone-shed broke even for the first time in 1890. AICP, *24th Report*, 1890, *25th Report*, 1891, *27th Report*, 1893.

20. *Morning Herald*, 22 Jan. 1891, AICP, *25th Report*, 1891.

21. AICP, *27th Report*, 1893, *28th Report*, 1894, *29th Report*, 1895; *Halifax Herald*, 22 Jan. 1895.

22. AICP, *27th Report*, 1893; SPC Case Book, 1892-96, 2 Apr. 1896, PANS, MG 20, vol. 513, p. 295.

23. *Morning Chronicle*, 1 Dec. 1885; *Acadian Recorder*, 3 Mar. 1897; AICP, *32nd Report*, 1898, *34th Report*, 1900; Simey, *Charitable Effort in Liverpool in the Nineteenth Century*, p. 115.

24. City Prison Records, Registry of Inmates, 28 Nov. 1879, PANS, RG 35-102, Series 18B, vol. 3; *Acadian Recorder*, 12 Jan. 1889.

25. *Morning Chronicle*, 1 Dec. 1877, 10 Jan. 1885; *Halifax Herald*, 8 Mar. 1893.

26. AICP, *3rd Report*, 1869, *4th Report*, 1870, *6th Report*, 1872, *7th Report*, 1873; *Morning Herald*, 18 Dec. 1877, 16 Jan. 1884, 22 Jan. 1891; *Morning Chronicle*, 13 Feb. 1878.

27. *Morning Chronicle*, 9 Jan. 1885; *Morning Herald*, 22 Jan. and 28 Nov. 1891; AICP, *25th Report*, 1891.

28. *Morning Herald*, 20 Feb. 1889.
29. AICP, *25th Report*, 1891, *32nd Report*, 1898, *33rd Report*, 1899, *34th Report*, 1900.
30. SPC Case Book, 1892-96, 2 Apr. 1896, PANS, MG 20, vol. 513, p. 295.
31. SPC Daily Journal 1885, 19 Jan. 1885, PANS, MG 20, vol. 516, No. 6; SPC Daily Journal 1888, 23 Feb. 1888, PANS, MG 20, vol. 516, No. 8; SPC Daily Journal 1889, 26 Feb. 1889, PANS, MG 20, vol. 516, No. 9.
32. SPC Daily Journal 1894, 9 Dec. 1884, PANS, MG 20, vol. 516, No. 5; *Acadian Recorder*, 22 Dec. 1884 from PANS, MG 20, vol. 519, No. 1, p. 100.
33. SPC Case Book, 1896-98, 27 Jan. 1897, PANS, MG 20, vol. 514, p. 71.
34. SPC Daily Journal 1889, 24 Jan. and 2 Mar. 1889, PANS, MG 20, vol. 516, No. 9; SPC Case Book, 1892-96, 15 Jan. 1894, PANS, MG 20, vol. 513, p. 172.
35. Naylor to Doull, 1 Mar. 1881, 9 Jan. 1882, PANS, MG 20, vol. 516, No. 1, pp. 300, 347; *Evening Mail*, 6 Jan. 1882, from PANS, MG 20, vol. 519, No. 1, p. 91; Naylor to Relief Committee, AICP, 5 Jan. 1886, PANS, MG 20, vol. 516, No. 1, p. 485.
36. SPC Journal 1889, 25 Feb. 1889, PANS, MG 20, vol. 516, No. 9; undated press cutting, PANS, MG 20, vol. 519, No. 1, p. 13.
37. *Morning Herald*, 31 Jan. 1888.
38. Soup kitchens were subsidized intermittently between 1875 and 1892. AICP, *9th Report*, 1875, *10th Report*, 1876, *15th Report*, 1881, *16th Report*, 1882, *25th Report*, 1891, *26th Report*, 1892; *Morning Chronicle*, 10 Jan. 1879, 9 Jan. 1885.
39. AICP, *17th Report*, 1883, *18th Report*, 1884.
40. AICP, *18th Report*, 1884, *19th Report*, 1885, *22nd Report*, 1888, *24th Report*, 1890, *25th Report*, 1891, *26th Report*, 1892, *27th Report*, 1893, *30th Report*, 1896, *31st Report*, 1897, *33rd Report*, 1899; SPC Daily Journal 1889, 9 May 1889, PANS, MG 20, vol. 516, No. 9; *Halifax Herald*, 25 Jan. 1895, 4 Mar. 1896.
41. AICP, *26th Report*, 1892; *Morning Herald*, 13 Feb. 1888; *Halifax Herald*, 30 Nov. 1892.
42. AICP, *28th Report*, 1894.
43. *Morning Herald*, 10 Dec. 1889.
44. *Morning Chronicle*, 1 Dec. 1887; AICP, *22nd Report*, 1888.
45. *Morning Herald*, 31 Jan. 1888.
46. *Morning Herald*, 2, 6, 16, 22 Feb. 1888, 8 Nov. 1890; *Morning Chronicle*, 21 Feb. 1888.
47. AICP, *23rd Report*, 1889; *24th Report*, 1890; *Morning Herald*, 25 Mar. 1890.
48. *Morning Herald*, 6, 13, 16 Feb. 1888. For a critical assessment of the Peabody Dwellings in London, see Jones, *Outcast London: A Study in the Relationship between Classes in Victoria Society*, pp. 184-8.
49. *Morning Herald*, 6 Feb. 1888.
50. AICP, *29th Report*, 1895; *Acadian Recorder*, 4 Aug. 1897.
51. AICP, *10th Report*, 1876; *Morning Herald*, 10 Sept. 1880, 31 Jan. 1890, 23 Feb. 1891; *Morning Chronicle*, 23 Dec. 1881, 29 Dec. 1882.
52. *Halifax Herald*, 15, 24 Dec. 1894, 4 Feb. 1896.
53. *Halifax Herald*, 12 May 1894; *War Cry*, 16 June, 6 Aug. 1896; J. Fingard, 'Evangelical Social Work in Canada: Salvationists and Sailors' Friends, 1890-1920,' in D.C. Platt (ed.), *Social Welfare in Canada, Australia and Argentina*, forthcoming.
54. *War Cry*, 16 June 1896.
55. *War Cry*, 24 Apr. 1897; *Acadian Recorder*, 10 Dec. 1897.
56. *Halifax Herald*, 25 Oct. 1894, 25 Nov. 1896; *War Cry*, 6 Apr. 1901.
57. *Morning Herald*, 12 Jan. 1891.
58. See *Morning Herald*, 18, 19 Oct. 1889.

# NOTES TO CHAPTER 8

1. On the American movement see Linda Gordon, 'Single Mothers and Child Neglect, 1890-1920,' *American Quarterly*, vol. 37, No. 2 (Summer 1985), 173-92, 'Child Abuse, Gender, and the Myth of Family Independence: A Historical Critique,' *Child Welfare*, vol. 64, No. 3 (1985), 213-23, 'Feminism and Social Control: The Case of Child Abuse and Neglect,' in J. Mitchell and A. Oakley (eds.), *What is Feminism?* (Oxford, 1986), pp. 63-84, and *Heroes of Their Own Lives: The Politics and History of Family Violence, Boston 1880-1960*; Pleck, *Domestic Tyranny: The Making of American Social Policy Against Family Violence from Colonial Times to the Present*. On the British movement see Margaret May, 'Violence in the Family: An Historical Perspective,' in J.P. Martin (ed.), *Violence and the Family* (Chichester, 1978), pp. 135-67; James Turner, *Reckoning with the Beast: Animals, Pain, and Humanity in the Victorian Mind* (Baltimore, 1980); Brian Harrison, 'Animals and the State in Nineteenth-Century England,' in his *Peaceable Kingdom: Stability and Change in Modern Britain* (Oxford, 1982), pp. 82-122; Behlmer, *Child Abuse and Moral Reform in England, 1870-1908*.
2. Neil Sutherland, *Children in English-Canadian Society: Framing the Twentieth-Century Consensus* (Toronto, 1976), part III; Andrew Jones and Leonard Rutman, *In the Children's Aid: J.J. Kelso and Child Welfare in Ontario* (Toronto, 1981); John Bullen, 'J.J. Kelso and the "New" Child-Savers: The Genesis of the Children's Aid Movement in Ontario,' a paper presented to the Canadian Historical Association, University of Windsor, 1988.
3. Naylor to Richey, 2 Aug. 1882, PANS, MG 20, vol. 516, No. 1, p. 369. The one study of the SPC is a superficial overview: Winifred M. Ross, 'Child Rescue: The Nova Scotia Society for the Prevention of Cruelty, 1880-1920,' M.A. thesis, Dalhousie University, 1975.
4. Naylor to Richey, 20 and 31 Mar. 1880, 18 Mar. 1881, PANS, MG 20, vol. 516, No. 1, pp. 173, 184, 317.
5. Account of meeting of the Dominion Humane Association in Toronto, PANS, MG 20, vol. 519, No. 1, p. 47.
6. Smith-Rosenberg, *Religion and the Rise of the American City: The New York City Mission Movement, 1812-1870*, p. 255.
7. *War Cry*, 12 Jan. 1907.
8. *Morning Chronicle*, 22 May 1884; *Halifax Herald*, 13 July 1895; *Acadian Recorder*, 28 Dec. 1906; *Morning Chronicle*, 29 Dec. 1906. The PANS SPC Collection in MG 20 is until 1900 virtually an autobiography of Naylor.
9. For opposition to Naylor, see Queen vs. P.S. Hamilton, 1880, No. 5, Halifax Supreme Court Papers, PANS, RG 39, 'c,' vol. 333; Hamilton to Binney, 8 Mar. 1880, *Acadian Recorder*, 27 May 1880, from PANS, MG 20, vol. 518.
10. Canada, *Sessional Papers*, 21 (1894), vol. XXVII, No. 12, Royal Commission on the Liquor Traffic—Minutes of Evidence, vol. 1 (Maritimes), 1893, p. 243.
11. Naylor to Woodill, 21 Apr. 1880, PANS, MG 20, vol. 516, No. 1, p. 197.
12. SPC Daily Journal 1884, 24, 30 June 1884, PANS, MG 20, vol. 516, No. 5.
13. Naylor to Baker, 29 June 1886, PANS, MG 20, vol. 516, No. 3, pp. 109-10.
14. These cases are compiled from the SPC Case Book, 1892-96, PANS, MG 20, vol. 513.
15. Gordon, *Heroes of Their Own Lives: The Politics and History of Family Violence, Boston 1880-1960*, ch. 8. Many of the Boston women Gordon deals with were in fact former Nova Scotians. *Ibid*, pp.9-10. On the failure of English women

to get separation orders, see Carol Bauer and Lawrence Ritt, 'Wife-Abuse, Late-Victorian English Feminists, and the Legacy of Frances Power Cobbe,' *International Journal of Women's Studies*, vol.6, No.3 (May/June 1983), 199. I discuss the SPC and wife abuse in 'The Anti-Cruelty Movement in the Maritimes,' a public lecture given to the 8th Atlantic Canada Workshop, September 1988.

16. For information on Doyle, see City Prison Records, Registry of Inmates, PANS, RG 35-102, Series 18B, vol. 2, 3, and Registry of Visitors, RG 35-102, Series 18H, vol. 1; County Jail Registers, PANS, RG 34-312, Series J, vol. 12-18; Police Court Minutes, PANS, RG 42, Series D, vol. 18-24; Stipendiary Court Records, PANS, RG 42, Series D, vol. 28-31; Poor House Records, PANS, RG 35-102, Series 33A, vol. 6, 8b; Victoria General Hospital Papers, PANS, RG 25, Series B, Section II, vol. 45, Section III, vol. 4, Section IV, vol. 18; 1881 Census, Halifax, Ward IV, Subdivision 2; *Morning Chronicle*, 11, 15 Oct. 1864, 9 Mar. 1865, 25 Feb., 19 Apr., 7 Sept., 13 Oct. 1866, 16 Sept. 1867, 13 Mar. 1869, 23 26 Nov. 1870, 22 Feb., 9, 30 Mar., 2 May 1872, 3 Apr. 1873, 25 May 1874, 1 Feb., 3, 4 Aug. 1875, 1, 6 July, 2, 4, 17, 18, 19 Oct., 3, 4, 21 Nov. 1882, 6 Jan., 2, 3, 19 Oct., 14 Dec. 1883, 2 May, 8 Oct. 1888; *Acadian Recorder*, 27 June 1868, 2 Oct. 1883; *Citizen*, 18 Oct. 1882; *Morning Herald*, 2 Feb. 1888.

17. *Morning Chronicle*, 2 May 1872.

18. *Morning Chronicle*, 13 Mar. 1869, 23, 26 Nov. 1870; *Acadian Recorder*, 2 Oct. 1883.

19. Medical Case Book, Victoria General Hospital, PANS, RG 25, Series B, Section III, vol. 4, pp. 423, 452, 469.

20. *Acadian Recorder*, 25 June 1887.

21. *Morning Chronicle*, 1 Feb., 3 Aug. 1875.

22. SPC Daily Journal 1888, 7, 9 Apr. 1888, PANS, MG 20, vol. 516, No. 8.

23. See SPC press cuttings on the John Brown case, MG 20, vol. 519, No. 1, pp. 129, 131-3, 138; Naylor to the Mayor, 6 Apr., 18 May 1888, Naylor to Silver, 6 Apr. 1888, PANS, MG 20, vol. 516, No. 3, pp. 286-7, 329; SPC Daily Journal 1888, 24, 27, 29 Mar., 12 Apr. 1888, PANS, MG 20, vol. 516, No. 8; Naylor to Hill, 16 Oct. 1882, PANS, MG 20, vol. 516, No. 1, pp. 383-4; Naylor to Mrs. Murray, 22 May 1893, PANS, MG 20, vol. 516, No. 4, p. 382.

24. For information on Thomas Norbury, see City Prison Records, Registry of Inmates, PANS, RG 35-102, Series 18B, vol. 2, 3, and Registry of Visitors, RG 35-102, Series 18H, vol. 1; County Jail Registers, PANS, RG 34-312, Series J, vol. 12, 14, 18; Police Court Minutes, PANS, RG 42, Series D, vol. 22-24; Stipendiary Magistrate Court Papers, RG 42, Series D, vol. 28; Poor House Records, PANS, RG 35-102, Series 33A, vol. 5, 6; Victoria General Hospital Papers, PANS, RG 25, Series B, Section II, vol. 45, Section IV, vol. 18; PANS, Halifax Marriage Registers, 1876, p. 152, No. 221; 1871 Census, Halifax, Ward III, Division 2; 1881 Census, Halifax, Ward IV, Subdivision 2; *Morning Chronicle*, 3, 9 Apr., 6 May 1868, 27 Feb., 1 Mar., 23 Aug. 1869, 20 Apr., 6, 27 May 1870, 19 Apr., 5 Nov. 1873, 27 Jan. 1883, 9 Jan. 1888; *Acadian Recorder*, 4 Apr. 9 May, 27 June, 3/4 July 1868, 23 Aug. 1869; *Morning Herald*, 26, 30 Jan. 1883, 12 Jan. 1891.

25. *Acadian Recorder*, 3/4 July 1868; *Morning Herald*, 12 Jan. 1891.

26. Police Court Minutes, 2 July 1868, PANS, RG 42, Series D, vol. 23; *Acadian Recorder*, 4 July 1868.

27. *Morning Herald*, 16, 30 Jan. 1883.

28. SPC Daily Journal 1887, 23 July 1887, PANS, MG 20, vol. 516, No. 7; SPC Daily Journal 1888, 4, 5, Jan. 1888, PANS, MG 20, vol. 516, No. 8.

29. SPC Daily Journal 1888, 7, 9, 11 Jan. 1888, PANS, MG 20, vol. 516, No. 8; *Acadian Recorder*, 7 Jan. 1888, from PANS, MG 20, vol. 519, No. 1, p. 121.
30. *Acadian Recorder*, 3 Oct. 1889.
31. 1891 Cenus, Ward 5i, pp. 33-34, No. 155; Naylor to Rev. Dr. Hole, 7 Jan. 1888, Naylor to Symons, 9, 11 Jan. 1888, PANS, MG 20, vol. 516, No. 3, pp. 233, 234, 237; Registry Book, St. Paul's Alms House of Industry for Girls, 9 Sept. 1888, 18 Mar. 1892, PANS, MG 20, vol. 1329, No. 2.
32. Minute Book, 14 Jan. 1887-18 Oct. 1898, St. Paul's Alms House of Industry for Girls, 25 Mar. 1890, 26 Jan., 23 Feb. 1892, PANS, MG 20, vol. 1326, No. 1, pp. 116, 181, 182-3.
33. SPC Case Book, 1892-96, 27 Nov. 1894, PANS, MG 20, vol. 513, p. 217; SPC Case Book, 1896-98, 31 Oct. 1896, PANS, MG 20, vol. 514, p. 49.
34. May, 'Violence in the Family: An Historical Perspective,' in Martin (ed.), *Violence and the Family*, pp. 158-62.
35. Canada, *Sessional Papers*, 21 (1894), vol. XXVII, No. 12, Royal Commission on the Liquor Traffic—Minutes of Evidence, vol. 1 (Maritimes), 1893, p. 241.
36. Naylor to superintendent, Halifax Band of Hope, [1880], PANS, MG 20, vol. 516, No. 1, p. 162.
37. DuBois and Gordon, 'Seeking Ecstasy on the Battlefield: Danger and Pleasure in Nineteenth-Century Feminist Sexual Thought,' *Feminist Studies*, vol. 9, No. 1 (Spring 1983), 11.
38. Naylor to Postmaster, Nottingham, England, 10 Jan. 1880, PANS, MG 20, vol. 516, No. 1, p. 122.
39. Naylor to Sister Angela, 27 Apr. 1888, PANS, MG 20, vol. 516, No. 3, p. 311.
40. Press cutting, Oct. 1893, PANS, MG 20, vol. 519, No. 1, p. 134.
41. Gordon, 'Feminism and Social Control: The Case of Child Abuse and Neglect,' in Mitchell and Oakley, *What is Feminism?*, p. 80.

# NOTES TO CONCLUSION

1. See the Reports of the Chief of Police in the *Annual Reports* of the City of Halifax 1893-4 to 1899-1900.
2. *Halifax Herald*, 11 Nov. 1892.
3. *Report of the Halifax Protestant Industrial School*, 1895.
4. *First Annual Report of the Committee of the Halifax Industrial School*, 1864.
5. *Halifax Herald*, 25 Sept. 1896.
6. Stansell, *City of Women: Sex and Class in New York, 1789- 1860*, p. 197.
7. Katz, *Poverty and Policy in American History*, p. 3.
8. Gordon, 'Feminism and Social Control: The Case of Child Abuse and Neglect,' in Mitchell and Oakley, *What is Feminism?*, p. 81.

# INDEX

House of Refuge 127-8, 136-7

infanticide 111, 122, 124
Infants' Home 122, 124, 143
Ireland 36-37, 78
Irish 19, 25, 48, 56, 91, 179

Jacob Street 25, 129, 164
Johnston, James W. 83
Jost Mission 24-25, 129

Kellum family 77-85, 88, 90-92, 95, 148-9, 158, 162, 165, 191, 206
Kings County 161
King's Daughters 142

larceny 42-46, 49, 78, 83, 144, 180, 182
laundries: women's homes 137, 142-3, 146-7; AICP 159
Lawlor's Island 49
lawyers 46
lieutenant-governor 47, 70, 107, 112
liquor law violations 21, 26, 28, 38, 64, 69, 81, 108, 112, 123, 161, 182
liquor legislation 26-27, 72, 82, 123, 173-4
Liverpool, England 158
Lockman Street (north extension of Barrington) 137-8, 142
Logan, Adam 129-31
Lockeport 144
London 36, 78, 119

MacGregor, James 25-26
MacGregor, P.G. 119-20, 123
Mackintosh, J.C. 164-5, 173
Maitland Street 130-1, 144
Maynard (City) Street 18, 20, 25, 27, 44, 56, 81, 83-85, 113, 120-1, 129, 155, 161, 164-5
Melville Island 21
Methodists 27, 121, 129, 131-2, 154, 191
military (British army and navy) 16-19, 21-22, 24-25, 33, 35-36, 40, 42, 44-45, 55-56, 61-72, 74, 96-103, 108-10, 113, 144, 150, 157, 161, 181; wives 22, 56, 97-99, 102, 111-12, 120, 125, 136
Montreal 62, 105, 136, 166, 171-2
Morton, Archibald 26, 119-21, 125, 128
Motton, Robert 70, 72
murder 44-45, 56-57, 176

Murray, William 52, 80-81, 90, 158, 180
Musquodoboit 99, 144

Naylor, John 130, 144-5, 160-1, 165, 173-8, 180-6
Neal, W.H. 157
needle trades 67, 99-100, 102, 158-9
Newfoundland 144, 161
New Glasgow 184
New York 20, 47, 155, 163
Night Refuge for the Homeless 166
Norbury family 127-8, 182-4
North End City Mission 129-31
North Street 87, 142
Northwest Arm 21, 137

offences 28, 31, 38, 42-45, 106; acquittals 33, 45-46, 86; locations 39-40; sentences 31-35, 41-42, 44-45, 50-51, 106-8 (see also specific offences)
Ottawa 146

Paris 109, 113
penitentiaries 21, 44, 57, 68, 83-84, 88
penny savings bank 125
Philadelphia 136-7
Pictou 25, 107
police 25-26, 33, 38-39, 44, 71, 79, 87-89, 92, 105, 111-13, 137, 142, 144, 178
police court (magistrate's court) 10, 20-22, 25, 28, 31-33, 45-46, 50, 52-53, 62, 64, 68-69, 73, 78-79, 82-84, 86, 89-90, 100-1, 105-6, 109, 112-13, 124, 127-8, 135, 139-41, 143, 145, 147, 178-9, 192
police station lock-up 21, 31-32, 50, 78, 80, 85-86, 88, 143
poorhouse (poors' asylum) 21, 34, 47-48, 54-55, 77, 79, 83, 86-88, 99, 106, 113, 137, 155, 157, 164, 180, 182
Poplar Grove Church 119
Porter's Lake 183
Potter, James 143, 165-6, 173
Presbyterians 27, 119, 128-9, 132, 154
Preston 104
Prince Edward Island 37, 57, 144
Prince Street 18, 69, 148
prisons (see bridewell, Rockhead City Prison, county jail, penitentiaries)
Prospect 36
prostitution 18, 19-20, 32, 36-37, 39-40, 42-43, 50, 61, 64-66, 74, 83, 86-87, 95-